D0255712

Round Moray, Badenoch and Strathspey

Walks and History

Boar's Head Press 002

Also in this series: Round Inverness, The Black Isle and Nairn

First published in April 1999
by Richard Gordon
at
Rosebank, Cairnfield, Buckie, Banffshire AB56 5EL, Scotland

Re-order from above address or tel. 01542-836087

ISBN 0 9533096 1 4

Note
Description or mention of walks and routes in this book do not guarantee or constitute a right of access. Permission for access should be sought as appropriate or if in any doubt whatever.
Every care has been taken to guarantee the accuracy of this guide but, given constant change in the physical landscape, road systems, telephone codes, etc., the author/publisher will not be responsible for any loss, damage or inconvenience caused by inaccuracies, nor for accidents incurred while using this guide.

Acknowledgements
Thanks are due to Bill Smith/Storycards for permission to use the original artwork as duplicated on the cover and internally. For Storycards catalogue/information contact the above address or: The Schoolhouse, Urquhart, Moray IV30 3LG

All photographs by the author

Scanning, typesetting and cover printing by
Posthouse Printing, The Park, Findhorn, Moray IV36 OTZ
Contents printing and binding by Short Run Press, Exeter

Contents

A rocky cove near Findlater Castle (**121**)

Foreword: How to use this book

Largely based on *The Complete Moray Rambler* (1992) and a sequel to *Round Inverness, The Black Isle and Nairn* (1998) this tour of Morayland offers more detail and walks than the original book, and also covers Badenoch and Upper Strathspey. With over 50 walks described, the opening chapters overlap those closing *Round Inverness*, this because the dramatic region between Culbin and Lochindorb demanded inclusion in both itineraries. Revised versions of some other chapters in *Round Inverness* (concerning Macbeth, General Wade, and the Moray Firth dolphins) are also included. The Banff and Buchan section of the original book, excluded here, awaits a sequel.

So, what's on the menu? Usually via back-roads and often on foot, this is a tour from Culbin to Cullen, Garmouth to Garva Bridge, the present to the past. It visits hills, moors, forests, waterfalls, gorges, rocky shores, cliff-hemmed beaches, mountain burns and gloomy passes, battle-sites, haunted places, fisher-towns, forgotten hamlets, ruined castles, museums and distilleries. Amid tales of bodach and kelpie we meet weird big black cats and the spooky Big Grey Man of Ben Macdhui. We meet Macbeth, the Wizard of Gordonstoun, Telford and Wade, the Bonnie Earl of Moray, Cluny Macpherson, 'Ossian' Macpherson, the fiddler-brigand James Macpherson; also villains like Black Sandy Grant and the Black Officer of Balachroan. The Wolf of Badenoch? He's everywhere - Elgin, Lochindorb, Ruthven, Loch an Eilean and Drumin all suffered his feral attentions.

In six sections (Forres and the Findhorn, 'Elginshire', Lower Strathspey, Upper Strathspey West, Upper Strathspey East, Old Banffshire), this tour doesn't have to be read or followed consecutively. Take it as you choose. For ease of cross-reference it is written in short chapters, each dealing with a specific route, walk, visit or subject. Cross-references to related sites or subjects are inserted as bracketed numbers in bold type - i.e., (**45**) or (see **45**) - meaning chapter-numbers, not pages. Gordonstoun's Round Square (**34**) is referred to Balachroan's round steading (**74**). Loch Gynack's fairy dogs (**73**) refer to (**92**), in which you flee the Big Grey Man and other grisly sprites out for your blood.

Of the mostly-circular walks, some explore high or remote ground, but few are strenuous. There are several Corbetts (hills over 2500 feet) but no Munros (over 3000 feet), this tour being for folk who prefer fresh air and discovery to heart attack or broken neck. It's also for those who enjoy unknown hidden places as well as better-known landscapes. Glen Feshie and Rothiemurchus are here, but so too are the Braes of Abernethy and Banffshire backlands – the Cabrach, Rothiemay, the Knock.

As to access, Scotland has no law of trespass, as such, but those owning or working the land see things differently to those seeking rural or wilderness recreation. Most people are reasonable, but a few can easily spoil it for others by leaving gates open, littering, failing to control dogs, and so on. So, please follow the country code and, though as far as I know walkers are welcome on all routes described, if in doubt ASK FIRST - especially during the stalking and shooting seasons. Many rely for a living on the land: it and they deserve respect. For further information on this vexed subject, contact the Scottish Rights of Way Society. Its address and phone number are given in the Gazetteer at the back of this book.

Also, especially in remote areas, wear good boots, dress appropriately, take food, and tell someone where you're going and when you expect to be back. If walking cliff-hemmed shoreline, check the tides first. The weather can change fast: a compass is always useful, and the 1¼ in.-1 mile (2cm-1km) Ordnance Survey map is essential. Map references cited are read from the top (eastings) first. In the text these are given both to pin-point sites and to clarify junctions. Heights are given both in feet and/or metres - personally I prefer feet, but the conversion (metric height x 1.0936 x 3 = height in feet) gets tedious.

Which I hope is not how you'll find what follows...

Note: Few photos are captioned. If their subject is ambiguous, inserted at the appropriate point in the text is (see photo) or (as shown below), etc.

As for Bill Smith's paintings (thanks, Bill), the cover shows Elgin Cathedral. On page 9 is Pluscarden Abbey, a 19th century Zulu drifter fights wild sea on page 35; page 59 shows the Telford Bridge at Craigellachie. On page 85 is Aviemore Station a century ago (much as now when the steam train operates). An osprey wings over Rothiemurchus and a red deer on page 111, while page 137 shows whisky smugglers crossing the Fiddich under ruined Auchindoun 200 years ago. The back cover photo is of Glen Feshie, with Coire Garbhlach in the background (see **86**).

1

The Findhorn and Forres Region

Culbin, Lochindorb, Findhorn & Pluscarden

1.　Introduction: Morayland

Once part of the Pictish kingdom of Fidach and extending from the Spey to Kyle of Lochalsh in the west, the Province of Moray (Gaelic *Moireabh*, from *mori-treb*, 'seaboard settlement'), remained semi-independent until the early Middle Ages, and still possesses its own strong identity, though now only an administrative district. Defined by the natural barriers of mountains to the south and by rapid rivers coursing northeast to the Moray Firth, Moray's remoteness from Edinburgh and Scone meant that the allegiance of its rulers could never be taken for granted, while its mild climate and fertile coastal plain (the Laich) encouraged settlement since the earliest times.

These days extending from Brodie east over the Spey (once county boundary) to Cullen in old Banffshire, and south to Strathavon and the Cabrach, Moray has had a human presence since at least *c*.5000BC, when Mesolithic (Middle Stone Age) hunter-gatherers camped at Culbin (**3**). Followed by Neolithic (New Stone Age) farmers whose cairns and stone circles are found throughout the northeast, much later (*c*.700BC), iron-working horse-riding Continental Celts began arriving. Ushering in an era of stone forts and *duns*, these artistic, headhunting newcomers survived the Romans, who named them *Picti* ('painted people'). With the promontory running from Burghead (**29**) to Kinneddar by Lossiemouth (**35**) one of their chief centres, by AD800 the Picts faced attack from both north and south. The Norse seized Burghead as the Scots (Latin *Scotti*, 'pirates') expanded northwest from their original base in Argyll, by *c*.850 conquering the northern Picts.

Finally expelling the Norse from Burghead in 1014, Moray was now ruled by Gaelic mormaers (stewards) like Macbeth (see **30**) who fought each other as well as the Norse and the House of Atholl further south. Gradually Canmore kings like David I (1124-53) asserted control, imposing feudalism and the Earls of Moray over the local Thanes, and the Roman Church over the older Celtic Church. Yet violence remained constant. With castles being built throughout the Province royal aggressors like the Wolf of Badenoch (**10**) wrought havoc; proud Edward's army invaded; Stewarts displaced Comyns; Gordons fought Stewarts (**6**); Covenanters wrecked cathedrals (**22**); Catholics hid (**44**); Jacobites fled with Cumberland on their heels – on and on it went, until at last Moray quietened down, so that today it's not another Clan Chattan raid or rebel heads displayed by the mercat cross we groan about, but council tax demands or local boundaries redrawn yet again.

As to which, in part defining this first section, the western boundary of Moray District (and Grampian Region) runs from the coast midway between Nairn and Findhorn south through Culbin Forest and over the A9 by Macbeth's Hillock. Following the Findhorn it cuts south through Darnaway Forest (**6**), then again paces the Findhorn past Randolph's Leap (**11**). Crossing Carn Duhie (312m), the Nairn-Grantown A939, and the Hill of Aitnock (413m), it reaches Lochindorb (**9**), its southernmost point. Breaking sharply northeast up the loch and Dorback Burn, it bears east over the moors between Carn Kitty (521m) and Carn Dearg (521m) south of remote Loch Dallas (**20**). Turning southwest down Glen Gheallaidh it crosses the Spey by Cragganmore (**58**), then tracks the ridge of the Cromdale Hills south past Bridge of Brown (**100**) to the summits of Cairngorm and Ben Macdhui.

This first section of the tour loops west from Forres to Culbin; south via Brodie and the Findhorn's west bank to Lochindorb, then north to Findhorn Bay, and so on east.

2.   Forres & Cluny Hill   (*History, Walk*)

Moray's most attractive town? Elgin folk may disagree, but Forres (pop. 9050) might claim this title, being well-sited, architecturally rich, historically resonant, and (vital nowadays) fully bypassed by the A96. With Grant Park's award-winning floral sculptures under the wooded folds of Cluny Hill, its streets and wynds have a long history. Possibly the Varris on Ptolemy's map, a royal residence by the 9th century (the castle stood at the west end of the High Street), it had its original charter renewed by James IV in 1496.

Always strategically important due to its site on the main Aberdeen-Inverness route, it occupies the first ridge above a fertile flood-plain a mile east of the River Findhorn's final meander into Findhorn Bay a mile to the north. With the Bay's gleaming flats closing in to a seaward neck where Culbin Forest (**4**) and Findhorn village (**14**) almost meet, Findhorn Foundation (**15**) caravans hug the east shore, a 'New Age' enclave oddly cheek-by-jowl with the Nimrods thundering up from the major RAF base at adjacent Kinloss.

At the northeast edge of Forres by the bypass, now encased within an unlovely tall protective glass-and-steel cabinet, stands Sueno's Stone (047596). 23 feet high, this is the last and greatest Pictish symbol stone. Or is it? Carved bands depict a bloody battle, with fleeing and beheaded warriors. Long thought to celebrate a Pictish defeat of the Norse, antiquarian Kenneth Jackson suggests it may instead be a propaganda coup by the first Scots king Kenneth mac Alpin (d.858), set up to remind the beaten Picts who now ruled the roost.

Most of the town lies west of Grant Park. The High Street, dominated by crowstep gables and the bizarre 1838 Gothic reconstruction of the medieval Tolbooth, remains traffic-bound despite the bypass. Service families, visitors to the nearby Findhorn Foundation, and retired southern settlers create an aura of prosperity. The town houses, hotels and villas hugging Cluny Hill's wooded western slope along the Rafford road are not dilapidated. Falconer Museum in Tolbooth Street (01309-673701) displays many items of local interest. The tourist information centre (01309-672938) in the High Street is open only in summer.

At the wooded summit of Cluny Hill is Nelson's Tower (see photo next page), erected in 1806 to honour the admiral who didn't know how to use a telescope. Open May-October (01309-673701) and housing a display on Nelson and local sites of interest, the easiest way up to it is from Grant Park. Start up the woodland tracks circling Cluny Hill, keeping left. Once there, don't abandon Cluny Hill.

Quiet avenues of Douglas Fir and other fine trees curve above grassy glades to Cluny Hill cemetery, peaceful amid its memorials and sculpted shrubberies.

Amid so tranquil an oasis it's hard to recall that Forres was long at the heart of the witch-madness. Best-known is the case of Isobel Gowdie of Auldearn, who in 1662 claimed to have slept with Satan, but there are others. When *c.*AD960 King Duff fell inexplicably ill on arriving at Forres from Scone, witchcraft was blamed. Three Forres women, dragged to the top of Cluny Hill, were forced into barrels set inside with spikes. With the lids nailed shut the barrels were rolled down the hill. Three boulders were erected to mark where they ended up. Of these 'Witches Stones', one is by Victoria Road, and a second near the railings in Grant Park. Such events helped persuade Shakespeare to site the witchcraft scenes of his Scottish tragedy (**30**) in and about Forres, which can also boast three regicides. For here in 908 King Donald was murdered; his son King Malcolm was slain nearby, maybe at Blervie Castle above Rafford (**16**); and here again, in Forres Castle, King Duff.

It's hard to credit such events today. Yet Moray's history is of instability and violence, both human and elemental. Of the latter type the 1694 Culbin sandstorm and the 'Muckle Spate' of 1829 (**12**), remain especially memorable; and it's with Culbin's 'Buried Barony' we now begin this journey through time and space.

3.   The 1694 Culbin Sandstorm   *(History)*

Culbin Forest covers a vast area of coastal sand-dunes between Nairn and Findhorn Bay; an area that in 1694 saw events more appropriate to the Sahara Desert than Moray.

The tale is that Alexander Kinnaird, Laird of Culbin, owned 3600 acres of fertile land with 16 farms, their tenants paying on average £200 Scots per annum in rent, plus 40 bolls of wheat, bere oats, and oatmeal. The climate was kind, the soil fertile, and the Findhorn swarming with salmon. Then came a sandstorm burying the mansion house and every farm but one, and forcing the Findhorn north to a new outlet. So it's said.

Yet the storm was no surprise. The Moray coast, much of it loose sand or shingle, has stranded beaches from Ardersier to the Old Bar east of Nairn. For years winter storms had driven sand inland. In 1663 the Laird of Brodie (5) wrote in his diary how Nairn '...was in danger to be quite lost by the sand and the water', and after 1676 Culbin fields were annually buried in up to two feet of sand. Then in autumn 1694 came the terrible storm, so sudden a ploughman left his plough in the furrow; reapers dropped their sickles and fled. All night the sand drifted, so when at dawn the gale died, folk had to break out of the backs of their houses to escape. In shock, they drove their cattle away. Amid a lull some came back for their goods, but then the storm returned. Blocked, the Findhorn burst north, engulfing the old village. Everything was buried, even the mansion house.

In 1698, Parliament refusing to revoke his debts, Kinnaird sold the ruined estate to Duff of Drummuir. Broken, he died in 1702, soon followed by his wife, and in 1743 by his childless son. Of the estate, only Earnhill Farm survived. Many years later shifting dunes exposed part of the old mansion. A man called down the chimney then fell back in horror, saying he'd heard a hoarse voice and ghostly laugh. Maybe he believed the old tale that Kinnaird, punished for working his tenants on Sundays, was still down there playing cards with Satan, trapped until Judgement Day. Sometimes other ruins appeared, their stone taken to build dykes for new farms; the fruit trees of vanished orchards blossomed when the sands released them; while smugglers burying brandy casks in the sands famously never found them again.

As for the tale, Kinnaird owned 1350 acres, not 3600 (the area of Culbin Sands); with six farms, not 16 - 16, the 1693 rental shows, was the number of tenants. Their rent and the land's wealth were also exaggerated. Seven times from 1691 to 1700 the Scottish harvest failed, causing famine and ruin. And with sand blowing since 1676, how by 1694 could Kinnaird have had 'highly cultivated fields with heavy corn' and 'extensive pastures with numerous crops'? After all, both his grandfather and father had died in debt: the estate was in crown hands. When Kinnaird inherited in 1691 he couldn't pay his creditors. Worse, he was a listed Jacobite rebel. The sandstorm was just the last straw, his appeal to Parliament encouraging the legend of the former wealth of the 'Buried Barony'.

In 1839 Grant of Kincorth began planting the desert, first with bent, then brushwood, then young trees. During the Great War vast harvests of fir were reaped. Then fire destroyed the new forest. In May 1920 a violent westerly blew the newly-released sand so old valleys became hills; hills were laid low; trees were buried.

In 1921 the Forestry Commission took over 2000 acres. Failing to hold the sand with marram grass, brushwood was tried, more successfully. Ultimately the FC planted 7500 acres, mostly Scots and Corsican Pine. In so doing, they also created a vast maze which can take days to explore…

4.   Culbin: Forest & Sands   *(Walks)*

Culbin Forest demands respect. Cloaking Britain's largest sand dune system, it hosts 550 flowering plants, many at their northern or southern limit, and over 130 species of lichen. Beyond it, a vast tidal lagoon and mudflats, machair and mussel-beds hide from the sea behind The Bar's marram-grassed dunes and miles-long beach. It's easy to get lost here, despite waymarked tracks from Wellhill and Cloddymoss. You'll need OS map and compass, also good boots, many tracks being rough or sandy. It also helps to mark your route in case you need to backtrack; and to take a piece to eat; while the Forest Enterprise leaflet with its outline map of tracks and sites of interest is useful - call 01343-820223.

The two main entry-points are at Cloddymoss (982600) nearer Nairn, and Wellhill (996614) by Kintessack, nearer Forres. A third carpark is at Kingsteps (912573) by Nairn. If heading west from Forres turn right off the A96 to Moy/Kintessack immediately after crossing the Findhorn (009583). Stay right, first east then north past Moy House, then west (left) to Kintessack at the Binsness-Kincorth junction (015608). Just east of the hamlet, turn north past Wellhill Farm 200 yards into the forest to a carpark. There is also access from Brodie Castle (**5**). From Nairn, access is via Lochloy Road north from the A96 (between river bridge and railway bridge on the east side of town: Culbin signposted).

The walks suggested here start from Wellhill, but Mavistown sand dunes (940600), 50 feet high with 1200-foot flanks, are best reached from Kingsteps or Cloddymoss, with its Educational Centre for school parties. Cloddymoss also offers the shortest route north to the intertidal flats of the Gut, part of an RSPB reserve, and to the Bar beyond.

From Wellhill four tracks depart, three from the pole-gate to the north; the fourth east into the wood. Here, of many possible routes, are three: (**1**) east then north round the forest fringe via Binsness and Findhorn Bay; then west past Buckie Loch to the tidal lagoon by Duck Island and the Gut's inter-tidal mudflats; (**2**) the straight path north to the sea, connecting with (**1**) then return or coastal routes west towards Nairn; (**3**) a forest circuit west towards Cloddymoss, then north (options various), and back east past Duck Pond.

(**1**) Starting east, the pleasant open track follows the forest edge two miles towards Binsness and Findhorn Bay, then turns north into deep forest. This turn leads (not all junctions on the OS map) to interesting sites. The Glade (017632: this and following references approx.) is an area of Lagoonal sediment amid tall Douglas Fir. The Buried Tree (018634) illustrates sand-movement since the forest began to grow, its partial excavation showing how deep others are buried. Lady Culbin (015644), one of the largest dune-systems, now stabilised by Scots Pine, is almost 100 feet high in parts. Shingle ridges further east (993634) support over 130 species of lichen. To find these sites obtain the outline map mentioned above.

Otherwise, leave the forest where the track swings north. Past a cottage, cut right to a track by Findhorn Bay's marshy tide-pools. Follow the shore east past

Binsness House, then north past Findhorn village, just over the seaward neck of the bay. Watch for seals on the spit beyond it (the Ee: see **14**). Follow the beach west two miles past Buckie Loch (mostly dry, with fields of wild iris and grotesque fungi) to the narrow-necked, broad tidal lagoon east of the Gut, maybe where the

Findhorn once met the sea. Mussel-beds and mudflats gleam, staked by poles erected to discourage German flying-boats during World War II. Tidal streams trickle out of the flat, anemone-rich machair past the old bothy on grassy Duck Island (983638) east of the lagoon. With fine views over the Firth to distant hills, and maybe yachts sailing in, it is idyllic. Yet here the tide is rapid, so don't get caught.

From here explore further west or return to Wellhill (see below). Note: on days of strong westerlies this nine-mile route is best done clockwise, unless you like trudging into a sandstorm. Either that, or take to the forest wherever breaks in the low sandy cliffs occur.

(**2**) For the direct, well-used route north to the sea, from Wellhill pass the gate to a large clearing and three-way junction. Follow the middle track along the forest fringe, tending left to (tall pine now both sides) a T-junction west of tadpole-rich Gravel Pit Pond (994618). Here cross the east-west track and continue north into the forest on an obvious sandy path, not shown on the OS or outline maps. Weaving up and down past old Scots Pine over dunes through a pygmy woodland of pine, silver birch and heath, mosses and delicate silvery lichens knitting the sand with fey colour, this path crosses a second east-west track and continues to a third.

Before crossing this third track on the increasingly sandy path, stop. Note where you are. Leave a marker - you may return on this track from the west and will need to be sure of your right turn onto the homeward, southbound path. Through a logged clearing up a pine-crowned dune the path crosses more logged dunes and a last east-west track to a final forest fringe and the lagoon. Here, turn east past Buckie Loch towards Findhorn (see route 1), return south to Wellhill; or head west via forest fringe and the Gut or outer beach towards Nairn. The first and last of these walks are lengthy. Check the tides and mark your route.

Turning west, you pass the start of a southbound track parallel to the path you just took. Intersecting main east-west tracks and at one point climbing steeply up and over the Forest's highest point (29m), it returns to Wellhill reliably and without confusion. If aiming for the Bar and tempted to cut over the tidal flats to the outer dunes, at low tide this is possible, but hard, with wide ditches and muddy black mussel beds. The easier roundabout route hugs the high-tide mark for a mile until, landward of the outer dunes, an abandoned bothy shows where to cut across. Also here, by a round gravel pond and lone tree (963616), a path on the left leads south via forestry track a dull two miles south to Cloddymoss.

The Bar is spectacular. At low tide the sands seem to stretch north almost to the Black Isle cliffs, and west to Nairn. Yet with tidal channels everywhere, without a tide-table don't be tempted to walk too far out. King Canute couldn't do it; nor can you or I.

(3) A third route from Wellhill runs west. Past the barrier at the three-way junction turn left then, 50 yards into the wood, left again onto a pine-needled path. This meanders southwest to a track that runs west to a logged-out T-junction, Kintessack visible to the south. Turn right (north) 100 yards, then left (west) at a second junction, back into the forest – this is all waymarked. The track, parallel to the forest's edge, leads to the 'species trials' (987606). Developed 1921-30 to learn which trees would grow best at Culbin, there are European (scruffy) and North Japanese Larch, Maritime (knotty and twisty), Western Yellow and Lodgepole Pine; and also the winners, Scots and Corsican Pine. At the junction beyond, turn right (north) 150 yards, then left to a logged clearing - a giant mess. At a third junction (signposted left: Cloddymoss 0.9m), keep curving northwest past another Cloddymoss turn through a young plantation. Briefly amid mature wood swing right to a main crossing. The track ahead leads seaward; the right turn (yellow marker) heads east. Soon re-entering mature forest, the track forks. Turn right under silver birch, a mossy bank to your left. Climb this to find Duck Pond (983615) - an old fire dam, now a wildlife habitat and secret place to enjoy. Here blue and great tits nest; pipistrelle and long-eared bats roost; Water Boatmen and Damselflies are at home, and mallard breed; hence the name. This is a fine place to relax. Beyond it the forking tracks converge to continue straight. Turn left at the next main crossing for the forest's highest point (see route 2 above) and the way to the lagoon. At the next junction it's straight on for the Gravel Pit Pond, left for the sandy path to the sea, or right 400 yards to Wellhill carpark.

Culbin is a wonderful place. For everyone's sake please respect it.

5.   Brodie Castle   *(Visit, Walk)*

Open daily Easter-30 September and October weekends Brodie Castle (979578: tel. 01309-641371) occupies wooded parkland by the A96 four miles west of Forres. From the A96 the signposted right turn north to Dyke and Kintessack is right before the hamlet of Brodie. If you miss it, in Brodie turn right over the railway then right again half-a-mile. Or, from Wellhill and Culbin, west of Kintessack turn left a mile to a T-junction, then right through Dyke, its kirk boasting a triple-decker pulpit, the better to preach hellfire from on high.

Built on land the Brodies got from Malcolm IV in 1160, this elegant lime-harled Z-plan towerhouse was Brodie-owned until the National Trust acquired it. A charter from the reign of Alexander III (1249-86) calls Malcolm Brodie Thane and royal tenant of Brodie and Dyke, but the first remembered Brodie is the 12th laird, Alexander, in November 1550 'put to the horn' (outlawed) for refusing to be tried after attacking his neighbour, Alexander Cumming of Altyre. He was unbowed: high up the southwest tower a carved stone is dated 1567 - the castle's oldest part. All other family records were lost in 1645 when, in the Civil War, the house was 'byrnt and plunderit' by Sir Lewis Gordon.

With conical turrets and coats of arms on the outer walls; French furniture, porcelain and paintings from far and wide within, the castle is approached by a beech avenue (the carpark route is less direct). Its best internal feature is in the rectangular block built after the 1645 disaster - the spacious 'Chamber of Dais', or drawing-room, built by the 15th laird, another Alexander. Designed to be 'all glorious within', with its richly-moulded plaster ceiling it suggests Dutch influence, perhaps because Alexander, a staunch Covenanter, was in the delegation at Breda in Holland in 1649 to negotiate Charles II's return to Scotland (see **41**).

During the '45 another Alexander supported the government yet died in debt due to the expensive good works of his wife, Mary Sleigh. In 1786 Brodie burned again and Lady Margaret Duff, daughter of the Earl of Fife, suffocated. Her son James having drowned, the next laird was her grandson William, who added the airy eastern end in the 'Gothick' style.

With adventure playground, picnic area, shop, and daffodil-rich gardens, Brodie is worth a visit. Walk the West Avenue past copper beech and lime trees over a minor road to the pond; from its hide watch heron and coot. Returning up the avenue, bear right before the castle to Brodie village. By the railway crossing turn left along the road to the main entrance, then up the drive past Rodney's Stone (985576), a 9th century Pictish symbol stone.

6.   Darnaway & the Earls of Moray   *(History)*

Between Brodie and Forres back-roads break south from the A96 through Darnaway Forest past Darnaway Castle (994551: originally *Tarnua*), long the seat of the Earls of Moray. The first road (988574: just east of Brodie opposite the

Brodie Castle turn) soon joins the second, which leaves the A96 a mile further east (998577: Darnaway 2). Through pretty woods past the estate's wrought iron north gates it runs over a crossing to a junction. Turn left (Conicavel 2; also to Whitemire and Redstone) over two crossroads. Wood gives way to fields, the massive facade of Darnaway Castle a half-mile east. Not open, the castle can be visited by appointment. Ring Moray Estates Office in Forres (01309-672213).

Behind this early 19th-century pile is Randolph's Hall. Later made 1st Earl of Moray by Robert the Bruce, in 1314 Thomas Randolph scaled the rock of Edinburgh Castle to rout the English, then at Bannockburn routed much of Edward's army from 'Randolph's Field'. Established at Darnaway, he was attacked by the evicted Comyns. Amid the ensuing slaughter only their chief, Alistair, escaped (it is said) by leaping the Findhorn at Randolph's Leap (**11**). Yet Randolph was more than just a brawler. As Bruce's envoy to the Pope he argued for Scots independence, concluding a treaty with France that cemented the Auld Alliance, so that until *c.*1900 all Scots had a right to French citizenship. When in 1329 Bruce died, Randolph became guardian of the realm, himself dying in 1332. With both his sons killed in battle, his daughter became known as 'Black Agnes of Dunbar' for her six-month defence of Dunbar Castle in 1337. 'She indeed laughed at the English,' claims the 15th-century *Book of Pluscarden*, 'and would, in the sight of all, wipe with a most beautiful cloth the spot where the stone from the engine hit the Castle Wall.'

James III (1460-88) stayed here and with Thomas Cochrane, Earl of Mar (**107**), built the old castle. In 1562 Mary Queen of Scots was here after her half-brother James Stewart defeated George Gordon, 4th Earl of Huntly, at Corrichie near Aberdeen. Stripped of the Earldom of Moray in 1550, Huntly had opposed Mary after her return from France in 1561. Hunted down after Corrichie, the Catholic Gordon died of apoplexy ('*...he sodenlie fawlethe from his horse starke dedde...*'), and the Protestant Stewart became Earl of Moray (**45**). So began a feud, even as the intrigues of Bothwell, Darnley and Mary led to her 1567 abdication and the coronation of her son, the infant James VI. Made Regent, in January 1570 Moray was assassinated at Linlithgow. His infant son, also James and 2nd Earl, is known to history as 'the Bonnie Earl of Moray'. His life was energetic but brief. The feud with the Gordons escalated. Amid dispute over Spey fishing rights and ownership of Spynie (**24**), tit-for-tat killings increased. George Gordon (6th Earl) was favoured by King James, whose Queen, Anne of Denmark, favoured Moray. Was James in on it? On 7 February 1592 Gordon's armed band surprised Moray at Donibristle Castle on the Fife coast. The indefensible 'castle' was fired. Moray fled to hide among the rocks, but two Gordon lairds found him, and:

'...Gordon of Bucky gave him a wound in the face: Moray, half expiring, said, 'You hae spilt a better face than your awin.' Upon this, Bucky pointing his dagger at Huntly's breast, swore, 'You shall be as deep as I;' and forced him to pierce the poor defenceless body.'

To Randolph's Hall nearly a century ago at last came home the gory portrait of the dead man, his wounds depicted, which his mother, Lady Doune, had commissioned to stir up popular indignation. Yet (the 'Bonnie Earl' had been well-loved), Huntly got away with it: seven years later James VI made him a marquis. Later the murdered Earl's son married Lady Ann Gordon, daughter of his father's killer; a marriage promoted by James VI to end the feud. Unsurprisingly, the new Earl avoided politics. As for the gory portrait, it lay in a chest at Donibristle for centuries. All that survived of the 'Bonnie Earl' was a later ballad:

Ye hielands and ye lawlands,
O where hae ye been?
They hae slain the Earl o' Moray
And lain him on the green.

The violence continued. In 1631 Clan Chartan invaded Moray. Ordered to exterminate the clan, leaving none alive except 'priests, women and bairns', the latter to be expelled to Scandinavia, the Earl's hesitation ended when the clan besieged Darnaway, plundering Dyke before retreating to the wilds. In pursuit, Moray took 300 prisoners, executing many on the spot. William Macintosh, brother of the escaping chief, was hanged and quartered at Forres, his head spiked on a cross at Dyke, and his body shared between Elgin, Forres, Auldearn and Inverness - both public warning and popular entertainment, the blood real, not reel-to-reel.

After the Civil War, when Randolph's Hall hosted Cromwellian troops, Darnaway at last knew peace. Francis Earl of Moray (1737-1810) built the present pile and planted 12 million trees, including the oak forest. His work was continued: in 1841 many miles of recreational walks were laid out. Of these, today open to the public are two fine circular walks above the Findhorn gorges, by Dunearn Burn on the west bank, and a mile further north at Sluie (**13**).

7.   Dunearn Burn at Conicavel   *(Walk)*

Scotland's most dramatic river? The Findhorn (*fionneren*, 'white water'), runs northwest from the Monadhliaths. Crossed by the A9 near Tomatin in Strathdearn, taking up the Fintack Burn from Loch Moy, its peaty waters run the bare gorges of the Streens to Carnach. Here it turns east then northeast before boiling under Dulsie Bridge *en route* to Randolph's Leap at Relugas where, during the Muckle Spate of August 1829 (**12**), it rose over 50 feet. Taking up the Divie, it roars past Logie House and Sluie then, more peacefully, winds past the Meads of St John and west of Forres to Findhorn Bay and the sea.

Spectacular in spring, when snow-melt adds to its white-foaming torrent, its banks offer dramatic forested walks, as at Dunearn Burn. Here the waymarked route comes in two lengths, 1.5 or 2.5 miles, much of it along the lip of the gorge.

From Darnaway, continue south through neat little Conicavel to a sign: *Dunearn Burn Walk 1 mile.* Continue through woodland to a left turn and carpark. The waymarked walk (green shorter, red longer) starts past tall pines into beechwood, then climbs a mossy bank high above the burn. Leaving the wood, a short detour leads to panoramic views east over Sluie and Forres to Findhorn Bay. The river below remains hidden, but a mile southwest above and across it is prominent, white-harled Logie House (**11**).

The path descends cut steps, the river louder. A sign warns: STEEP CLIFFS KEEP TO PATH. Suddenly you reach a railed viewpoint high above the junction of burn and river. Black waters boil over rocks below: dense forest over the ravine accentuates the giddy depth as the path continues south above the gorge, the drop so steep you can almost touch the tops of trees rooted below. Dangerous points are railed; there is no risk. Soon the path forks. The red route follows the edge another half-mile opposite Logie House up to an estate road then back to the carpark. Leaving the gorge, the shorter green route joins this road earlier. Either way, the track's final stretch offers stunning views of billowing woodland beyond the gorge. A last turn through a tall stately grove leads back to the carpark.

The road runs on south through craggy wooded land before (now in Highland Region) descending to a junction by the Findhorn. The left fork over the river via a fine old stone bridge climbs to the Carrbridge B9007 south of Relugas and Randolph's Leap (**11**). The right fork continues past Coulmony to the A939 (at 958473) just north of a turn southwest past Ardclach to Glen Altnarie and Dulsie Bridge – all close, and all worth a visit.

8.   Ardclach and Dulsie to Lochindorb   (*Route*)

West of the Moray boundary (see *Round Inverness*), Ardclach, its 1655 bell-tower above an old riverbend kirk, lies under the A939/B9007 Ferness crossroads three miles south of Relugas. If from Forres and Relugas, at Ferness turn sharp right north (A939). Over the river climb to the Ardclach-Dulsie road (960471: left). If from Coulmony, at the A939 turn left then first right on the minor Dulsie road. Either way, after a mile turn left by a swampy pool. Half-a-mile on above the river, a private road breaks left under a bell tower on its mound (955454). Built by Alexander Brodie of Lethen and his wife Margaret Grant, Covenanters who needed a watch tower, below it by the river is the old kirk: DANGEROUS ROOF NO ADMISSION, its burial ground still used, nearby the pillars of a vanished bridge.

From Ardclach continue five miles southwest, left at each junction, to Dulsie Bridge via Altnarie Falls (931435). In steep woodland, the Altnarie (*Allt na Airidh*) runs under the road bare yards before the junction with the old military road south from Cawdor to Dulsie. The Falls, well-regarded in Victorian times, lie back and down through the wood about 100 yards east of the road. At the junction the left turn descends to Dulsie Bridge (1764) built to carry the military road from Perth to Fort George. Below it, the Findhorn boils through an impressive gorge. Upstream amid moors, the Leonach and Rhilean burns combine to join the Findhorn in a fine glen southwest of Dulsie (921406).Continue past Dunearn Farm, above it an old fort (*dun-earn*, 'river-fort'). At a sharp bend (936405) a track departs southwest to ruined Lynemore steading (925399), the Leonach's fine cascades beyond.

This road east from Dulsie Bridge soon intersects the B9007 at a minor crossroads (947403), the moorland track opposite continuing past the Hill of Aitnoch to the A939 north of Lochindorb. Here, turn right on the B9007, south through bare land towards Carrbridge. After three miles turn left, east, on a little road (950350) to Lochindorb - a strange wild place appropriate to the myth of the Wolf of Badenoch, his chief lair crumbling on the isle amid it.

9.   Lochindorb Castle   (*Island Castle Visit*)

Lochindorb is also reached by driving south from Nairn (A939) or Forres (A940). Soon after these roads meet at Dava (phone-box, little else), a minor road (004383) breaks west two miles over heather heath to the bleak glacial trench containing this shallow, allegedly kelpie-haunted (see **92**) 'Loch of the Little Fishes'. Passing the castle, the road continues past Lochindorb Lodge up to the B9007 (as above).

There is a desolate beauty here, and few trees. Pine screens the lodge, a fringe of forestry crowns rocky Craig Tiribeg (486m) above, old ash trees stand amid the ruined 13th-century castle 300 yards offshore; but all else is bare. Other than lodge and castle the only sign of human presence, ancient or modern, is a rust-red roofed byre at Terriemore under the Hill of Aitnoch to the north.

Yet there the castle is, its still-solid outer walls the focus of romances like Maurice Walsh's 'The Key Above the Door' (1926) and Thomas Dick Lauder's 'The Wolfe of Badenoch' (1827). Comyn-built, occupied by Edward I in 1303 and later by the Wolf, in 1455 James II ordered the Thane of Cawdor 'to raze and destroy the house and fortalice of Lochindorb.' This was done.

From Lochindorb Lodge (355970), having rung 01309-651270 to book a boat, you can row 1200 yards north to it. 'The depth goes from about fifty feet to just two or three,' the underkeeper may warn, indicating choppy white-capped black water. 'You'll probably ground and have to push off at least twice.' And you may find, as a friend and I did one brisk May day, a stiff breeze holding you back. It took us a while to round the isle to dock at a tiny inlet on the north side, this under a gap torn through the 20-foot-high old wall. Best choose a calm day.

Inside, the old Comyn buildings are gone, leaving an uneven grassy quadrangle. On the east side huge ash trees sprout between outer and inner wall. By the water-gate (the original iron yett taken to Cawdor Castle in 1455) the stonework is pitted, as if by hostile fire. A 1993 survey found five stone balls in the loch 25-30 metres offshore, probably slung by a trebuchet (siege-engine) used by Sir Andrew Murray during his 1335 assault. A submerged ridge this east side suggests a causeway to the shore but is natural, yet the isle was certainly built up to support the walls. Masonry drowned off the north side may be from a harbour, or the walls of an earlier fortress pillaged to build the 13th-century castle.

Oddly, for a place so haunting from the shore, it held no morbid presence. Yet it was a May afternoon, white clouds scurrying above. I'd not want to visit on a wild November night with the banshee in the blast...nor meet the Wolf of Badenoch in a bad mood.

10.   The Wolf of Badenoch   *(History)*

Upper Strathspey is easily flooded, and so Badenoch, 'the drowned place'. And in 1390, with Scotland 'nocht governit', Alexander Stewart, fourth son of King Robert II, was on the rampage. Also called Alasdair Mor Mac an Righ ('Big Alexander, Son of the King'), and Ridire Ruadh ('Red Knight', for his red hair), his vicious nature and buck teeth got him his best-known title, the Wolf of Badenoch - a slur on wolves?

Born *c.*1343 to Robert's first wife Elizabeth, he seized titles, property and power as he could, but made little of any of it. His father had been a golden youth yet, when crowned in 1371 aged 54, slack-witted Robert had 'bleared' red eyes, and was widely reckoned as past it. Granting 'our dearest son...our whole lands of Badennach...with the castle of Lochyndorbe...', by 1374 he'd made Alexander Earl of Buchan, King's lieutenant from 'Moray to the Pentland Frith [sic], and within the whole county of Inverness.' So the Wolf did as he pleased. Besides Lochindorb obtaining fortified lairs at Ruthven (**82**), Loch an Eilean (**88**) and Drumin (**105**), in

1382 he married Euphemia Countess of Ross to get the earldom, then abandoned her for a mistress, Mariott Athyn, who bore his five sons.

In 1384 admitting his incompetence, Robert gave power to John, Earl of Carrick. Though kicked silly by a horse in 1388, in 1390 John became king as Robert III, so invoking the name of the Bruce and denying the misfit name 'John' to sidestep the Balliol claim: he was neither John I nor John II. Derided as John Faranyeir ('Yesterday's John'), he told his wife Annabella Drummond he desired burial in a dunghill under the epitaph: 'Here lies the worst of kings and the most miserable of men.' Declared unfit to rule even before he was crowned, his brother Robert Earl of Fife became Governor of the Realm. The royal finances and laws of the realm fell into vicious farce, as epitomised by the Wolf's anarchic ventures.

These led from his claim to Church lands by Kingussie (**71**). When in 1380 Bishop Burr of Moray proposed switching protection payments to the Sheriff of Inverness, the Wolf was outraged. The dispute simmered until in February 1390 Burr excommunicated him for abandoning his wife. Thus provoked, in May and June of 1390 with his 'wild, wikkid heilandmen' the Wolf roared out of Lochindorb to torch Forres, Pluscarden (**17**), and Elgin Cathedral (**22**). These attacks led Burr, now hiding at Spynie (**24**) near Elgin, to write Robert III a pathetic letter of complaint. In time the Wolf did formal penance, and after he died at Ruthven *c.*1405 was royally buried at Dunkeld.

It's said the night he died a tall man in black came to play him at chess. After many hours the stranger rose, saying 'checkmate'. Instantly, thunder, hail and lightning struck the castle. Next day the Wolf's men were found dead and blasted outside the walls; he was found dead in the banquet hall, unmarked, the nails of his boots torn out (see **82**). When the funeral procession started out, another storm was quelled only by removing his coffin to the rear.

The lesson? Crime pays, if you're of royal birth and live in medieval Scotland. Some find the Wolf romantic: basically he was an antisocial incompetent. Gaining the Earldom of Ross, he lost it by so obviously deserting Euphemia that both marriage and earldom were annulled. *'Inutilis fuit communitati,'* he was called by the Scots Council-General two years before his attack on Elgin – *'He was useless to the people.'*

11.   From Dava to Randolph's Leap   *(Routes, History, Walk)*

From Lochindorb two routes run south to Badenoch and Strathspey. To the west, the B9007 crosses barren moonscape then descends to the Grantown-Carrbridge A938 a mile east of Carrbridge (**64**), itself bypassed by the main Perth-Inverness A9. East of Lochindorb from Dava the A939 crosses the bare land some miles to descend through woodland past Castle Grant's baroque lodge into Grantown-on-Spey (**59**).

Now returning north towards Forres via Relugas and Sluie, at Dava turn left on the A939 half-a-mile to a fork. *En route* to Nairn the left fork (A939) crosses the B9007 at Ferness (964451) above Ardclach (**8**); from Ferness the B9007 follows the

Findhorn to Relugas and Randolph's Leap – the longer but scenically-preferable route. The right fork (A940 to Forres) runs north under the broad bare Knock of Braemoray (456m) into broken land and forestry. Crossing the Divie it runs high above the river and Dunphail Castle (007481), a crumbled Comyn stronghold besieged in 1330 by Thomas Earl of Randolph, nearby it Dunphail House (1828).

A mile on the A940 takes up the B9007 (010504), a turn easily missed. If taking this route to Relugas and Randolph's Leap (001495), look out for the sharp

left turn downhill, past the drive to Logie House and Steading (006505: 01309-611378). With tearoom, a gallery of local arts and crafts, and working craft-shops, Logie Steading is open much of the year; the tall, white-harled house beautifully-sited above the Findhorn. Continuing down, cross the Divie to park higher up the wooded brae opposite the sign to Randolph's Leap.

If from Ferness, where the B9007 descends past minor junctions (uphill right then downhill left via a fine old bridge over the Findhorn to the Darnaway-Ardclach back road: see **7**), slow down on entering thick forest. Just beyond Relugas lodge and driveway on the right and round a bend, on the right is parking-space: over the road, a sign under the trees indicates the path down to Randolph's Leap. Follow steps down into lush beechwood to a viewpoint above rocky spurs below. Bare yards apart, they form a narrow gate through which the river foams into the gorge. This is Randolph's Leap (**6**). Somehow Alistair Comyn (Cumming) made the jump from the far side to this. Nothing like spears at your backside to encourage a champion leap.

The narrow, twisting woodland path turns downstream, the river below foaming over huge boulders, the dizziest sections guard-railed. Ending at a rocky spur below which Findhorn and Divie meet in a vast dark pool (an idyllic spot where salmon leap), to the right a steep path climbs the wooded east bank of the Divie back to the B9007. It's a wonderful place, with another surprise too. Either end of the gorge there are two marker stones, each under an iron grille. The first, deep in the wood some 50 feet above the river where it enters the gorge between the rocky spurs of Randolph's Leap, is worn, its inscription hard to read. The legible inscription on the second, 50 feet above the confluence of the rivers, states: 'The Findhorn and Divie met here in flood, August 3rd & 4th 1829'.

12.   Thomas Dick Lauder & the Muckle Spate   *(History)*

On Saturday 1st of August 1829, after months of unnatural heat, sudden downpours and weird atmospheric effects, a huge black pillar of cloud appeared over the Moray Firth. Joining sea to sky it whirled inland. Early on Sunday morning, it broke on the Monadhliaths. For three days and nights rain poured. Swollen rivers inundated the Laich of Moray. Bridges on the Findhorn, Lossie, Spey and Deveron collapsed. The ruin was immense.

The disaster was recorded by Sir Thomas Dick Lauder, an aristocratic eccentric from Lothian who by marriage had come to live at Relugas, another old Comyn seat with a vitrified fort (The Doune of Relugas) in the grounds. Thin, restless, voluble, devoted to the wild Relugas gardens, he'd published romances like 'The Wolfe of Badenoch', but had never found his true metier. Cushioned by wealth, he had remained aloof from local life.

Then the deluge began. The Findhorn and Divie rose with awesome speed. Late on August 3rd, after 36 hours of rain, Lauder was roused from dinner to find the Divie up over the strawberry beds. The waters were surging: 'with a strange and alarming flux and reflux, dashing over the ground 10 or 15 yards at a time.' Tall trees, undercut on the banks, leaned dangerously. Worst was the noise: '...a distinct combination of two kinds of sound: one, a uniformly continued roar, the other like rapidly repeated discharges of many cannons at once.' Lauder's description continues: 'Above all this was heard the fiend-like shriek of the wind, yelling as if the demon of desolation had been riding upon its blast...'

Describing stripped leaves whirling by as trees like terrified beasts groaned before breaking, he adds: 'There was...a peculiar and indescribable lurid, or rather bronze-like hue, that pervaded the whole face of nature, as if poison had been abroad in the air.'

Next day the Findhorn was up 50 feet. By the marker-stone above Randolph's Leap the Relugas butler caught a salmon in his umbrella. Aghast, Lauder watched his gardens vanish as tall ancient trees plunged into the flood. 'Never,' he wrote later, 'did the unsubstantiality of all earthly things come so perfectly home to my conviction.'

Outraged yet energised, he decided to record the wider ruin. For months he travelled every flood-struck river and burn from source to sea - a journey of some 600 miles. He gathered eye-witness reports, then in 1830 published a masterpiece of investigative journalism; *The Great Moray Floods of 1829*, now back in print (see bibliography).

Even more awesome than the chaos caused by the Spey (**52**) was the Findhorn's inundation of the Plain of Forres. Some 80 miles from source to sea, the Findhorn has less volume than the Spey, but is pent up in narrow gorges (Dulsie, Relugas, Sluie), while its flood-plain is broader than the Spey's. So a huge head of water burst over a vast area. Surging through the narrow neck at the Red Craig of Coulternose near Mundole, the torrent swept away the three-arched Bridge of Findhorn, then drowned over 20 square miles under up to five feet of water. From Mundole two miles west of Forres to Findhorn village four miles northeast the land was consumed. Forres folk retreated up Cluny Hill as the area north of Moy (Culbin Forest side of the A96) was cut off. 'Nothing could be more strange than to behold a sea of water from whatever window of the house one looked,' a witness reported.

A Dr. Brands, looking over the Broom of Moy, saw only a few roofs above the flood. With steadings, beasts and houses destroyed, many folk drowned, but more were saved by boatmen risking their lives to reach the stranded. Even so, there was humour. One rescuer, a Sergeant Grant, was offered a second dram to warm him. 'Na, I thank ye, Sir,' he said, eyeing it askance. 'I like it ower weel; an' if I tak it I may forget mysel', an' God kens we need to ha'e a' our wits aboot us the day. But an we get a' the poor fouk safe, I'se no say but I'se get fou.' And a man called Monro complained to Lauder: 'Was it na' hard that after a' that we had done, thay idle, weel held-up loons, the Preventives [Excisemen] gat a' the praise i' the newspapers, while we poor fisher bodies were never mentioned at a', although the lazy lubbers never pat their noses oot ower the door the hale day.'

Above the confluence of Findhorn and Divie you get some idea of the enormity of the torrent. As for Lauder, he was so heartbroken by the ruin of his estate that he returned to Edinburgh, never coming north again.

13.   The Findhorn at Sluie   *(Walk)*

Just north of Dunearn Burn (**7**) on the Findhorn's east bank is a fine walk above the gorge at Sluie. From Relugas, cross the Divie and climb past Logie House (see above) to the A940. Turn north towards Forres. After a long mile through woodland look for a small roadside sign, 'Sluie Walk' (014525). Turn left by the lodge into a carpark under the trees. Of two tracks converging below the lodge, take the lower one bearing right (west) towards the river, not yet visible. Start downhill between wood and pasture, bearing left to a steading. The long low building here, now a ruin, once housed five salmon fishermen and their families.

To reach the gorge directly keep left (east) of and above the steading into the wood. Yet also worth a look is the river north of the gorge, its placid shingle-banks under a ruddy, tree-crowned cliff. Turning right through the steading to a gate into pasture, stay above the wooded riverbank. Where the Findhorn bends almost back on itself, riverside access is easy.

Under steading and gate a track, no longer 'official', climbs steep left through beechwood. Suddenly, just before joining the higher path from the steading, appears a sight to make you gasp.

Unexpectedly far below, dark waters swirl between steep banks sprouting stunted silver birch. The well-made path with its rustic viewpoint benches follows the lip of the gorge through a deep cool forest of larch and Scots Pine. Douglas Fir, planted c.1870, tower overhead, creating a cathedral atmosphere. There is no danger. But take care if with children, or dogs, or if you don't like heights.

After nearly a mile the arrowed track reaches a clearing and turns sharp left, climbing away from the gorge into the wood. (Further along the gorge is a gate with the request: PLEASE GO NO FURTHER: one look at the steep wooded bank ahead and you may agree.) Following the forest track northeast, ignore a left turn and continue 400 yards to a T-junction. Bear right to a clearing past a derelict croft, then swing hard left and, now parallel to the A940 above through the trees, return to the carpark past more derelict crofts in the pasture to the left.

About three miles, there's no hard climbing and the path is fine all the way.

14.   Forres to Findhorn   *(Route)*

Two miles north of Sluie the A940 passes the pretty Loch of Blairs (fishing permits: 01309-672936), hidden behind woodland on the right, then a turn (9019559) to Dallas Dhu/Rafford, also on the right. Try this wooded back road, from which (025563) soon a track departs right to the lochside. Continuing to a junction (Forres left, one mile), turn right to Dallas Dhu (035567; 01309-676548). On the Whisky Trail and in care of Historic Scotland, at this former distillery you can learn in detail how whisky is produced. Continue east via the winding wooded road to Rafford, a scattered hamlet on the B9010 southeast of Forres, with on-going routes east to Pluscarden-Elgin (**16**) and south to Dallas-Knockando (**20**). The scenic Pluscarden road in particular is a good way to head east while avoiding Forres and the A96.

Back to the A940: it continues north, past a loop road to Mundole and the Findhorn, into Forres. Past a right turn to Dallas Dhu and a second right turn to town carparks and the Rafford B9010, cross a roundabout north to the A96 bypass (left to Culbin and Nairn). Turn right past the industrial estate and football park to the A96 roundabout northeast of Forres.

From the roundabout by Sueno's Stone the A96 runs east nine miles over farmland via Alves to Elgin (**22**), a route intersected by minor roads crisscrossing fertile coastland or climbing south via forests and moors towards Speyside. Alves, a hamlet flanking the A96, offers a ruined kirk (fine old tablestones) on the back road to Burghead (**29**); also nearby the Knock of Alves, said by some to have been where Macbeth (**30**) met the witches.

Also from this roundabout the B9011 runs two miles to Kinloss, site of a major RAF airbase which, like nearby RAF Lossiemouth (**35**), takes advantage of the Laich's flatness and mild climate. Since 1970 chief base of the Nimrod maritime anti-submarine squadrons, the end of the Cold War has led to cutbacks, but most days the Nimrods still lumber up into the sky then bellow down again, attracting planespotters. Here, where the B9011 breaks north, in a field south of the continuing B9089 is ruined Kinloss Abbey (065615). Founded in 1150 by King David I after a ghostly white dove guided him out of a forest where he was lost, it was abandoned after the Reformation, but not before the monks, famous tipplers, had founded an 'Ailhous' near Keith's Strathisla Distillery (**111**).

Turning north up the east side of Findhorn Bay with Culbin Forest (**4**) the far side, the B9011 runs four miles past Kinloss runways (stop lights when Nimrods take off or land), the Findhorn Bay Nature Reserve, and Findhorn Foundation to the picturesque coastal village of Findhorn. Now a conservation area at the sandy tip of this windswept peninsula and its three very different communities (military, 'New Age', and local) the present village is the third. The first, mentioned in 1189, was, like its successor in 1694 (**3**), lost to sea and sand. Once a trading and ship-building port, later a fishing village, today this yachting and holiday centre draws windsurfers, water-skiers, naturalists and geologists.

Between village and firth, curving almost over to Culbin, the sandbar called the Ee is, along with Galloway's Ae, Scotland's second-shortest name - the prize goes to the River E in Stratherrick, southwest of Inverness. Here seals bask on estuary dunes, bottle-nosed dolphins (**42**) sport offshore; waders, oystercatchers, widgeon, shelduck, cormorants and curlews, redshank and dunlin stay all or part of the year: in summer ospreys fish at low tide. The area, its geology a storybook of coastal erosion (**39**), hosts many fungi and lichens. Extensive dunes to the east offer interweaving walks: the sandy, forest-flanked shore continues to Burghead. With the Findhorn Village Heritage Centre (01309-690349/690659) open in summer; Culbin Forest dark and dense over the shallow bay, and fine views over the Moray Firth to the Black Isle and the mountains beyond, Findhorn is a must.

And close by is one of Moray's more unusual communities...

15.   The Findhorn Foundation   *(Visit, History)*

In the 1960s tales emerged from Scotland of how, on a bare, sandy site by the Moray Firth, grew a garden rivalling Eden. From California to Kabul 'New Age' seekers heard how in 1962, persuaded by the mediumship of their friend Dorothy Maclean, hoteliers Peter and Eileen Caddy had moved from Cluny Hill Hotel in Forres to a caravan park by Findhorn Bay. They were following, Dorothy claimed, the orders of nature spirits she called *devas* ('architects of the plant kingdom': apparently from the Sanscrit for a 'shining being').

So, *deva*-aided (no hard work involved?) soon – on allegedly poor shoreline sand and gravel - grew blooms so fine and cabbages so huge that scientists, it's said, were amazed. By the mid-1970s seekers, most from the USA and Northern Europe, were flocking to this Paradise Regained. Some stayed. The Californian 'human potential' movement came to the fore, marketing expensive therapies. The tales got taller. By 1979 a feature-length documentary played in US repertory cinemas, the camera dwelling on wild sky, bare land, and quaint locals (dialect subtitled) bemused by these emissaries from the developed world, or maybe from outer space. In 1981 noted French director Louis Malle made an art-house movie, *My Dinner with André*, in which *deva*-dazzled New York theatre director André Gregory tells sceptical actor Wallace Shawn how the roof of the community's Universal Hall - an elegant structure hosting world music and other events open to the public - had been levitated into place by the community's combined mind-power...

So by the mid-1980s the *devas* were back seat to a business now with annual turnover in the millions. Today, with thousands of visitors a year and a core of long-term residents, the Foundation (a registered charity) still occupies the caravan site. The caravans surround new eco-correct houses, some adapted from whisky vats. Emphasing the arts and holistic health, with residential courses and workshops for those willing and able to afford them, there is also a shop well-stocked with luxury foodstuffs (the bread baked on the spot is excellent), craftware, and 'alternative' titles, some published by the Foundation press.

With claims that the community is: 'a centre from where the forces of light will emanate to counteract the forces of darkness throughout the world,' the irony of the Foundation's proximity to the barbed-wire perimeter of Scotland's largest military airfield goes unmentioned in its publicity. And far from being barren, as the globally-marketed myth suggests, the locality is fertile, the climate mild, and the soil mostly good. With twenty hours of summer daylight, growth-rates can be fantastic, with or without *devas*.

16.   Forres via Califer Hill to Pluscarden   *(Routes)*

The most scenic route from Forres to Elgin is via Califer Hill and the Benedictine Abbey in the lovely Vale of Pluscarden, with an alternative route via Rafford.

First, from Kinloss the B9089 runs east over flat Laich fields, back-roads cutting right (south) over an open rise to a rural east-west route between and parallel to the A96 and B8089 via Coltfield, Standingstone and Westfield. A road on the left (114647) leads north a half-mile to Roseisle Forest Walks, less impressive than those at Culbin (**4**). Past Roseisle Maltings at a crossroads (124657) the B9089 forks left two miles to Burghead (**29**). The right turn leads to Alves (**14**); the road ahead meets the Burghead-Elgin B9013 at College of Roseisle (an early Celtic Christian settlement: 138665), a minor road continuing 200 yards to a fork - right northeast to Duffus, Gordonstoun and Lossiemouth; straight on up over bare Clarkly Hill and down, with fine Firth views, to the B9040 at Cummingstown (**28**)

For Califer Hill from Forres: at the roundabout by Tolbooth Street and South Street turn south (B9010) up St Leonard's Road past Leanchoil Hospital and Cluny Hill College, which is part of the Findhorn Foundation. Just past the 30-mile limit the road forks. The B9010 curves right to Rafford; the road ahead runs up then down to a crossroads (073575: left to the A96; right to Rafford past Blervie Castle, a crumbling 16th-century Z-plan towerhouse visible nearby).

Continue over the crossroads up Califer Hill's steep, twisting brae to a carpark and viewpoint at the top on the left. From here, with a rangefinder to identify distant hills, on a clear day you can see at least 60 miles in three directions – a fine spot! Continue east a mile to a junction (097577). For Pluscarden turn right, up over forested Heldon Hill and down to another junction. Turn left two miles down the long wooded brae, with views east to the Bin of Cullen (**122**), into the lovely 'Vale of Rest', Pluscarden Abbey prominent ahead to the left.

For the alternative Rafford route; if from Forres on the B9010 continue through this quiet mile-long residential dormitory; if on the A940 from Dallas Dhu (**14**) turn right on meeting the B9010 in the village. A mile past the last houses (Moor of Granary) a minor road breaks right (south) to Dallas (**20**). 200 yards on, a left turn (091556) zigzags uphill, at the crest picking up the road from Califer Hill (108557) then descending to Pluscarden. As for the B9010, it continues past a second turn south to Dallas, then follows the River Lossie past Kellas to regain the Pluscarden road just southwest of Elgin.

17. Pluscarden Abbey   *(Visit, History)*

The lovely vale of Pluscarden, below Heldon Hill to the north and the Hill of the Wangie to the south, demonstrates how medieval monks so often chose the best locations for their retreats. Descending into this broad fertile vale you see, a mile ahead over lush fields nestling under forested slopes, the restored roof and walls of Pluscarden Abbey, its grounds offering a tranquil stroll.

Pluscarden wasn't Moray's first monastic foundation. Besides early Celtic Christian colleges like Roseisle, Kinloss Abbey hosted Cistercians from 1150, and Benedictines from Dunfermline colonised Urquhart Priory (**38**) in 1136 - both founded by David I (1124-53). It was Alexander II (1214-49) who in 1230 invited the Valliscaulian order to establish houses both here at Pluscarden and at Beauly west of Inverness. Wearing white as with other Benedictine reform movements like the Cistercians, and named after their order's base in the Val des Choux ('Cabbage Valley') in Burgundy, they led a rigorous life. Daily at 2am they rose for a 90 minute service: Matins and Lauds. Daily they laboured and ate big meals (save amid fasts between September and Easter) between further observances: Terce, None, Vespers and Compline. They had no modern distraction. Yet controversy, commercial lawsuit and rumour of unmonkish desires accompanied Pluscarden's growth. Growing remote from its French mother house as the Wolf of Badenoch terrorised the area, in 1454 Pluscarden joined the black Benedictines.

After 1560, with monasticism suppressed, the Abbey would have become another old ruin save for the 3rd Marquess of Bute and his son, Lord Colum Crichton-Stuart. Born in 1847, in 1868 Bute, an orphaned earl, 'defected' to Roman Catholicism. In 1897 he bought Pluscarden from the Earl of Fife. When he died in 1900, his youngest son inherited it. 48 years later, the Abbey buildings were reoccupied by five Benedictines from Prinknash in Gloucestershire. Known as the 'Pluscarden Pioneers', they wore not the black Benedictine habit, but the white of the original Valliscaulians. History takes time to work out its cycle.

Today there is a working community at Pluscarden, its buildings restored through public appeal, with new stained glass in the north transept. The symbolic designs are modern, and appropriately so, but the surroundings are ageless - definitely a place to stop, maybe as prelude to a longer walk…

18.   Torrieston Forest & Heldon Hill   *(Forest Walks)*

From the Abbey turn east towards Elgin. A few yards on, under mature trees by Pluscarden Parish Church (1898), a lane on the right curls up the north flank of the Hill of the Wangie, then down to the Rafford-Kellas road. The high pastures and forestry offer no easy walking. Continuing east through the valley, past a second lane climbing right the road turns north over the Black Burn under Monaughty Forest slopes, then turns sharply east. Soon, before leaving the woods for farmland, on the left is Torrieston Forest Walks carpark (164588).

An information board tells how from 1819 James 5th Earl of Fife planted these slopes with larch, Scots pine and beech. With the mature wood felled 1899-1920, this became the Forestry Commission's first Scottish plantation. As for the waymarked walks (see a Forest Enterprise pamphlet, 'The Forests of Moray & The Deveron Valley': 01343-820223), you can follow these, or explore further. If the latter, take compass and map – though amid this maze the map may confuse. Tracks range miles along the spine of Heldon Hill – steep to the south, less so on the north (Monaughty Wood). Some aren't mapped; some that aren't there. Many intersect or wind confusingly: on a sunless day you can get lost. It takes time to decipher this maze, which has entry-points other than at Torrieston.

One is at Garrowslack on the hill's north flank. Here, with the slope mostly clear to the ridge, open views make it easier to work out connections. To reach the entry track (149602), from Torrieston continue east a mile to the hamlet of Miltonduff with its 1824 distillery. Turn first left (before the war memorial) by a school, and soon first left again past bungalows under the wooded hill. After over a mile park under a house where the road turns north to Carden Hill. Hug the verge: timber-trucks manoeuvre the tight turn from track to road. Another way to identify Garrowslack: red deer are pastured under the wood.

As for Torrieston, though rarely exciting (if ideal for marathon runners in training), especially along the ridge there are unexpected glades, views, stretches of heath, and hidden dells. And who knows, you may even meet a big black cat...

19.   Moray's Big Black Cats   *(Natural History, Folklore)*

In 1985 near Dallas eight miles southwest of Elgin, by the Hill of the Wangie ('wildcat'), a big cat was shot as it stalked pheasants. Jet-black and long-legged, spaniel-sized (36 inches long) with a long bushy tail, it stumped the experts. Unlike a lynx, puma, or any other big cat, it was not the Scottish wildcat, *Felix silvestris grampia*, nor was this the first shooting.

In 1983 a 42-inch cat had been shot at nearby Kellas after a spate of odd livestock killings. Walking cheetah-like with unretracted claws, it was stuffed and examined at London's Natural History Museum. A second 'Kellas Cat' was shot in 1984 at Revack (**97**) by Grantown, and a third in 1985 at Advie (**58**), one of these labrador-sized. The beast shot by Dallas (the fourth, and second locally) was examined by a vet and by the editor of the *Forres Gazette*, which has since reported other sightings, several in suburban Forres gardens.

Other large puma- or panther-like cats appear to prowl Ayrshire, Sutherland and the Inverness area. In 1980 a puma, 'Felicity', was caught in Strathglass. Oddly tame, she went to the Highland Wild Life Park (**69**) near Kingussie. Such reports go beyond Scotland. The 'Surrey Puma', the 'Beast of Exmoor' and other X-filed felines have padded into the news since the 1960s. Some sceptics try to pooh-pooh it all as on a par with Nessie or UFOs but, here at least, they're out on a limb.

Have some of these cats, like Felicity, been secretly released from private zoos? Have feral cats and wildcats interbred, or bred with imported big cats? How to explain the size, long legs and unretracted claws. Zoologists and biologists remain silent - and, interestingly, such reports are not new.

Back in January 1927 a wave of mystery predation round Inverness was attributed locally to big black cats of unknown origin, while 16th-century chronicler Ralph Holinshed, source of Shakespeare's *Macbeth*, remarks oddly that: 'Lions we have had very many in the north part of Scotland.' The possibility that for centuries unknown beasties have lurked in Highland forests may be reinforced (I like to believe it, anyway) by the folk-tale of Ailean nan Creach ('Alan of the Forays') and the cats. The following is one version:

Living by the River Lochy at the south end of the Great Glen, in old age this violent Cameron chief, a killer of many men, so feared for his soul that he asked a local witch to help him. She, apparently a devotee of the ancient divinatory rite of *taghairm*, told him to spit and roast his housecat live. He did so, but its screams attracted a horde of other cats to the open slope where he'd lit the fire. Not attacking, they watched the now-terrified old man. Soon came a gigantic black cat with fierce yellow eyes. Scattering the fire, it glowered at Ailean, then said: 'We will not kill you because you are a stupid and credulous man. But we will spare you on one condition only' – which was that he should build seven churches, one for each of his murderous forays, where no church had been built before.

Still think I'm telling a tall one? Then ask big-cat hunter Di Francis, who moved from Devon to Forres to study the Kellas Cats then tried to breed and domesticate them. Read her *Cat Country: The Quest for the British Big Cat* (1983) and *My Highland Kellas Cats* (1993) – the latter a sad tale in that, to date, these cats do not seem to thrive in human company.

20. Loch Dallas & Glen Lossie   *(Routes, Walk)*

This 14-mile circular hike round Loch Dallas and back by Glen Lossie offers solitude and fine views, but is exposed, so check the weather forecast.

From Forres take the B9010 past Rafford to a right turn (085545) seven miles through high wooded land to Dallas, or follow the B9010 to a T-junction (127530) under the Hill of the Wangie, and turn right to Dallas. From Pluscarden turn left then right over the Hill of the Wangie to the B9010 at Edinvale: turn left one mile to the T-junction, as above.

From Elgin, take the Pluscarden road a half-mile to Pittendreich (194613) and turn left to Dallas (10 miles) via the River Lossie's west bank, past back-roads to Miltonduff, also past a left turn (199584) east to Birnie Kirk (**27**). Past the whitewashed roadside cottages of Kellas continue under the forested Hill of the Wangie to a T-junction (127530: see above). Here turn left past a ruined towerhouse half-a-mile into Dallas, a remote single street hamlet. At the war memorial turn left to Knockando (right if from Forres/Rafford). By the school before Lossie Bridge turn right past Dallas kirk then, over the Lossie, left. Follow the riverbank road a mile south past Craigroy. Park at a four-way junction (121499) by a wooden bridge over a burn on the left and start southwest to Auchness Farm (signposted).

The first mile climbs past Auchness (shut the gate: there are ponies about) via an old drove road past a waterfall. Leaving the glen, head southwest over heather moor then, after a mile, west through a narrow pass under crags past a ruined croft and broken bridge. Continue west over a vast flat, planted as far as the eye can see, with no easy way south over deeply-ditched ground and up the scarp. The track improves, but this three-mile slog west above the plantation is tedious. Views briefly open up before, at last, a passage through mature forestry enters open moor above the Findhorn, so reaching a Y-fork (064481).

Turn left, southeast, towards a white house (Rochuin) visible on the moor a mile away. Cross a locked gate onto the track through the young plantation. Beyond a second gate over a crossing, pass the turn to Rochuin. With forestry left and open moor right, the track climbs east for a mile. Leaving the wood, it curves north past a track to the glacial sink of Loch Dallas (088471). Swing right here on the south-east edge of the next new plantation a half-mile to double gates, a new forestry road to the left. The OS map shows only a path running due east, not the new road.

Take this new track round a small hill, down a bare glen, and curve up past a blocked access, Loch Dallas below, to a new junction,. Keep right (east) over the broad crest of Carnachie (359m). The trees planted here don't yet block a view from over the Firth to Ben Rinnes (**55**) and the Convals. This view lasts the next two miles, wide over forestry and bare hills. Ignoring all junctions, descend to and cross the young Lossie in its shallow tree-fringed glen. Its sound, besides that of the wind, may all you heard in the last ten miles.

Bear left (northwest) onto the main track east of the river, up and out of the glen. Keep left at the next moorland junction (124469), and left again onto an older, grassy track, a few yards on. Here the map may again confuse: only one junction is shown. If you reach a quarry (fresh views of Ben Rinnes), you missed the turn.

Now east of and above Glen Lossie, follow the older track north as views open up. Past ruined Torwinny by a shattered plantation, the track descends through silver birch to the mouth of the glen, crossing the Lossie above Ballachraggan. Walk the metalled farm-road northwest a mile back to the bridge where you began.

Footsore? Of course. Happy and thirsty? Hopefully.

Next is Elgin, world capital of the whisky trade. First, as we'll not be here again, the route southeast seven miles from Dallas to Knockando (**57**) above the Spey's west bank.

Crossing the Lossie this narrow road climbs a wooded brae to high heath and moor before crossing the Burn of Corrhatnich, a Lossie tributary. After two miles of forestry (east of this last walk), the road reaches open moor with wide views over the Spey to Ben Rinnes and the Convals. From here, with deer-fences and locked gates discouraging walkers, the road descends rough pasture over Knockando Burn to the hamlet of Knockando, Tamdhu and Cardhu (**56**) distilleries nearby. A B9102 left turn here runs northeast to the Elgin A941 just south of Rothes (**49**). The right turn (the scenic Speyside route) continues southwest to Grantown. All of which soon.

2

'Elginshire'

Elgin to Burghead & Lossiemouth

21.   Introduction: Elgin & The Laich

Moray, as Sir Robert Gordon of Straloch in Aberdeenshire noted in 1640, 'much exceeds our other northern provinces. The air is so temperate, that when all around is bound up in the rigour of winter, there are neither lasting snows, nor such frosts as damage fruits and trees; proving the truth of that boast of the natives, that they have forty days more of fine weather in every year than the neighbouring districts.'

Clearly a skilled publicist, Sir Robert had a point. Moray has many charms, and among them is Elgin (pop. 20,000), an old cathedral city occupying fertile ground five miles south of the coast. Bisected by the A96 and by the Lossie, which burst its banks in July 1997, this busy commercial and administrative centre is named, perhaps, after Helgy, a 10th-century warlord, or maybe from the Gaelic *elg*, 'Little Ireland' – suggesting early settlement of the area by Irish Gaels.

Either way, Elgin once gave its name to the old county which, later Moray, after 1974 absorbed much of Banffshire east of the Spey.

After exploring Elgin and Spynie Palace nearby, this section circles the area round Elgin, avoiding where possible the main A96 east to Fochabers (**45**), where it forks: east (A98) past Buckie (**115**) and southeast (A96) through Keith (**111**).

South of Elgin, the A941 runs through Fogwatt (**25**), where fields give way to rising moors before at Rothes (**49**) it joins the main Speyside route south. With Dallas to the southwest and Pluscarden to the west, to the north the ports of Burghead and Lossiemouth, seven miles of cliff-hemmed shore between them, are linked by the B9040. Passing through Cummingstown and Hopeman, a popular holiday resort, east of Hopeman the B9040 sheds the B9012, which breaks south through Duffus past Gordonstoun (**34**) to Elgin. The B9040 continues east to Lossiemouth, five miles north of Elgin via the A941. East of this road and between the A96 and the coast, back-roads run through rolling fields and woods past the Binn Hill to Garmouth and Kingston-on-Spey (see **39**; also next section).

22.   Elgin's 'Lantern of the North'   *(History, Description)*

With a rich history, fine architecture, and a well-preserved medieval street plan, Elgin was made a royal burgh by Alexander II (1214-49), in whose reign and after 1224 a magnificent cathedral was built as the seat of the Diocese of Moray.

Sited by the Lossie east of Cooper Park amid what was once the Chanonry (a walled ecclesiastical mini-city, four-gated and in circuit over half-a-mile), enough of the 'Lantern of the North' survives to suggest its former splendour. Yet its history is full of misfortune. Torching it in 1390, the Wolf of Badenoch (**10**) was not the only vandal. Rebuilt by 1460, in 1506 its central tower collapsed. Again rebuilt, with a new tower and spire 198 feet high, in 1560 (the income for its upkeep 'expropriated' by Patrick Hepburn, Moray's last Catholic bishop) it fell into disuse. In 1567, the Earl of Moray stripped its roof of lead to pay his soldiers. Dismissed as 'a piece of Romish vanity, too expensive to keep in repair,' its decay was hastened by Covenanters destroying the rood screen in 1640. On Easter Sunday 1711 the tower collapsed, wrecking the north transept and nave arcades. For years thereafter the ruin was used as a quarry and 'receptacle of filth and rubbish' before, in 1809, a wall was built round it and a keeper appointed. Excavations by John Shanks, keeper from 1825 to 1842, led to money being raised for its preservation.

Now restoration work continues, aided by Historic Scotland. With the adjacent remains of the Bishop's Palace (1406), and a small shop, it's open most of the year (01343-547171).

A poignant tale connects it with a large, solid 19th century building in South College Street - Anderson's Institution, named after General Andrew Anderson, whose mother-to-be Marjory Gilzean fell for a soldier, Andrew Anderson of Lhanbryde (**38**). Marrying him in 1745, she followed him to India, but in 1748 returned, alone and destitute with an infant - the future general. Disowned by or avoiding her family, she sheltered in the cathedral, in a room still with roof, chimney, walls and window, using an old ceremonial basin as crib. So, 'baptised in tears and cradled in stone', the boy grew, his food and clothes provided by charity. Schooled as a pauper as Marjory travelled about spinning linen, he paid for his education by cleaning the schoolroom. With a bed of straw and a door of bundlings of broom, his mother remained in the ruin. 'I'm not afraid of the dead,' she once said, 'they are very quiet neighbours, it's the living - if they would let me be.'

Joining the army, in India Andrew prospered. Visiting Elgin in 1811 with his mother 20 years dead, he arranged for the foundation of the 'the noble and useful institution...opened in Elgin in 1832, for the Education of the Young and the Support of Old Age.' Did he have a bad conscience about his mother?

Though in 1784 one critic reckoned that Elgin 'in filthiness exceeded all the towns of the north-east,' by 1840 the burgh, with New Elgin developing to the south, was transformed by the new wealth of returning colonials. Notable amid that era's neo-classical architecture and dominating the now-pedestrianised High Street is austere St Giles (1825-8), a fine example of Scotland's Greek Revival. In a wynd off the High Street, which also features the arcaded façades of buildings like Braco's 1684 Banking House, is Thunderton House, now a pub, once a royal residence and townhouse of the Earls of Moray. West of the High Street, atop Lady Hill (site of the old castle) the 1839 column commemorates the 5th and last Duke of Gordon (**68**). Amid Cooper Park is Grant Lodge, built *c*.1750 for the Earls of Seafield; while nearby at Newmill is Johnston's Cashmere Visitor Centre (01343-554099). Elgin Museum (01343-543675: by the Little Cross at the head of the High Street), displays Pictish remains, including two of the Burghead Bull stones (**29**), and fragments from what may have been a Pictish royal court at nearby Kinneddar (**35**). Lastly, nearby and also in the High Street is the tourist information centre (01343-543388), alone in the district in being open all year.

23. Quarry Wood   *(Walk)*

The congested main A96 and A941 siphon traffic through central Elgin past the St Giles Centre, but the bustle is easily avoided. After exploring the centre, Cathedral and Chanonry grounds, from Cooper Park cross the A941 west to Lossie Green to follow the riverbank behind the football ground and Mansion House Hotel. A footbridge by Haugh Road crosses to Ladies Walk on the north bank: a little further along this wooded path a second footbridge (Mary Well Bridge) recrosses the river, the path continuing to fields round Old Mills – a working water-mill with a wood-turner's shop, as shown here. The mill is open to the public: tel. 01343-540698.

For a longer hike, Quarry Wood (416 feet) just northwest of Elgin offers pleasant exercise. Served by a carpark (called Quarrelwood) by the 30mph limit on the B9012 northwest to Hopeman/Burghead, it can as easily be entered by continuing from Old Mills. With Elgin Academy over the river to the right, keep north over Bow Brig (1630-35: the Lossie's oldest stone bridge). Cross Morriston Road. Bear left then right up Brumley Brae 100 yards to Oak Wood and a sign: 'Pedestrian Paths'. (If driving west from central Elgin, from the A96 Bilbohall roundabout turn right up Old Mills Road past Old Mills, as above.)

At wood's edge, take the higher of two paths, keeping left at a fork. Continue southwest along the bank above houses to a path crossing, where oak gives way to silver birch. Turn right uphill into forestry by a bridle path sign burned into a tree-stump. Cross a clearing under power-lines, then a forestry road, and carry on 200 yards to a crossing at the edge of the wood (194634). With the Laverockloch animal by-products plant over open ground to the right, follow the wood's edge gently uphill and northwest for a half-mile.

At the ridgetop views open up north, from Duffus Castle (**33**) and Covesea Lighthouse to the Bin of Cullen (**122**) twenty miles to the east. Turn left (west) along the ridge-top track into the wood. At a crossing after 200 yards stay left; the rough track ahead dead-ends at a quarry. Continue through the pines to a clearing, then on along a broad, dull forestry road. Where views west open up a main left fork turns hard back to a turning-circle. From that a faint path descends south through the wood, not far, to the east-west path on the hill's south flank, parallel to and above the A96. This is the short option: see below.

For a longer walk, ignore the fork. Keep west and downhill 300 yards. Just after a path by a fence to the right, a path descends left (south) into the wood. At a fork after 200 yards turn left (east) along the south slope. With A96 traffic audible below, contour along the wooded slope to a clearing with fine views south past Heldon Hill (**18**) to the moors, and west past York Tower (**28**) to Forres, the Black Isle and the hills beyond Inverness.

Passing the junction with the faint descending path (short option above) continue southeast downhill over three path crossings. At a junction not far above the now-audible A96 turn left onto a broad path and over other crossings, bearing left above Elgin until back where you turned right on the bridle path. Having come full circle, return as you came.

24. Spynie: The Palace of the Bishops   *(History, Visit)*

Entering forestry a mile north of Elgin on the Lossiemouth A941, with cleared ground on the right look for a Historic Scotland sign to Spynie Palace (231659), once Scotland's greatest ecclesiastical palace after St Andrews. Abandoned in 1686, this vast, semi-restored ruin tops a bank above swampy woodland where sea-going ships once anchored. Yet soon after the palace was deserted sandbars blocked the sea; Spynie's tidal reach became a marshy loch; Lossiemouth became Elgin's new port, and rooks inherited the palace begun some 400 years before by the Bishops of Moray. As for the loch, it was mostly drained by 1812, when the remarkable engineer Thomes Telford dug the canal to Lossiemouth (**35**).

A palace? With Scotland's largest towerhouse, it looks more like a fortress. Here in 1390 Bishop Burr fled after the Wolf of Badenoch sacked Elgin Cathedral. The arms of Bishop John Innes (*c.*1406) decorate the gateway; but the massive, five-floor bulk of Davy's Tower dominates. Named for Bishop David Stewart (1461-77) who began the work when the Earl of Huntly swore to 'pull him from his pigeon-hole', it was completed by William Tulloch (1477-82). As for the gunports, installed at a level to make your stomach knot, they were the work of Bishop Patrick Hepburn (1535-73), who had reason to fear attack.

Governing Moray like a Machiavelli and seizing church revenues for his own use, twice at Spynie he welcomed his infamous great-nephew: James Hepburn, 4th Earl of Bothwell. That he welcomed Bothwell's second visit in 1567 suggests he thought blood thicker than holy water. Shocking Scotland more by marrying

Mary Queen of Scots than by blowing up Lord Darnley, with his army melted away Bothwell had fled the wrath of the Lords. Declared traitor, with Mary jailed at Loch Leven, this suspected warlock fled via Huntly and Spynie to Orkney. Turning pirate, he was hunted through Norway to Denmark, where in 1578 he died in jail. No wonder his great-uncle was Spynie's last Catholic bishop.

With a visitor shop and picnic area, Spynie Palace is open daily 1 April-30 September; weekends only the rest of the year (01343-546358).

Unseen from the palace, a remnant of Loch Spynie survives. Flanked to the west by the old railway track south from Lossiemouth past Spynie Palace, from which Old Spynie Kirk is visible above fields 400 yards to the south, this hidden water hosts swans, gulls, heron, mallard, coot and oystercatcher. On autumn nights up to 7000 greylag geese from Iceland rest here before moving further south. Now down to about 100 acres, the loch continually decreases due to plant succession at its verge. An SSSI (Site of Special Scientific Interest) part-managed by Scottish Natural Heritage and on private ground, for access to its waterside hide apply to Pitgaveny Estate Office, Elgin, Moray IV30 2PQ (tel: 01343-551436).

Old Spynie Kirk, the burial place of Ramsay Macdonald (**36**), is reached via Linksfield Road, a minor road leading from Lesmurdie Road in Bishopmill on the northeast side of Elgin. With many old tablestones on its mounded rise, the kirk here was replaced in 1736 by New Spynie Kirk (182643), above the Laich off the B9012 two miles west of Elgin.

Next, the area immediately southeast and south of Elgin, leading to a walk round Millbuies Country Park, then exploration of the Birnie-Glenlatterach back-lands.

25.   Southeast of Elgin   *(Routes)*

East from Elgin the A96 runs ten miles to the Spey through rolling farmland inter-sected by minor roads. The coastal area north of the A96 is explored later: here I outline routes boundaried to the north by the A96; to the south by the A941 to Rothes.

A mile east of Elgin past a lane north (left) to Elginshill the A96 is inter-sected by the B9013 from Lossiemouth. Via a staggered crossing this route (now the B9103) continues south to Cranloch/Rothes past Coxton Tower (262607), a 1644 Innes towerhouse: to visit, call Mrs W Christie: 01343-842225. Crossing the Fogwatt-Lhanbryde back-road, a mile on and hidden behind woodland opposite the Strypes/Teindland turn is peaceful Lochnabo (fishing permits: 01343-842214). Climbing to open heath past a left turn to the Animal Country Hotel (a monocled cigar-smoking Scottie in a deck-chair?) in three more miles the B9103 joins the Mosstodloch-Rothes B9015 at Inchberry (310550).

Continuing east past Lhanbryde (**38**), with left turns at the bypass round-abouts leading north to Urquhart, Garmouth and Kingston, the A96 takes up the Fogwatt road. A half-mile on, before a left turn to Urquhart, the old main road breaks right past Loch Oire, rejoining the A96 west of Mosstodloch, a mile-long Elgin dormitory. Here the B9015 crosses, south to Rothes, north to Garmouth. A little way on, by the Ben Aigan pub, the Essil road starts north past the Red Kirk, also to Garmouth (41). Finally, on the Spey's west bank opposite a southbound lane to Dipple and Inchberry, is Baxters of Speyside, a well-known family business producing speciality foods. With gifts, crafts and a woodland walk, the visitor centre is open daily (01343-820393). On the far side of the Spey is Fochabers (45).

Save by detouring south to Boat o' Brig (48), the A96 Spey crossing is unavoidable. From Elgin, eastward routes avoiding the A96 a few miles at least run north and south of it. A longer, quieter southern route to Lhanbryde starts from the roundabout at the bottom of Moss Street. Crossing the railway on the southbound A941 (signposted Perth), at a second roundabout by the mart, with New Elgin ahead, turn left onto Linkwood Road, leaving Elgin past Linkwood Distillery. Two miles through rolling land leads to the Fogwatt-Lhanbryde road (255597). For Lhanbryde turn left a mile to the B9013, then left and immediately right to the A96 at Lhanbryde bypass. The right turn leads to Fogwatt and Millbuies – our next stop.

From Elgin the A941 runs south to Fogwatt/Millbuies. Crossing the railway follow New Elgin Road out past the Birnie turn (27) by the 30mph limit. The A941 continues three miles past Benriach Maltings, Longmore Distillery, another Birnie turn, and Glen Elgin Distillery to the hamlet of Fogwatt. Here, with the A941 climbing on through Glen Rothes past a trout fishery then the 1893 baronial extravaganza of Rothes Glen Hotel, turn left (Lhanbryde 4), then after 100 yards right as indicated, uphill to Millbuies Country Park

26.   Millbuies Country Park   *(Natural History, Walk)*

Millbuies is a miniature wonderland of flora, fauna, and peaceful woodland walks round the side of a mile-long artificial loch in a deep trench.

This trench between upland moors and coastal plain was created by the event that made Britain an island and Scotland habitable: the global warming ending the last Ice Age. The Laich was created by debris dumped by glaciers retreating west. Before this, the huge volume of water pouring from the hills, ice-blocked, cut a path down the ice. As the flood fell, its debris formed a lateral moraine by the ice. Later, with the ice in final retreat, the meltwater cut in behind the moraine, so creating the Blackhills Meltwater Channel (also see 89).

Dammed *c.*1900 by Millbuies' then-owners to create a fishing loch, on retiring to Lossiemouth in the 1930s Singapore tea-planter George Boyd Anderson brought the estate. Planting many rare trees and shrubs, in 1956 he gifted it to Elgin via the Town Council. In 1975 Moray District Council took it over, maintaining the policy of planting rare species.

From the carpark by a rhododendron trail above the valley the walk offers fine views north over Elgin; the 'Tree Trail' leaflet identifying the exotics - Grand Silver Fir, Violet Willow, Atlas Cedar, Western Hemlock and others - on the banks under the commercial forest. The placid, narrow loch has paths both sides. Halfway along it a stone causeway and rustic footbridge join the opposite banks. Near a majestic Wellingtonia - the giant Sequoia which in California grows over 350 feet high over two millennia - a turf-roofed cabin invites a picnic, or simply a gaze over the water. There are some 30 species of rhododendron here; the 'Plant Trail' leaflet identifies rare exotica like the Mountain Pepper plant. Swans, mallard and tufted duck float; sparrowhawks hover and buzzards sail; and you may see roe deer.

This is a delicate environment. There is no swimming, canoeing or camping, but there are picnic and barbecue facilities, while from April to mid-October rods can be hired to fish for trout. The loch is stocked fortnightly; for two in a boat the current charge is £16 daily; for OAPs, £6. Scrambling and mountain bikes are discouraged, as is horse-riding; the paths are easily damaged. Dogs under control are welcome; either bin your litter or take it home. An orienteering map is available at Elgin Tourist Office. Visited annually by over 20,000 people, prettiest in summer, Millbuies is open daily dawn to dusk. (Warden and bookings: 01343-860234; Glenlatterach fishings are also booked from this number.)

27.   Glenlatterach, Shougle & Birnie   *(Routes, Walk)*

Above the Lossie between A941 and the Elgin-Dallas B9010 (**20**) is an area easily missed. Climbing the moors, it's reached from New Elgin by the Birnie road south past the golf course. A mile on, with a belt of forestry to the left, is a right turn to Birnie Kirk (206587), a 12th-century seat of the Bishops of Moray. On an old mounded Culdee site, this plain but robust parish church with Romanesque apse was dedicated to the Irish saint Brendan the Navigator (*c.*489-583). The claim, long disbelieved, that Brendan reached America in an ox-hide coracle was proved possible when in 1976-7 explorer Tim Severin made the same voyage in a replica of Brendan's boat as described in the medieval *Navigatio*. Severin's account, *The Brendan Voyage*, is required reading for all armchair travellers.

The road continuing west joins the B9010. Returning to the junction above, turn right south past the Glen Lossie distillery complex and, at nearby Thomshill,

Andrew Brown

Moss Street

Keith .

engine
driver

junction (214567: left to the A941; see
)s right to a second junction (209553).
)ast Glenlatterach water treatment plant
ire moor. Opened in 1957 to provide
buies), this is a dreich spot, the sloping,
narrow channel carrying run-off into a
ich, the Lossie Basin's biggest waterfall
, is another fall. The burn, running north
).
00 yards to Shougle steading, there pass-
scattered crofts to Bardonside, where the
Moss of Birnie down the western fringe
Iannoch to Cardhu Distillery (**56**) by
an means 'fairy hill'.)
gotiates scrappy woodland then the north
h over Elgin to Covesea Lighthouse by
:nds left then right to thick forestry and
941 at Fogwatt a mile further on.
'560) a broad track with a sign asking you
. With room to park, the track breaks north
he Fogwatt-Birnie road (222570), gaining
ng of a weak bridge ahead, this lane bears
len Lossie Distillery. The entry to the track
it lies a mile west of a turn from the A941

n a mile to a junction at Birnie (214567: see
t up the lane to Glenlatterach/Shougle, then
)lete this quiet back-road circuit.

(Routes)

n (B9010 to Dallas; the Miltonduff road to
ribed (**16, 18, 20**), and needs no more notice
it farmland between Miltonduff and the A96.
duff road just after the B9010 turn south to
Dallas, runs west to Arves, c.. . 70615) crossing a lane north from Miltonduff
to the Elgin-Forres A96. The latter joins the A96 by Toll Cottage (1821) with its
blue-pillared Doric porch and Tudor chimney-stacks.

Dominating wooded Knock Hill above this junction is York Tower
(163630). Three-storeyed and octagonal with bricked-up windows, over its locked
door is a plaque with the legend YORK TOWER JAN 5 1827, and by it an iron-

fenced memorial to members of the Forteath family. Visible over much of the Laich, it commands fine views, northeast to Covesea (**32**), south to Ben Rinnes (**55**), up Glen Rothes to Ben Aigan (**51**), and west to Forres. It stands within a large prehistoric fort, sections of the ramparts surviving.

West of Elgin under Quarry Wood (**23**) the A96 passes what used to be the Oakwood Motel (1932: 185627); a tree-framed log roadhouse with timber shingles, its style more Montana or Manitoba than Moray. Continuing past a turn north to New Spynie Kirk (see below), after three miles and just past Toll Cottage it sheds the B9013. Running northwest to Burghead, after 200 yards or so this road passes Newton House (1852; a turreted, crowstep-gabled baronial confection) on the left, then continues straight over flat Laich farmland past College of Roseisle and the B9089 from Kinloss (**16**).

Almost as direct a route to Burghead from Elgin, with better views and more interest, is the B9012 via Duffus and Hopeman. Leaving Elgin from the A941 through Bishopmill north of the Lossie, passing turns west to New Spynie Kirk (**24**) and east to Duffus Castle (**33**) it weaves through Duffus to the coastal B9040, which runs through Hopeman and Cummingstown to Burghead - a place of weird atmosphere, tradition, and history.

29.   Burghead - Well of the Past   (History)

Jutting northwest into the sea like a bull's horn, Burghead (pop. 1420) may be the 'Winged Camp' (*castrum alatum*) noted by Ptolemy after the Romans rounded Britain in AD86. Famed for its annual fire festival (**31**), the town is named after the old Norse 'borg' or fort on the rocky seaward promontory. Carbon-14 dating of charred wood from the site suggests an earlier Pictish fort *c*.400, three stone ramparts 240m long once guarding an enclosure 300m deep. Long after Irish Christians established the College at Roseisle nearby Sigurd Earl of Orkney and his Norsemen arrived, felling forests to build the 'borg'. They named the place Torfness for the 'torf', local peat they exported to Norway. Though driven out by the Scots in 1014, their victory here in 1040 led to Macbeth (**30**) gaining the Scottish throne.

From the coastal B9040 the first sight of Burghead is wrecked by the incredibly ugly concrete maltings dominating the grey, grid-plan 19th-century promontory streets, these flanked by slated freestone houses. West of the harbour (1807-10, extended 1881) and its large stone granaries, the broad beach, good for winter birdwatching, curves five miles to Findhorn (**14**) under Roseisle Forest. As for the old fort once on the seaward point, little is left - but under its perimeter, reached by green-banked steps, is a spooky subterranean grotto - the 'Roman Well', or St Aethan's Well. Rediscovered in 1809, later rebuilt, in this barrel-vaulted chamber is an ancient, spring-fed square stone tank, the narrow walkway round it sometimes flooded. You can get the key from Mrs Main, 69 King St., Burghead (tel: 01343-835559). If she's not in, it's in the porch, above the well's visitor book.

So, how old is this weird and mysterious place? And how was it used? A

Christian baptistery after the Pictish conversion? If so, what of the bull-carving found there? Dated *c.*500 and one of several locally, it suggests ancient bull-cults as in the myth of Theseus and the Minotaur ('Bull of Minos'), and surviving church dedications to St Taur in the Languedoc and Spain, land of the bull-fight. Celtic druids identified bulls with the sun; pagan Ireland's great epic, *Táin Bó Cualnge* ('Cattle-Raid of Cooley'), was about a war to steal a famous bull.

With bull-worship went well-worship. Celts (including the Picts, Welsh/Brittonic P-Celtic speakers as opposed to Q-Celtic speaking Gaels) believed that oracular spirits lived in wells, demanding sacrifice for health or good luck. Not pennies but severed human heads once dropped into wishing wells, the Celts believing that by taking your enemy's head you got his soul-strength. As Sueno's Stone (**2**) suggests, this gory custom endured. Erected in 1812, the monument to The Well of the Seven Heads by Loch Oich in the Great Glen recalls a feud between the Macdonnells of Keppoch and Glengarry. Glengarry men beheaded seven Keppoch brothers. Washing the heads in the spring *Tobar nan Ceann*, the bard Iain Lom gave them to Macdonnell of Glengarry as a mark of the 'summary vengeance' taken.

Were folk ritually drowned in the Burghead Well? Sculptor's Cave at Covesea (**32**) suggests child sacrifice in the early Bronze Age, four millennia ago, long before the well. The truth is, nobody knows, any more than it's clear when Burghead was first fortified, nor how many battles were fought here, the most crucial of them in the year 1040...

30.   Meeting the Real Macbeth   *(History, Speculation)*

Little in Shakespeare's 'Scottish tragedy' (few actors dare name it in fear of the curse on it since its fated London premiere in 1606) relates to the real Macbeth

(Maelbaetha or Mac-Bethad, 'Son of Light': King of Scots 1040-1057). He probably never met three witches, was not a tyrant or wife-ridden usurper, did not slay Duncan at Inverness, and he died at Lumphanan in Mar, not Dunsinane in Perthshire. Yet maybe he *was* fooled by an advancing wood – the way a Scots army had earlier fooled the Norse at Portknockie (**119**).

To portray 'that dead butcher and his fiend-like queen', the Bard used the *Chronicles* of Scots 'historian' Ralph Holinshed. These (via Aberdonian Hector Boece) were negatively influenced by the 233 year-long rule of the dynasty birthed by Macbeth's nemesis, Malcolm Canmore - Canmore meaning 'Great Head' or, as some have it, 'Bighead'.

The Canmores had good reason to malign Macbeth. Kin of the slain Duncan, they were long plagued by his descendants, the unruly men of Moray.

Macbeth was son of Findlaech mac Ruaidri, Mormaer ('Great Steward') of Moray. Murdered by the sons of his brother Maelbrigte in 1020, in the *Annals of Ulster* Findlaech is named *ri Alban*, meaning a (not the) king in Scotland. The House of Moray was highly-placed, and in constant conflict with the southern House of Atholl. Born in 1005 near Spynie, or maybe at Dingwall, Macbeth spent most of his life in Moray, even after his coronation. Records of Celtic monks of the old College of Roseisle call him their friend and near neighbour. By birth he was Thane (*ri*) of Ross, becoming Thane of Moray by marriage to Lady Gruoch, daughter of Boedhe, a son of King Kenneth IV (995-1003). Another tradition has it that, after killing Duncan, he married Duncan's widow, 'Dame Grwok'.

As to Duncan's death and Macbeth's succession, accounts vary, but a 'history' may be suggested as follows. At Torfness (Burghead) on 14 August 1040 the Scots under 'the pure and wise' Duncan engaged the Norse Earl Thorfinn the Mighty. Of the House of Atholl and High King since 1034, that year Duncan had already failed in attacking Durham, and Thorfinn had just whipped him at Deerness: Duncan was already in flight. The chronicler Marianus Scotus says Macbeth was Duncan's general yet maybe, given their later friendly relations, Macbeth and Thorfinn were allies. Duncan was Macbeth's cousin, but so was Thorfinn. Macbeth and Moray men had no reason to support this unpopular, incompetent High King who saw Moray as foreign. One tradition says the battle was between Duncan and Macbeth, Duncan trying to invade Moray from the sea.

With the battle lost, Duncan fled, to be slain *a suis occisus est* ('by his own people') at Pitgaveny near Loch Spynie, or in a shed above nearby Hopeman. Did Macbeth deal the killing blow? Marianus Scotus says so. Certainly Duncan's three sons fled the kingdom after his victory. Yet the 'usurper' ruled so successfully that for 14 years there is no tale to tell, save that, by 1050, Scotland was at peace and Macbeth went as a pilgrim to Rome. Hardly a case of 'uneasy lies the head'. But in 1054 Malcolm Canmore invaded from England and defeated him at Dunsinane, then in 1057 slew him at Lumphanan.

As for Duncan: the Scots assumed the right to kill a bad king. Poor rule meant common misfortune. Yet of Macbeth, within a generation of his death it was written that 'in his time there was fertility' (*fertile tempus erat*). If truly a tyrant, he'd never have lasted so long. As Shakespeare also assassinated the character of Richard III to legitimise his Tudor and Stuart patrons, so he and Canmore chroniclers maligned Macbeth - the last great champion of Moray as a kingdom.

29. Burning the Clavie   *(Visit, History)*

Get to Burghead's Granary Street (the Old Manse Dyke) by 6pm on January 11 each year (if January 11 is on a Sunday then a night earlier) to join in one of the most exciting of the few remaining midwinter/New Year fire-festivals still celebrated in Scotland – the Burning of the Clavie; a ceremony by which Burghead folk (Brochers) have long seen in the New Year.

Similar festivals occur in Stonehaven (January 1st), and at Lerwick's Up-Helly-Aa, where the last Tuesday in January a replica Viking longship is torched. Yet the Clavie may represent the purest continuity of a rite once universally celebrated each New Year.

But why January 11th, not January 1st?

In the 1750s the old Julian Calendar was replaced by the more accurate Gregorian Calendar. Eleven days were lost. Throughout Britain folk rioted, demanding back their lost days. But the Brochers stuck to January 11th as the true New Year, and ever since, save during the World War II blackout, they've celebrated a fiery New Year on January 11th.

Once the Clavie was a herring barrel filled with tar and packed with staves. The barrels came from Archangel on the White Sea. In the 1960s creosote replaced tar, and iron-hooped whisky barrels began to be used, but in 1998 the current Clavie King Dan Ralph built a replica Archangel barrel. Flatter-sided than a whisky barrel, and with hazel hoops, it was a success, as usual being nailed on a carrying-post; as usual with the same nail, a granite boulder hammering it in from the inside.

Lit by a peat from the hearth of an old Burghead Provost and with fire now leaping, the crew of ten or eleven local men (usually from the fisher families of More, Main, Davidson and Ralph) set off. Taking turns to carry this burden (over two hundredweight when full) they walk a time-honoured route clockwise round Burghead's streets. At houses where prominent citizens once lived, bits of burning Clavie are thrown into the doorway to bring the inhabitants a year's good luck. As pieces fall from the flaming barrel, the pursuing crowd (bigger every year, news crews present) scrambles to grab their own piece of the coming year's fiery good luck. Burghead's three pubs also get pieces of the Clavie...

With stops to refuel the barrel, the hour-long tour finally reaches the stone altar atop the Doorie Hill. On the ramparts of the old fort, this may once have been a beacon point. Set up here, the Clavie has another barrel hoisted atop it, then in the dark January night the crew hurl fuel, nowadays diesel, onto and about it until the entire hill is ablaze. Leaping 30 feet high and visible far over the firth, briefly this roaring inferno drives back winter.

Elsewhere the Kirk successfully banned such festivals, but in Burghead the Clavie endures. Both a rite of the sun's return and a trial of strength for the young men who carry it, it is impressive. Our ancestors had no electricity, no gas fires: they had to keep the hearth fire going all year long, and the Clavie ceremony reminds us of those hard times. Plus it's great fun.

Best organise a taxi to get home afterwards, or persuade a teetotal friend to drive. And next day, to get over the hangover, why not walk the cliff-bound cave-wormed coastline from Clashach by Hopeman just east of Burghead, to Covesea a mile west of Lossiemouth?

32.   Coastal Caves: Burghead to Lossiemouth   *(Walk)*

The 30 miles of coast east from Inverness is mostly low, sandy, and forest-fringed. At Burghead it changes dramatically, huge sandstone cliffs overhanging the rocky, pot-holed shoreline for most of the seven miles to Lossiemouth, after which sand and shingle fringes the long curve past Spey Bay to Buckie (**115**).

From Burghead you can walk east, first via the old railway track to the neat holiday village of Hopeman (founded 1805), then by or below Hopeman golf course to Covesea and Lossiemouth. If planning to take on the rocky shore past old smuggling caves and coves, first two *caveats*. Often on tumbled, seaweed-slick rock, this trek is hard on the feet and demands good boots. And be sure of the tide. If not well out or on the ebb, don't try it. There is quite a way to go, with some stretches so cliffbound that retreat may be impossible.

For a shorter circular route past the finest caves and stacks and back via the clifftop, drive the B9040 east through Hopeman and on a half-mile to the B9012 Duffus-Elgin turn south. Take the rough track opposite, north towards the sea. With Hopeman golf course to the left, park by the gate (158698) signposted DANGER: CLASHACH QUARRY.

Start northeast up the track beyond the gate. Soon, with fine sea views and the clifftop path bearing inland past the quarry, a gap in the gorse leads to the crumbling cliff-edge and steep sandy paths down to Clashach Cove. Bear right above the beach to a long narrow cave, then duck through a natural arch east onto the rocky shore. Head east through a maze of sea-carved, pot-holed tidal rock onto rock slabs past quarried rubble to a heathery path under the cliffs and Clashach Quarry. Hereabouts raised beaches and fossil cliffs show how the sea was once some 17 feet higher. The weed-slick rocks, from the Permian-Triassic era, are a mere 225 million years old. Skid on over them to a giant cave, huge smooth boulders on its sandy floor, then emerge by a low, narrow, second exit into a cliff-hemmed cove - Seagull City. There's a fine beach, with raucous cormorants on the sea-rocks beyond hanging out their wings to dry.

Round the next point a path escapes to the clifftop as the beach gives way to tumbled boulders needing care, above them a cave halfway up the cliff - the entry to the tunnel said to run a mile to Gordonstoun (**34**)? This tricky section rounds yet another point to a grassy bank and the ugly barbed-wire entry to the recesses of Sculptor's Cave (175708), its smooth inner walls bearing ancient graffiti. In human use since at least the Bronze Age and possibly as far back as 5000BC, this gloomy hole may have seen ritual human sacrifice of children during the Bronze Age. Much later Pictish artists carved the symbols - some crude, like the crescent and V-rod near the west entrance; others more stylish, like the triple oval and flower on the roof above - that give the cave its name.

Next, the going still rough, appears the triple entrance to another huge cave ('Sir Robert's Stables': also **34**). Here a friend asked drily: 'Would you take your Granny on this walk?' Continuing under the coastguard lookout, soon a ladder in a cleft allows hard access up the now-lower cliff to the path above. In the next cove, steps carved in the rock also allow escape up a gully to the path. The initial three-foot step is difficult.

Further on is a grand bouldered cove, a freestanding two-legged stack inviting entry to caves and hollows in the cliff. Beyond it, an easy path up a grassy bank joins the clifftop path, Covesea Lighthouse ahead (204704) – the name apparently from *Causie*, the causeway once under Loch Spynie. From here on to Lossiemouth is mostly sandy beach, but if your car is at Clashach, it's from here you start back the easy way along the rising clifftop path, a vast panorama all about and, far below, the rocks you cursed but hopefully enjoyed.

For the short way to Smuggler's Cave and the others, midway between Hopeman and Lossiemouth the B9040 passes a small plantation on the left. At its eastern edge (179701) a gated, surfaced road breaks north. Park by the gate and follow this road past a transmitter station, then down a grassy slope to the coastguard lookout. Turn right along the clifftop path to descend via the path to the stone steps and cove described above.

Again, please check the tides and take care.

33.   Duffus Castle   (Visit, History)

Unique in Scotland atop its steep Norman motte, ruined Duffus Castle (188673) dominates the plain that was once under Loch Spynie (**24**). A mile southwest of RAF Lossiemouth, reached by turning east off the B9012 (see **21**) a mile south of Duffus, it is rarely quiet, with shark-like jets roaring over its roofless keep. This is appropriate. Warplanes now rule the air as warriors once ruled the land. Picts, Gaels, Vikings and others fought to call Moray their own. Duffus Castle is a relatively new addition to that long history of fierce attack and desperate defence.

The site was probably first fortified *c*.1150, not long after the Scots crushed the Picts then drove off the Norse. Yet before we get nationalistic, who were the Scots? Ulster Gaels, certainly, migrating to Argyll after *c*.450AD. And who were they? The Irish *Lebor Gabala* ('Book of Invasions') describes five invasions, more myth than history, but suggesting a constant Celtic influx from the early Iron Age on; i.e., from *c*.800BC, and from all over Europe. The final arrivals, the Children of Mil, had allegedly come from Milesia, meaning Spain - but where had they been before that?

From *c*.1400BC the Urnfield (cremated ashes buried in urns) and Hallstatt (iron-working) Celts inhabited a region between Bavaria and Bohemia, long thought their original home. Yet Celtic place-names (like *nemeton*, 'grove') exist in central Turkey, while Celtic marriage customs, poetic conventions and religious beliefs parallel those of India's ancient Brahminical culture. The Gundestrup Bowl, dug out of a Danish bog and 2000 years old, suggests Indian workmanship. It seems proto-Celts emerged from central Asia *c*.2000BC, moving both east and west. Flamboyant, poetic, sentimental, credulous, quarrelsome, generous, superstitious yet subtly-spoken, they were fierce in war but always feuding and fatally unable to sustain their gains. Sacking Rome in 386BC and Delphi in Greece a century later, they were divided, first by Romans, later by Germans and Anglo-Saxons, and so driven to the 'Celtic Fringe' - Brittany, Cornwall, Wales, Ireland and Scotland.

Of course, the Scots gene-pool isn't Gaelic alone. The earlier Picts and Britons probably interbred with descendants of the Beaker folk, who'd probably done the same with the megalithic folk, who...and so on. The Norse, themselves Indo-European, were also part of the story by the time Pictland became Scotland *c*.850 while (to further confuse matters), a century before Duffus Castle was built, Normans from France, originally Norse, invaded England (a Celtic land seized by

Germanic Anglo-Saxons) then came north to Scotland.

Which brings us to Freskyn, who first fortified Duffus. A Fleming, from what is now Belgium, and Norman by culture, he held land in West Lothian, before David I encouraged him to settle at Duffus. With other strongholds in Strathnairn and on or by Loch Flemington near Inverness, this he did, building a wooden fort atop the motte. A generation later, his son William - a popular name after 1066 - took the title 'de Moravia' - 'of Moray'. By 1200 the house of de Moravia was the strongest in north Scotland. When the male line perished c.1270, the de Moravia heiress Mary married Sir Reginald le Chen (from Aberdeenshire, not France), who as an Anglo-Norman supported the Anglo-Norman king Edward's attempt to annexe Scotland. So Scots patriots burned down his wooden castle at Duffus.

Early in the 14th century a stone keep replaced it. It seems nobody knew of the old saw about castles built on sand. The northern wall, notably the latrine-block, subsided to its current angle; and the keep was abandoned for more comfortable quarters below.

Taken over by the Earls of Sutherland (Freskyn's descendants) c.1305, the castle was held by them until 1705. Later the Duke of Sutherland, the Most Noble George Granville Leveson-Gower, second Marquess of Stafford and as Scottish as they come, became known as the 'Great Improver' due to his success in replacing folk with sheep. His vast effigy still looms a hundred feet high above the summit of Ben Bhraggie near Golspie and Dunrobin Castle. As for Duffus Castle, its ruin is now maintained by Historic Scotland, and is an excellent place to meditate on what is or is not 'Scottish'.

Curried haggis, anyone?

34.   The Wizard of Gordonstoun   *(History, Folklore)*

The famous boarding-school Gordonstoun (185690) lies amid woods east of Duffus and near RAF Lossiemouth. Founded in the 1920s by a pioneering German educationalist, Kurt Hahn, its mixture of study with strenuous outdoor activities has, some say, helped to form the character of the present British royal family.

Originally a keep built by the Marquis of Huntly to consolidate Gordon power, for centuries this 'ghostly old palace' (as a 19th-century author put it) was the home of lairds with an evil reputation. Of them all, the most notorious was the 17th-century architect of Gordonstoun's Round Square - Sir Robert Gordon, alias the 'Wizard of Gordonstoun'.

Known as '...the wisest o' warlocks, the Morayshire chiel/The despot o' Duffus and frien' o' the deil,' this gloomy, reclusive scholar was feared as a satanist. Studying mechanics and chemistry in Italy, on return to Scotland he retired to his vast library, shunning daylight and human company, the night-time glare of his forge attracting superstitious comment. It was said he lurked indoors because Satan had stolen his shadow; that he'd built the Round Square so the Devil couldn't catch him in the corners (see **74**); that a fire-imp in his furnace told him forbidden secrets; that witches and warlocks attended his weird revelries. It's told how he'd ordered his coachman to take a short-cut over ice-bound Loch Spynie, insisting all would be well if the man rode over the thin ice without looking back. Yet near the far shore the coachman had turned, to see not the laird but a great raven perched on the carriage. The demonic bird had taken off, shrieking, and the coach had sunk. As to the Wizard's fate, of course it was hideous. Fleeing towards Birnie (**27**), he was caught and mauled to death by two hell-hounds directed by a rider on a coal-black horse.

Such tales, eagerly believed, typify an era of witch-trial and fear. Sir Robert's studies and correspondence with Sir Robert Boyle and other great thinkers impressed local opinion no more than his sea-pump. Of this the diarist Samuel Pepys, then Secretary of the Admiralty, says that it was: '...tried in the fleet and highly approved of, and found far to exceed anything of the kind then known...' As for his elegantly Italianate two-storeyed Round Square, kirk-ridden zealots saw it only as evidence of how much the Wizard feared his Infernal Master.

Yet Gordonstoun lairds were hated with reason. From the start they'd grabbed land and despoiled tenants, brutally asserting their claim to pit and gallows. The Water Dungeon, a hole in which semi-tidal sea-marsh rose to torment captives, was especially feared. Along with the 'hoodie craw' and the 'gowd' (a yellow weed that choked cornfields), this family was one of '...the three worst ills that Moray e'er saw.' Such popular hatred bred insecurity. The old mansion was riddled with secret passages, sliding panels, and refuge-holes, many made by the Wizard's son, also Sir Robert, a gloomy tyrant said to have spirited contraband from Covesea's caves to Gordonstoun via a now-lost tunnel. In one cave, 'Sir Robert's Stables, he hid cattle and horses during the '45 (**32**). Though briefly imprisoned, he held

Gordonstoun for 70 years, succeeding only in further blackening the name of his father and family. The conclusion? Maybe the Wizard should have stayed in Italy...

35. Lossiemouth: Home of the Zulu   *(Description, History)*

On a promontory above broad sandy beaches five miles north of Elgin, this resort town with its golf courses and RAF base dates from the 1690s when the old port at Spynie silted up (**24**). With a new harbour built at the mouth of the Lossie and Old Lossiemouth later laid out on the west bank in 1764, a fishing community at Stotfield to the west worked from the Hythe. This ended on Christmas Day 1806 when 21 men and boys out at sea in open boats perished in a storm. After that, Stotfield men fished with the 'Doggers' of Seatown or 'Dogwall'; so-called due to its inhabitants' use of dogskins as floats or buoys.

Growing wealth from herring led to a new harbour (1837) and, above it, the town of Branderburgh, founded by Colonel Brander of Pitgaveny (see **38**). Gradually the three communities merged into the present town (pop. 7350). At first, with fishing done from 'scaffies' and 'fifies', Lossiemouth was just one of many working ports, but here in 1879 the first 'Zulu' drifter (named after the Zulu wars) was designed by 'Dad' Campbell. Until 1900 built from Nairn to Fraserburgh and with five local shipyards turning them out, they put Lossiemouth on the map, landing their catch as far south as Lowestoft. In 1900, the steam drifter arrived; and in 1928 the first modern seine-net vessel was designed, again in Lossiemouth.

The Fisheries Museum (Pitgaveny Street; Easter-September: 01343-813772) and booklets by local man William Stewart (Pilot) explain all this. Also in the museum is a reconstruction of the study in his Moray Street house of Lossie's most famous son - Britain's first Labour Prime Minister, James Ramsay MacDonald (see below).

Today a holiday and golfing centre, Lossiemouth is best-known as the home of RAF Lossiemouth, one of Britain's most important front line stations. Housing three RAF Tornado squadrons, this base just west of Stotfield is often in the news for the air-sea-mountain rescues conducted by its Sea King helicopter crews.

Two roads run south towards Elgin; the A941 (Elgin Road) and, from the B9040 by Stotfield, the B9135. Past the airbase, a mile before joining the A941, the B9135 passes Kinneddar Churchyard (223694). With Birnie (**27**) and Spynie (**24**) this was a seat of the Bishops of Moray before Elgin Cathedral (**22**) was built. Maybe among the first local sites of Pictish Christianity, Kinneddar was certainly a religious centre by 934, being associated with the oratory (or death) of St. Gerardine/Gervadus at Kenedor. Here, it's said, this Pictish evangelist hid from the Norse. Later Lossiemouth incorporated in its coat of arms an image of Gerardine patrolling the shore on a stormy night, seeking wrecked mariners to rescue.

Besides the kirkyard there's little at Kinneddar now, but St Gerardine's High Church (1901), red-roofed and Italian-styled high on Prospect Terrace, is visible miles away.

36.   Ramsay MacDonald & the Moray Golf Club   *(History)*

The Moray Golf Club course at Stotfield is rarely peaceful. The B9040 to Burghead winds through, while the roar of Tornados touching down on adjacent runways can be incessant. Yet the racket is minor compared with the furore of 1916 when some club members called for the expulsion of Ramsay MacDonald, claiming that his membership demeaned the club. Born at Gregory Place in Lossiemouth in 1866, in 1894 joining the Independent Labour Party, in 1906 this local loon made good became Leicester's Labour MP, and in 1910 party leader. Enjoying his golf, when staying at 'Hillocks' in Moray Street, the house he built for his mother, he played at Stotfield. One day in 1913 he was out with Liberal PM Herbert Asquith who, married to Margot Tennant of the family owning Innes House (**38**) near Elgin, had holidayed locally since 1905. Nearing the 17th green with MacDonald, Asquith was attacked by two suffragettes, one allegedly Christabel Pankhurst. Though charged with breach of the peace and briefly jailed, they went on spoiling his holiday.

Worse was the storm that hit MacDonald when the Great War began. A pacifist, on resigning the Labour leadership he was attacked in the press as a pro-German public enemy. In 1915 the jingoistic magazine John Bull called him 'Traitor, Coward, Cur', then descended still lower by calling him the 'illegitimate son of a Scotch servant girl.' Such slurs should have got him loyal local support. Yet one noble band of golfing patriots could not tolerate him. Ignoring the fact that he'd visited the Front in 1914 to report for the ambulance corps, which was closer to the action than any of them had been, in 1915 they tried to eject him. The motion failed, but in a 1916 meeting in Elgin, a London barrister, Noad, again moved to expel him. With new members drafted in to vote him out, the motion was carried 73-24, despite much disgust at what MacDonald, writing to the club secretary, called the 'political prejudice and spite' involved. At the time, the club had 564 members, 239 of them women without a vote. Deciding not to sue, MacDonald removed his game to the Spey Bay links (**41**).

Even more amazing, when in 1924 he became Britain's first Labour Prime Minister, a motion to reinstate him (though carried 55-45) failed, a two-thirds majority being required. Only in 1929, when again Prime Minister, did the club agree to reinstate him. Refusing to reply, MacDonald wrote to James Brander Dunbar, Laird of Pitgaveny, that the club had been humiliated, not he, and that he would stick with Spey Bay. There it ended, though George Bernard Shaw's reference to a 'stupendous collection of golf snobs' is not forgotten.

This is told in John McConachie's 'The Moray Golf Club at Lossiemouth 1889-1989' (Moravian Press, Elgin 1988). The best biography of MacDonald (he died in 1937 and is buried in Spynie churchyard) is David Marquand's 'Ramsay MacDonald' (1977).

37.   The Lossie Estuary   (Walk)

East of Lossiemouth sand-then-shingle beach runs seven miles to Kingston-on-Spey and the Spey estuary. Before exploring that, here is a six-mile route from the estuary via the river's south bank southeast through the woods to Arthur's Bridge, then back on the north bank.

A quiet stream winding north from Glen Lossie and Dallas (**20**) through Elgin to the sea, the Lossie attracts anglers seeking flounder, eel, finnock and brown trout. Yet lately its luck has been poor. In 1983 spills of Protim wood preservative, a toxic organochlorine pesticide, killed its fish and contaminated its eels; and in July 1997 the river burst its banks after a deluge, causing huge damage in Elgin and flooding the farmlands about.

While in Lossiemouth climb Prospect Terrace on the steep bank above the Seatown, St. Gerardine's Church prominent at the head of School Brae. Enjoy the view over the Seatown and estuary to the forests and hills beyond, then descend to park at Gregory Place by the Seatown, near Ramsay Macdonald's birthplace. Follow the river's south bank past the East Beach footbridge to the caravan site.

At the far end (parking here too), the road ends by a gate. Beyond it, a pebbly track or the riverbank leads to the woods ahead. The estuary, rich in birdlife, is easily waded at low tide. Where stunted spruce begins, the track becomes a sandy path along the forest's edge, curving gradually away from the river. (The riverbank path, at first vague, in time leads to Coral Cottage (253681), there leaving the river to join the route described below).

Leaving the river to follow a ditch through tussocky grass and gorse, the track enters the wood. A plantation leads to mature wood and a track intersection. Bear left over a larger track, the B9013 to the right, Coral Cottage in the wood to your left. Continue parallel to the road through heathery open Old Scots Pine. Where faint paths crisscross on a bank above the (hidden) River Lossie, bear right to the road at Arthur's Bridge (253673). Ignore the rough path on the river's west bank: it ends on meeting the Innes Canal.

Over the bridge follow the road round a bend some 200 yards to an unrailed bridge across the canal opposite Inchbroom steading. The rough track left over the bridge leads in 100 yards to two houses at the edge of Lossie Forest (257671). Here, with the main forestry road continuing east gated and locked, turn left past a Forestry barrier (Walkers Welcome sign) onto a mossy track running north along the edge of the wood. The track meets and follows the canal.

Ignoring all right turns, keep left into deeper wood, in a mile or so emerging by the river where the canal joins it. With Lossiemouth visible ahead the river nears the estuary, forest falling away as between river and sea broad East Beach with its broken shells and less lovely debris takes over. If the tide is out you can explore the estuary flats. If not, follow the outer dunes back to the rivermouth and footbridge over to Seatown, noting a sign by the footbridge warning of strong currents and the danger of bathing here.

38.   Urquhart & Lhanbryde to Garmouth   *(Routes)*

Just before the Lossiemouth 30mph limit on the Elgin A941 the B9013 to Fochabers breaks left into Lossie Forest. Crossing the old railway track then Telford's 1812 Spynie Canal, the road, at first straight, twists through sharp woodland bends three miles to Arthur's Bridge (see above) over the Lossie. By a gravel quarry just before the bridge a minor road (253674) breaks right over flat farmlands four miles to Elgin, *en route* passing Pitgaveny, a mansion amid rich woodland built in 1776 for Lisbon merchant James Brander, his family prominent in Lossiemouth history. Pitgaveny may also have been the site of Duncan's murder (**30**).

Beyond Arthur's Bridge and the track over Innes Canal into Lossie Forest, the B9013 crosses flat land past RAF Milltown's aerial arrays. On a disused airfield, these arrays monitor ground-to-air and ship-to-shore radio communications.

Amid a beech copse just beyond, a left turn (256649: signposted Milltown/Urquhart) by Leuchars House leads past Milltown's council houses to a woodland crossroads. Here a right turn leads to the hamlet of Elginshill; the left turn to tall, elegant, L-planned Innes House (1640-53: 279660), long home of the Tennants. The heart of Innes Estate (*inis*, 'island': in 1157 Malcolm IV gave marshland between the Lochs of Cott and Spynie to Berowald the Fleming), its walled garden is open to the public in summer. The continuing road and the Elginshill turn rejoin in a half-mile at another crossroads (276637); the quiet village of Urquhart (site of a vanished Benedictine Priory founded in 1136: see **17**) on a rise a half-mile southeast; the route northeast passing Urquhart Stone Circle (289641) by another crossroads. From here it's south to Urquhart; north past the hamlet of Lochhill to Lossie Forest; or straight on a mile on past the southern flank of wooded Binn Hill with its many tracks (park at 306648 where the road meets the wood: see below), and so on over rolling coastal farmland to Garmouth.

Back on the B9013 by Leuchars House and continuing south, in 400 yards a minor turn right (to Kirkhill) crosses the Lossie over a humpbacked bridge by a large steading. This leads to Elgin, picking up the Pitgaveny road (see above) at the 30mph limit before meeting Newmill Road in Elgin.

The B9013 continues south over a crossroads (Elginshill east, Elgin west) to a large roadside kirk (255619): here a lane breaks east to Darkland and Urquhart. Yards further on the B9013 meets the main A96 before, via a staggered crossing, continuing south as B9103 past Coxton Tower (**25**) towards Rothes and Speyside.

Running east, the A96 bypasses Lhanbryde via roundabouts either end of this now-peaceful village (pop. 2050). Named after the enigmatic Celtic saint (see **76**), enlarged by new housing estates, Lhanbryde has a churchyard full of old table-stones, including the effigy of Innes of Coxton. From Lhanbryde two roads break north. One, from west of the village, crosses the Darkland-Urquhart route to meet the Elginshill-Garmouth road; the other, from amid the village, heads past Muir of Lochs four flat farmland miles to Garmouth with, after a mile, a left turn through Urquhart to Lochhill and Lossie Forest.

This backland maze is mostly flat, in places fertile, often wooded, and annually subject to fierce sandstorms...

39.   The Unstable Coastline   *(History, Walk)*

Shaped and fertilised by glacier, river and sea, the Laich is prey to natural disasters. In AD1010 and again a century it was inundated; in 1694 the Culbin sandstorm forced the Findhorn east to its present exit (**3**) even as the sea-mouth at Spynie silted up. In 1829 came the Muckle Spate (**12, 52**), while recent years have seen floods almost as catastrophic.

East of the Lossie, when Beorald the Fleming gained what became Innes Estate he got more swamp than land. In time the Loch of Cott and the marshes were drained, creating new farmlands east to the Spey estuary.

Wind, wave and sand...the tight-packed spruce of Culbin, Roseisle and Lossie is unlovely, but holds the sands in check. Every year after inland fields are sowed spring gales whip up violent sandstorms. Dun clouds hide the Binn Hill as topsoil swamps roads then blows out to sea. This awesome waste annually suggests the Laich's instability - and so does the seven-mile shoreline walk from Lossiemouth to Kingston.

Starting from Lossiemouth's East Beach, after two miles the broad sands give way to vast shingle-banks piled high by Spey Bay tides. The dunes behind are forest-hid, but clearly this coast is precarious. World War II concrete tank-traps starting near the Boar's Head Rock (188679) and continuing almost to Kingston suggest a danger greater than mere human warfare. Graffiti-rich gun-emplacements facing the sea from the forest's sandy edge also carefully watch the pounding sea, driven back from this land just 10,000 years ago. The Boar's Head rocks (and the boiler of an old wreck nearby) are visible only at low tide, but flocks of gulls and eider duck betray their presence. The nets of salmon fishermen who worked this point for years are gone, though their bothy lies not far into the wood.

The shoreline route on to Kingston can be varied. By the Boar's Head, where two tank-traps lie dragged aside for tractor-entry (the shingle here is quarried), turn south on a sandy path up a straight forestry cut. Cross two east-west tracks to the Innes Links – an open hollow, 50 yards wide and running east to west. Paralleling the shore for three miles, this may be an old riverbed. Keep south to the forest's edge, the Binn not far to the east, the farm-track ahead continuing south through open fields to Lochhill and Urquhart.

Here (284671) turn east on the broad track just inside the forest. Ignoring left turns, continue east a mile past a derelict cottage into dense forestry under the Binn's steep north face. Reaching a rifle range, pass behind the firing-point – on the shoreline track red flags warn when the range is in use.

The Binn, the only hill hereabouts and so a landmark, is not to be confused with the higher, more elegant, equally coastal Bin of Cullen (**122**). Yet like the latter it offers many woodland paths, and fine views from its northern ridge. It is best approached by parking two miles west of Garmouth on the minor Lochhill road (306648: see above).

Beyond the range, a broad open gravel-course meets scrubwood, broken ground, and acres of shingle - The Lein, Scotland's largest shingle system, and a Wildlife Trust Reserve. Here the shoreline has often shifted. Each of the many ridges was once a beach; each offers many habitats; marsh, swamp and heath. Up to 30 feet deep, the shingle runs almost a mile inland and most of the way west to Lossiemouth. Now, amid dense undergrowth, return to the shoreline path for the final lap into Kingston by the Spey, and to a very different region.

*The Spey Estuary looking inland (see **42**)*

3

Lower Strathspey

Garmouth to Aberlour & Grantown

40.   Introduction: The River Spey

Often impetuous, as rich in scenery and history as in the malt whiskies associated with it, Britain's fastest river flows 98 miles northeast from Loch Spey (1143 feet) in the bare Monadhliath highlands to Moray's coastal flatlands and the sea. *En route* passing the Cairngorm plateau, it fertilises the forested haughs of Strathspey, inhabited long before the Romans (who named the river Tuessis) here found a folk they called the Vacomagi.

Today, with the ancient Caledonian forest (see **89**) mostly gone, Speyside hosts an economy embracing tourism, farming, forestry, distilling and outdoor sports: from skiing and climbing to hunting, shooting and fishing. With large tracts of this famed salmon river and the land about privately owned, demands made on both by rival interests at times cause dispute, with areas where walkers are definitely unwelcome.

Speyside is famed for its salmon fishing, but more so for its *uisquebaugh*, the Water of Life. 'Freedom and Whisky gang thegither', Robert Burns wrote 200 years ago, celebrating the illicit distillation which so flourished after the '45 that the Revenue Men, unable to stop it, instead licensed and taxed it. Now there are so many distilleries that north of Grantown on the A95 to Elgin few miles pass without one, on or off the 'Whisky Trail'. Yet 'Speyside' malts are distilled less by the Spey itself than its tributaries - Fiddich, Dullan, Avon, Livet, Lour and others. 'Speyside' embraces an area broader than the strath (wide valley) of the Spey alone; just as 'Glenlivet' is now hyphenated to the names of malts distilled as far from Glenlivet (**104**) as Elgin.

'Speyside' also means the 'Speyside Way', a 46 mile (58km) walkers' track which (via riverside paths, back roads, abandoned railway, forest and moorland tracks) follows the river as best it can, given geography and private objections, southwest from Spey Bay to the Avon-Spey confluence at Ballindalloch, there turning southeast over the moors past Glenlivet to Tomintoul (**100**). From Craigellachie a spur (**53**) follows the Fiddich to Dufftown; a coastal spur runs east from Spey Bay. Some of the walks soon described follow the Way, but only in part: most are circular; the Way is one-way.

As for the term 'Strathspey',besides referring to the Spey Valley alone it evokes Gaelic music, dance, history, culture; it implies the ancient Vacomagi, the fierce Wolf of Badenoch and the confederation of Clan Chattan; it resonates with battles fought for lost causes - Glenlivet in 1594 (**103**), Cromdale in 1690 (**58**), and Cumberland's pursuit of the Jacobites in 1746 (**43**); it summons up the ghosts of redcoats, excisemen, outlaws like Sheamus-an-Tuim (**101**), and mistier beings - kelpies, bodachs, witchesand warlocks, the fey folk in their knowes, and grislier beings high in the misty hills (**92**).

But first things first. Let's start with Speymouth.

41.   Garmouth & Kingston   *(Routes, History, Walk)*

Facing windblown Spey Bay on the east side of the Spey estuary, the west bank villages of Garmouth and Kingston are reached from Lhanbryde (**38**), or by the B9015
from Mosstodloch (**25**) on the A96 west of Fochabers, or via the prettier Essil road.
Starting 200 yards east of the B9015 by the Ben Aigan pub, this route passes the
distinctive Red Kirk (1733) and Essil Cemetery's 18th century tablestones, some
with skulls and crossbones, then joins the B9015 in Garmouth (pop. 350).

Settled by the 12th century and made a Burgh of Barony in 1587, here in
1650 this old village of crooked wynds and houses built of shoreline boulders saw
the return from European exile of the future King Charles II, this a year after his
father was beheaded in London. Carried ashore by one 'King' Milne, he was made
to sign the Solemn League and Covenant, which he later repudiated. A plaque on
the wall of Brae House by the Loanies marks the site. Later exporting grain and
manganese and importing coal and glass, Garmouth lost this trade when the 1829
Muckle Spate (**52**) altered the river's course and estuary. Here, the last Saturday
every June, is held the Maggie Fair, so-named in 1681 to commemorate Lady
Margaret Kerr, wife of Sir James Innes.

With the Binn Hill (**39**) two miles west on the Lochhill road, from School
Brae in Garmouth a footpath crosses fields half-a-mile north to Kingston-on-Spey
(pop. 250). Formerly the Port of Garmouth, the village is named not after Charles
II but Kingston-upon-Hull in Yorkshire, home of a Mr Dodsworth who, along with
Osbourne of York, here developed a timber-export and ship-building business after
1786 (see **89**). With timber rafted down the Spey from Inverdruie, seven shipyards
arose. Long superseded by Clydeside yards which by 1850 built cheaper iron-clad
vessels, these yards have vanished. Either end of this exposed village's two parallel east-west streets, carparks by the shingle banks cater to the Spey Bay Wildlife
Reserve (Scottish Wildlife Trust). To the east (right), at the head of the B9015 from
Garmouth, 'Birdwatch Corner' overlooks swan-rich lagoons which, until 1989,
adjoined the estuary, now by Spey Bay on the east shore. To the west, at the end of
Beach Road, a second carpark serves the shingle-banks, flora and wildlife of the
The Lein (see **39**).

The oldest building here, Dunfermline House, was founded by the monks of
Urquhart Priory (**38**), itself settled from Dunfermline Abbey. Later renamed Red
Corff House, then again the King's Barn, it contained an almshouse, the Blue
Anchor Tavern, and (appropriately) a lock-up for drunks from the tavern.

To get from here across the estuary to Spey Bay by road means returning to
the A96 at Mosstodloch, turning east over the river, then taking the B9104 north:
10 miles or so. Why not walk it instead, via the 1886 railway viaduct? From
Garmouth Hotel take the Lemanfield (Essil) road 100 yards south to the bridge over
the old railway track, embanked above the golf course one side and flat pastures the
other. Here, amid the Muckle Spate, the Spey ran a mile wide. As for the viaduct,
two years after it was built the Spey again changed course, which is why you're

almost over before meeting the main stream. On the far side, follow the track 200 yards to the Speyside Way. Turn north to windy Spey Bay, where in 1989 a new river mouth was cut to draw the flow away from Kingston. As a result, new shingle banks now run 200 yards further north into the sea than before. These formed in three years, and now the unpredictable Spey again seems to want to go west.

42.   Spey Bay: Moray Firth Dolphins   *(Wildlife, Boat-trips}*

With a hotel by the links to which Ramsay Macdonald (**36**) took his game, Spey Bay's estuary carpark is usually busy, even in winter. With a summer exhibition on local wildlife and salmon-fishing, the old Tugnet ice-house is graced with animal mosaics made of river pebbles by pupils of Milne's High School in Fochabers, and by David Annand's fine bronze of an osprey taking a salmon. Nearby the Moray Firth Wildlife Centre (01343-820339: open daily March-October; weekends November-December), caters for lovers of osprey and other wildfowl and waders, also of otter, seal, and harbour porpoise. But its special focus is on the bottlenose dolphin (*tursiops truncatus*), sadly now threatened by Moray Firth pollution.

Several herds, maybe 130 individuals in all, of these magical creatures range the firth from Kessock and Cromarty to open sea off Aberdeen. Descended from a warm-blooded mammal which some 70 million years ago (about when the dinosaurs perished) returned from land to sea, they're often seen offshore between Findhorn (**14**) and Findochty (**116**), especially between June and September. Travelling fast in search of cod, herring, salmon or mackerel, up to four metres long and 350 kilos in weight, these very smart mammals, once inaccurately called 'The King of Fishes', navigate by echo-location, can stay submerged up to 20 minutes and may live 40 years or more.

Tales of dolphins rescuing drowning mariners by guiding or towing them to land led many early folk to believe them semi-divine. In ancient Greece they were associated with the goddesses Aphrodite and Thetis, also with the sea-god Poseidon. Thought to guide the souls of the dead to the otherworld, it was a capital offence to kill one even by accident. Venerated by ancient Celts, Hindus and Sumerians, more locally and lately along the Banffshire coast they were called 'lowpers' or 'lowper dogs'. It's said that in the 1950s a herd chased a school of her-ring into Burghead harbour and onto the beach, providing the Brochers (**29**) with a welcome free fish supper.

Often seen bow-riding pilot whales or large ships, with its short, prominent beak and sickle-shaped dorsal fin the protected bottlenose is the Moray Firth's best-loved denizen. Yet at least four other dolphin species visit the Firth; sperm whales have lately grounded by Cullen and near Nairn; a hump-back whale was seen off Lossiemouth in 1983, and an orca (killer whale) off Hopeman. The grey or common seal is often seen; also the shy harbour porpoise, bullied and even sometimes killed by our friend the bottlenose - behaviour more human than we might care to admit...

To learn more, visit the wildlife centre, where the daily movements of the dolphins are recorded, or contact The Friends of the Moray Firth Dolphins (Pete MacDonald, 4 Craigview, Findochty, Banffshire AB56 4QF: 01542-833867: call to book dolphin-spotting boat trips). Karl Neilson (Benbola, 21 Great Eastern Rd., Portessie), also runs dolphin-spotting trips: contact him at 01542-832289.

43.   Speyside Way: Warren Wood & Romancamp Gate   *(History. Walk)*

The first Speyside Way section covers four flat miles between Spey Bay and Fochabers, mostly by a good riverside and woodland track, though the last mile to Fochabers follows the narrow B9104. With the high wall of Gordon Castle (**45**) grounds hugging the east verge and dense wood crowding the riverbank to the west, this is an uneasy stretch.

Between Spey Bay and Fochabers a circular walk is found as follows.

If on the A96 from Elgin, on crossing the Spey turn north nearly a mile up the Spey Bay B9104. Passing a marker indicating the Way's return to the riverbank, then a rough roadside parking area, just before a right-hand bend a rough track on the left (347605) enters the wood, leading almost to the edge of the river. (If heading west from Fochabers on the A96, the B9104 turn-off is just after the 30-mile limit and the castellated entry to Gordon Castle).

Parking, follow Speyside Way markers north along the pebbly track by Warren Wood, or take the riverbank path to a flood-strewn peninsula just before the river sweeps east. Here in 1746, opposite Bellie ('Mouth of the Ford') Cumberland's army forded the river in pursuit of the Jacobites. Amid the broad stream is a shingle isle on which, from May to July, terns nest. Black-backed gulls, oystercatchers, and ospreys are seen here, and the overgrown banks form a fascinating maze. From here the main riverbank track follows the edge of Warren Wood

past a fishing bothy, where a path enters the wood, allowing a loop return for a shorter walk. Again, at the north end of the wood, just before a sign: Finnock Fishing Upper Limit, another track into the wood curls south, back to the start.

For a longer walk, stay with the banked riverside track, open fields to the right. Entering Culriach Wood, the Way swings east then north, the hamlet of Bogmoor visible over flat fields. After half a mile, just before the old railway viaduct to Garmouth, a track branches right to Bogmoor and the B9104, here straight and open, approaching traffic easily seen. Turn right, south, past the art gallery in the old schoolhouse (01343-821432) then past the Upper Dallachy turn almost a mile to a left turn up the Portgordon road. 50 yards up this road is a track on the right at Romancamp Gate (359619), where pottery shards suggesting Roman presence were found a century ago.

Follow this pleasant track south half a mile through fields to Den Farm. By the steading a right turn onto a surfaced farm road descends 400 yards west to Bellie Cemetery, with its old tablestones and the Ionic-columned mausoleum of Duchess Jean Gordon (d.1825: see **68**). Continue downhill to the B9104 at Bellie Lodge, then turn left a quarter-mile south back to Warren Wood and the riverside track where you parked.

A longer (or separate) circuit from Romancamp Gate via Auchenhalrig and the long-disguised Catholic chapel at Newlands of Tynet is described below.

44.   The Secret Church   (History, Walk)

Of 2205 confessed Catholics recorded in 1677 as living in Scottish lowlands from Galloway to Moray, almost half were in western Banffshire, where the 'Gudemen o' the Bog' (the Dukes of Gordon) protected them. In particular, the Braes of Enzie south of Portgordon were 'papistical country', while the Parish of Rathven near Buckie (**115**) birthed eight Catholic bishops in the three post-Reformation centuries. In 1690 there was a Catholic chapel at Preshome above Clochan: this and the Chapel of the Craigs above nearby Cairnfield were sacked by Cumberland's men. Both were later restored. Preshome (St. Gregory's Church: 409615) survives; the Chapel of the Craigs does not.

At Newlands of Tynet, by the Speyside estates of Gordon Castle and 200 yards north of the A98 near the old county boundary at Mill of Tynet, St Ninian's (378614) is Scotland's oldest post-Reformation Catholic Church still in use. Built as a sheepcot then made into a church, the sheepcot disguise lasted until persecution declined. In 1779 the building was extended, glass replacing straw in the windows. The sheep, having provided a puddled floor plus disguise, were removed. Later the 1832 Reform Bill emancipated Catholics and gave them (men anyway) the vote. Renovated in 1957, with services held in summer, this long low white-washed building testifies to intolerant times.

To begin or continue this six-mile circuit from Romancamp Gate (see above), adapt the following description, which starts at Mill of Tynet.

From Fochabers, take the A98 Buckie road past the Winding Walks (**46**) through dense forest for three miles. Just after the forest ends a right turn leads to Newlands of Tynet. 200 yards further on at the old Moray-Banffshire boundary the A98 reaches Bridge of Tynet (384614), by it the Mill House Hotel; a sweet factory before it became a mill. Parking here, cross the A98 and start up the minor road to Spey Bay. After 50 yards turn left onto a track through fields to forestry. At a crossing just inside the wood before a house with a large garden, turn left 200 yards to the chapel at Newlands of Tynet. Back at the crossing (the path on the right leads to Auchenhalrig: see below) continue west past the house, howling hounds penned nearby. Half a mile on through the wood a wide logged-out clearing rises left. Ignoring a left turn, continue past a new plantation to a second track on the left. Here, just before a stone bridge, a sign at the pole gate says 'Walkers Welcome'. Take this track (364613).

For a shorter circuit with wider views, continue over the stone bridge and down past high-hedged fields to Den Farm (356609), then turn north to Romancamp Gate.

The left turn climbs south to mature forestry and a Y-fork. Bear right, south, gently down then up to open woodland, a new plantation blocking views to the west. At a T-junction (365599) by the crest of the low hill, A98 traffic audible but unseen ahead, turn right (west) 300 yards, then right again at the next fork. Descend through mixed woodland and glades to a turreted, pink-harled lodge with fine gardens – one entry to Gordon Castle. Turn right (north) along a rhododendron drive to.a Y-fork by cottages before Den Farm. Here the track mentioned above (over the bridge) joins the drive.

Continue north past steading and the left turn to Bellie cemetery half a mile to Romancamp Gate and the Portgordon road. Turn right a half-mile to the first crossroads, with care: some drivers use the road as a 'rat-run' to avoid the Fochabers A96/A98 bottleneck. At the crossroads (left to Upper Dallachy, right to Auchenhalrig: wide Firth views) just beyond Upper Dallachy reservoir, turn right (south) a half-mile to Auchenhalrig. Through a steading and past cottages on the left, opposite a phone-box turn second right, between two cottages, then left via a small concrete footbridge over a ditch. Keep straight, southeast, first between cottages, then via a gated, fenced footpath through rough pasture into dense forestry. Soon the straight track reaches the crossing by the House of Barking Dogs. Head straight on for Newlands of Tynet; for Bridge of Tynet turn left, then right over the A98 to the hotel carpark. This walk should take about two hours.

45.   Fochabers & the Gordons   *(History)*

From the west the A96 crosses the Spey by a modern bridge alongside the 1854 three-rib cast iron arch, which replaced the 1804 Fochabers Old Bridge, damaged in the 1829 flood (**52**). Past the B9104 and the driveway to Gordon Castle (not open) the road enters Fochabers (pop.1500: Pictish *Foth-opir*, 'marshy land').

Made a Burgh of Barony in 1598 and after 1776 resited to allow expansion of the Gordon Castle estate, the High Street of this rectangular planned village is a juggernaut bottleneck, talk of a bypass still just talk. Traffic crawls through The Square under the spire of Bellie Church (1798), then past crenellated, turreted Milne's High School (1846) - working at Gordon Castle, its benefactor Alexander Milne (1742-1839) emigrated after the Duke of Gordon objected to his long hair, and made a fortune in New Orleans. At the east end of the village, under Christies Garden Centre and Whiteash Hill, the road forks – the A96 southeast to Keith (**111**), the coastal A98 northeast past Buckie (**115**).

The home of Baxters of Speyside (**25**), in recent years Fochabers has annually hosted the Speyfest, highlighting Celtic music. With the Folk Museum in a converted church in the High Street, the village also hosts a number of antique shops. What exhaust fumes do to the antiques is anyone's guess.

Fochabers has a long Gordon association. Leaving place-names like Gourdon in southern France, this family was given Border lands by Malcolm Canmore (1057-93). In 1313 granted Strathbogie by Robert the Bruce, Sir Adam Gordon's descendants on one side were Jock of Scurdargue and his brother, Tam of Ruthven: most northern Gordon branches come from these two. On the other, the late 14th century marriage of Elizabeth Gordon to Alexander Seton birthed the Seton Gordons, after 1445 the Earls of Huntly (Old English *hunta leah*, 'huntsman's wood': a Borders name). In Huntly building a castle on an old riverbank site fortified since early Norman times and covering the Moray-Aberdeen trade route, the Earls became powerful governors of the Northeast. Then came the Reformation. Losing the Earldom of Moray in 1550 to Protestant Stewarts, the Catholic 4th Earl died after his defeat at Corrichie. Feud between the Gordons and Stewarts escalated, culminating in the 1592 murder of the Bonnie Earl of Moray (see **6**). Meanwhile civil war raged; victory for Huntly and Erroll at the Battle of Glenlivet (**103**) in 1594 led to their exile, James VI destroying their castles. Allowed home, Huntly completed a new castle in the 'palace' style in 1602, but defeat of the royalist, Catholic cause in the Civil War 50 years later caused its abandonment.

The Gordon power-base moved to Fochabers, where *c*.1480 the 2nd Earl of Huntly had begun building Castle Gordon on the Bog of Gight. His successors (the 'Gudeman o' the Bog') prospered, maintaining their Catholic faith (44). After 1769 Alexander, 4th Duke and 18th Gudeman extended the Castle into what has been called 'the most magnificent edifice north of the Forth', or, 'a tedious quarter-mile of two storeyed crenellated regularity': take your pick. Later it was a home to Duchess Jane Maxwell who helped raise the Gordon Highlanders by offering recruits a kiss and a shilling, though she preferred Kinrara (**68**) near Aviemore.

As for the Duchess of Richmond, wife of the 6th Duke, she too lived here, and is commemorateded by a monument atop Whiteash Hill, our next destination.

46. Fochabers: Whiteash Hill   (Walks)

By the A98 500 yards east of Fochabers a forest carpark (357586) serves Whiteash Hill's waymarked 'Winding Walks', with routes to the 1973 gazebo above the village at the 'Peeps'; or up to the monument near the top (264m.), where wide views make up for logged clearings; or up a dramatic, steep-sided linn, a burn gurgling through it.

Under old Scots Pine carpark information boards tell how, a century ago, the Duke created these walks amid ornamental woodland, to be enjoyed by all. Restored in 1972 by Gordonstoun pupils and extended in 1990, they're offered as four colour-coded routes. Here is a three-mile circuit, covering most of what Whiteash Hill has to offer.

Start south through the swing gate to two broad, climbing tracks. The left turn goes direct to the top but, for a more scenic route, swing right past a pond to the mouth of the wooded linn, entering it at the 'Winding Walks' marker. (For the 'Peeps', continue on the main (red) trail up to a right turn (yellow) through regimented forestry. On return, continue up the red trail or join the Winding Walks below). The exotic woodland path up the narrowing gully crosses a burn then zigzags up a steep, guard-railed slope, in time climbing out of the ravine by the junction of two higher, broader, flanking tracks.

Now united, the track (blue markers) crosses a forestry road to an unlovely path. Starved spruce one side and a logged clearing the other leads to Ranald's Grave; once camp-site of a tinker-king executed here for robbing travellers on the old Aberdeen-Inverness road. A stern cairn emphasises his fate. The track continues to the pyramid memorial at the devastated hilltop (374575). 30 feet high, erected by Fochabers folk in memory of local benefactress the Duchess of Richmond (d.1887), it was lost in forestry until recently uncovered again. From here it's said you can see ten counties: a range-finder marks distant heights and sites, from the Convals by Dufftown (**106**) to Wick (95km) in Caithness far to the north.

To return: follow the blue marker north downhill through logged clearings and uniform forestry. At a junction after zigzags (steep linn right), an arrow points left ('to pond': green marker) to a clearing, peaty pond one side, wide views the other. Another ten minutes leads to the head of the 'Winding Walks'. Turn right, down the main (red) track to the carpark. An odd walk, in parts lush, in parts desolate, but worthwhile.

47.   Fochabers: Earth Pillars and Jean Carr's Stone   (Walks)

South of Fochabers Slorach's Wood and the Wood of Ordiequish are flanked to the east by the A96; and to the west, above the Spey, by a back road carrying the Speyside Way. Leaving Fochabers via East Street (by the fish'n-chippy opposite the museum), this road past Milne's High School climbs a wooded bank under Slorach's Wood two miles to the Earth Pillars carpark (339562). From Fochabers or this point there are several options.

For a circular six-mile walk from Fochabers via the Earth Pillars start from East Street or the roadside park between village and river. If the latter, park opposite the Spey Bay B9104 turn. Follow the riverbank south past the cricket pitch via Speyside Way markers to a bridge over a burn. Turn left up a shady burnside path past gardens, Bellie Church spire visible, then right, over the burn up The Innings past Woodside Road, to a waymarked fenced path. Passing the west (river) side of Milne's High School, this continues past a fir-hedged field, down steps into scrub-wood. Bear left at the marker, over a footbridge along a wood-fringed linn to steps up a bank on the right. Reaching the rising Ordiequish road, turn right as views open west over the Spey. With forestry rising left, follow the road a mile past steadings and a rough track turning left under pylons to Slorach's Wood carpark. Here, on the right, is Earth Pillars carpark and a path.

Winding under old Scots Pine above a deep gorge, this path reaches a railed viewpoint, the Spey below running north from Boat o' Brig (**48**), and Ben Aigan (**51**). As for the Earth Pillars, you're above two of them. Best seen from the west bank, you can sight one of these weird pudding-stone towers by descending carefully a few feet one side of the viewpoint. Protected by their capstones as the earth about them erodes, they erupt like red sentinels, frozen giants.

Back at the road, start up the track to the edge of Slorach's Wood. For a shorter circuit, turn left (north) into the wood through an open, broken gate. The track follows the edge of the wood to a Y-junction. Bear right into dense forestry along a pine-needled avenue. Cross a wide cut under the pylons into dark wood above the Burn of Ordiequish in its deep mossy linn to the right. With the track petering out, bear left on a faint path to the apex of an open field then swing right, following the path steeply down the bank and over the burn. Follow the burn's wooded north bank along then up to the edge of a field, Fochabers visible beyond. At the junction here, take the main path left to more open, mixed woodland, then descend to the Ordiequish road. Turn right and return as you came.

For a longer circuit via Jean Carr's Stone (see opposite) and the gorge higher up Ordiequish Hill, follow the Slorach's Wood turn half-a-mile to the forestry
carpark with its information board and route-map of waymarked tracks. Bearing
east then southeast, the first mile of this route (green waymarker) is dull and devastated, but improves. In time, on a long straight stretch, left of the track an information board indicates 'Jean Carr's Stone' (approx. 355556) – a conglomerate
boulder, silver birch sprouting from it, with a tin box containing notebook and pen-
cil for visitors' comments. Chained by her father as a child, when he died in the 18th
century Jean Carr took to the road. Unmarried, she had a child. Authority seized it
and jailed her. Released but further maddened, she stole other women's children.
Outlawed, she slept, lived and died under this stone, her only home.

100 yards on at a main track turn left 400 yards to a Y-fork. Keep left up
under the pylons to another fork. Turn left back into the wood, a red-earth ravine
opening below to the left, the Burn of Ordiequish far below. Again turn left, on a
wooded path high above the burn's steep northeast bank. With occasional far views,
the path winds through dark forestry then climbs away from the linn. Crossing
another open cut, soon you have the option: red waymarker right, green straight on.
The right turn (heather, lichen, light forestry) descends to a main junction and a left
turn, northeast, A96 traffic audible through the trees. At the next downhill junction
keep straight on (north) out of the wood back to Fochabers.

Ring Forest Enterprise (01343-820223) for a pamphlet with outline maps of
Slorach's Wood and Winding Walks routes, and take map and compass for this one.

48.   Speyside Way: Ordiequish to Craigellachie   *(Route, Walk)*

From the Earth Pillars the Speyside Way continues five miles south on the back
road, offering wide views before dropping steeply past Cairnty and Delfur Lodge to
Boat o' Brig (see photo next page) under Ben Aigan. Here the first bridge over the
Spey was built *c.*AD1232, but later fell, leaving only a ferry. With carpark and
information board under the railway bridge, here the Way meets the B9013 Keith
road, up which walkers are directed half-a-mile east. With its blind bends this *Go towards*
wooded brae demands care. On open ground atop the brae and just before *the old*
Auchroisk Distillery, a track on the right (325514) turns hard west towards *Toll*
Bridgeton Farm. Before the steading, a left fork (gated: if starting from here park *House*
by the track junction) passes a firing range then swings right along the forest fringe, *and up*
running west nearly a mile under Knock More by open pasture above the river – *the step*
very pleasant. *to meet*

Entering forestry, the track climbs south up Ben Aigan's wooded north flank *the...*
via the deep, north-facing gully carrying the Allt Daley. Joined by another main *Bridge-*
track then crossing the burn it breaks back, still climbing, before levelling off to *farm*
descend over and climb up above the Sandyhill Burn. This section offers only one *road.*
good viewpoint north (302494), and no easy way up Ben Aigan's higher slopes. A
way can be forced but involves tedious scrambling over squelchy ditches under

young trees liable to poke your eyes out: not recommended. The approach is much easier from the southeast (**51**).

Past the Sandyhill Burn the track descends to the road above Arndilly. The dead-end right turn runs north a mile past Aikenway to a castle ruin on an open point by a sharp bend in the Spey (512292): another lost site. The left turn winds two miles south past Arndilly House, a 1750 Jacobean confection, to join the A95 by Craigellachie's Fiddichside Inn just yards before the River Fiddich joins the Spey. Turn right over the narrow bridge. Here on the left is Fiddich Park, once Craigellachie railway station yard, now start of the Speyside Way's Dufftown spur route (**53**). Passing under Craigellachie and the A95/941 where the latter crosses the Spey by the old Telford bridge, the main Speyside Way continues south past Aberlour (**54**), Carron (**56**) and Blacksboat to Ballindalloch (**58**), where it leaves the river and breaks over the hills to end at Tomintoul (**100**).

Next, before walking up Ben Aigan, a visit to and walk above Rothes.

49.   Rothes: Distillery & Castle   (*Visit, History*)

From Elgin ten miles to the north this Speyside distilling centre (pop. 1400) is reached via the Glen Rothes A941; or from Mosstodloch by the B9015 (**25**); or via the Speyside Way route from Fochabers (dawdlers and walkers only). Joining the B9013 at Boat o' Brig, dawdlers turn right over the Spey to the B9015, thence left two miles to the Vale of Rothes under Ben Aigan's dark-wooded, deep-cleft bulk.

Rothes (in 1819 poet laureate Robert Southey disliked the 'mournful solemnity' of its 'neatly built cottages') is functional. Dominating the northern entry to the long main street is a huge animal feed factory. The pungent odour comes from draff - a barley residue left in the mash tuns early in the whisky distillation process, and used for feed. Next, at the A941/B9015 roundabout, comes a slip-road to Glen Grant Distillery (tel. 01542-783318). Founded in 1840, this Chivas subsidiary is on the Whisky Trail. Open mid-March to the end of October, you can sample the malt, then enjoy the woodland walks, log bridges, and exotic plants from round the world in Major Grant's Garden.

Established in 1766, the village's only connection with the castle, its remaining wall on a mound above the A941/High Street, is probably its name. Of several derivations, most likely is *Rath-ess* ('fort by the river' or 'by the waterfall'). Long before any village existed where the Burn of Rothes meets the Spey, the castle guarded a crucial strategic highway. By this riverside route the Danes poured south from the sea in AD1010, to be routed at Mortlach (Dufftown: see **106**). Not much later, Norman barons built a vaulted hall several stories high with drawbridge, portcullis and moat – a fine site from which to watch for danger approaching from north or south.

The ancestor of the Earls of Rothes, wardens of the Castle from 1296 until it was fired in 1660, was a Hungarian nobleman, Bartholomew, who settled the Garioch in Aberdeenshire in the time of Malcolm Canmore. Just as David I encouraged the Fleming Hugo Freskyn to settle at Duffus (**33**), so Malcolm promised Bartholomew land-rights for a mile about wherever his north-driven horse collapsed. This happened at Leslie in the Garioch; thus the name of the Rothes lords; for in 1296, by marrying the heiress of Rothes, Sir Norman Leslie got the Castle. A love-match?

That year Edward 1 came north to hammer the Scots. Leaving Elgin with his army to start his homeward march, on Sunday 29 July he was received at Rothes by Sir Norman, who'd done him homage in Aberdeen. A good move: Leslie's descendents held the castle another 350 years. In 1513 Earl William died with King James IV at Flodden; in 1546 his son George was acquitted of plotting Cardinal Beaton's murder but, sent to France to witness the marriage of Mary Queen of Scots to the Dauphin, died at Dieppe, possibly poisoned. George's son Andrew helped plot the murder of Mary's secretary David Rizzio, and was later among the peers to acquit Bothwell of Darnley's murder. Andrew's great-grandson carried the Sword of State when Charles II was crowned at Scone in 1651. Soon after the castle was fired by John Innes, a Covenanting zealot, then demolished by local folk: 'to prevent its continuing to be a refuge for thieves and bandits.' Wearied by such fuss, the Leslies moved to a new palace by Glenrothes in Fife.

50.   Rothes: The Wood of Conerock   *(Walk)*

To visit Castlehill then enjoy a circular walk past the Linn of Rothes and round the Wood of Conerock, turn west off the High Street towards Rothes Golf Club. 200 yards up the lane is a carpark by the castle's surviving wall.

Start either by walking on up the golf club road, which is simplest, or by taking the path from the back of Castlehill atop the wooded bank above the Burn of Rothes, distilleries and the cemetery below, a field on the left. A path leads down to the burn: for this walk keep going until the banktop path fails just below the golf course. Bear left to the road and turn right . At the clubhouse swing left uphill on the now-rutted track; fairways to the right, sheep-pasture to the left, fine views behind, forestry ahead.

A left fork at the forestry's edge is how you'll return: keep straight on, west, past the top of the golf course and a second fork left. Climb gradually on through mixed open forestry past a third fork, right. Now, with a wooded ravine dropping steep on the right and open heath and forest-clad hills ahead, there is a broad T-junction. Before taking the left-hand track up the forest edge, detour some way down to the right, to a horseshoe bend where (258484), you'll see the rocky waterfall of the Linn of Rothes – more visible in winter than summer when foliage hides the view.

Return to and continue left up the western flank of the Wood of Conerock past derelict Dounie Cottage – was there once a fort or *dun* here? Keep on left into the forestry, still steadily climbing the broad track. At the first woodland junction (260177), turn hard left, northeast, a hundred yards or so, then right at the next junction, southeast. Soon this track leads to a T-junction (265475) by open heath and cleared ground near the top of the hill, with good views east to Ben Aigan.

Turn left downhill along the forest fringe, keeping straight on past the first fork to a broad, muddy T-junction. Here (267478) the OS path shown as forking right may be confused with a track breaking up the hill; the path itself is all but gone, and there have been fellings since the survey. Safest to bear left on the muddy main track, back into the wood. In a half-mile or so, on reaching a main track at the wood's northern edge, keep left to the original track up from the golf clubhouse. Turn right, downhill, enjoying the fine views, and so continue back as you came to the Castlehill carpark.

By the way, anyone interested in helping to develop a footpath network locally can contact Mr Ray Brumby at 22 New St., Rothes (01340-831588).

51.   Craigellachie: Up Ben Aigan   *(Route, Walk)*

Two miles south of Rothes the B9102 breaks right from the A941, climbing west past Macallan Distillery (visits by appointment only) through Archiestown and Knockando to Grantown-on-Spey (**59**) 24 miles away, at first over scrappy high pasture with views southeast over the Spey to the Convals and Ben Rinnes (**55**). We pick it up soon, via the Carron-Cardhu route (**56**).

Just after this turn the A941 crosses the Spey. With Telford's 1814 bridge on the right and Craigellachie (pop. 480) to the left, at the Craigellachie junction the main road on south through Aberlour (**54**) becomes the A95, the left turn through Craigellachie past Ben Aigan to Keith likewise. The A941 becomes the Dufftown road, 300 yards further on.

The salmon-fishing centre of Crachellachie (stress on second syllable) occupies terraces above the confluence of Spey and Fiddich. Mostly late 19th century, its name, meaning 'Swan's Rock', 'Boundary Rock', or (*creag ealach*), 'crag of the rocky place', is shared with the rock above Aviemore (**66**) from which Clan Grant once shouted its war-cry. Nearby on the Dufftown road is the award-winning Speyside Cooperage Visitor Centre (294443: 01340-871108), where you can see coopers at work.

For Ben Aigan ('Mountain of the Gorge': 1546ft, 471m), from Fiddich Park in Craigellachie and the start of the Speyside Way Dufftown spur (see **53**), drive up the steep A95 brae a mile or so to Wester Gauldwell. By a cream-walled house (313455) turn left up the minor Belnagarrow road, bearing right to the forestry edge. Park on the left where a rough track starts up through silver birch and spruce (314466), Balnacoul Farm is ahead and below to the right. If you drive on into a deep gully, you've gone too far.

With its bald dome, forested slopes, and the transmitter mast atop adjacent Knock More (386m), Ben Aigan is no beauty. Yet, as the last big hill before the sea, or the first big hill before bigger hills, it commands fine views. The up-and-down walk is simple, but can be extended.

Taking the rutted track, bear right at a fork not far up, and climb on through the plantation. The trees are still young, with views south to the Convals and Ben Rinnes. Steep at first, the slope eases. Reaching open heather, the main crossing track continues northeast to the mast atop Knock More. A lesser path breaks left over a low brow to Ben Aigan's summit. When it peters out, cross wiry heather to the trig point at the windy top.

On a fine day, the view rewards. North, the Spey's final run past to Fochabers to the coast, Sutherland hills beyond; northeast, the Bin of Cullen. Below, the huge green Chivas bonded warehouses at Mulben; Keith to the east; Dufftown southeast, the Cabrach beyond. The Spey winds south past Ben Rinnes to Ballindalloch and Glenavon, Craigellachie below. Steam rises from the animal feed-plant at Rothes; Glen Rothes leads to Glenlatterach *en route* to Pluscarden, Dallas, Forres and the Findhorn.

Waymarked bike trails and other tracks up Ben Aigan and Knock More begin from a forestry carpark (335495) by the A95 a mile southwest of Mulben crossroads (353506). From Wester Gauldwell follow the winding A95 through Maggieknockater ('Plain of the Hilly Land'?), where a road turns south above the Fiddich to Dufftown via Kininvie (319441); a white L-plan 16th-century Leslie towerhouse. Two miles further on the Belnagarrow loop-road (see above) rejoins the A95 just before the carpark. Sited above the road and the hidden house of Auchlunkart (1700), it is gained by a bulldozed track. Start here if you want, but it's a long slog up the spruce-dark hillside.

But however you get there, Ben Aigan's summit is a good spot to reflect on the devastation caused by the Spey in the Great Flood of 1829.

52.   The Muckle Spate & the Spey   *(History)*

In 1992 and 1997 huge damage was caused when, after heavy downpours, rivers inundated the coastal plain. Far worse was the Great Flood or Muckle Spate of

1829. The Findhorn devastated the Forres area (**12**), but the Spey and its tributaries caused as much or more damage, again as recorded by Sir Thomas Dick Lauder.

Looking south from Ben Aigan the Spey may look placid, but imagine instead a raging monster devouring the Plain of Rothes below, having already caused chaos further upstream. With the Insh Marshes (**68**) between Kingussie and Aviemore turned into a mile-wide torrent, not only the Spey but its feeder-streams wreaked havoc. Glenfeshie (**85**) folk fled for their lives; the Dulnain (**64**) swept away the Bridge of Curr; and in Abernethy (**96**) 13 bridges plus sawmills and mealmills were destroyed. A sea-captain from Counakyle who lost most of his land said he 'could have sailed a fifty-gun ship from Bellifurth to Boat of Garten, a distance of seven or eight miles.' At Ballindalloch (**58**) the Avon roared into the Spey having destroyed farms and forced new channels: an avenue of oaks normally high above water was torn up and carried past Aberlour, where the Knockando burn grew 'to a size equal to that of the Spey in its ordinary state.' A man called Cruickshanks, swept down the Lour Burn on a makeshift raft, caught hold of a tree to avoid being lost in the Spey. With every attempt that night to reach him failing; 'he began to shout for help in a voice that became every moment more long drawn and piteous.' Next day his body was found five miles downstream.

At Dufftown the Fiddich and Dullan joined in destroying a woolmill: further downstream a plantation was uprooted and two bridges swept away. Everywhere, loss of cattle and sheep was immense. At Craigellachie, Telford's 1814 bridge survived because Telford, heeding local warnings, had pitched it higher than originally planned. The flood boomed a foot under the arch even as one of the Ballindalloch oaks came to rest on the Plain of Rothes, where the corn-stacks of the 1828 crop 'were carried off like a fleet of ships.' Rothes itself was flooded, 15 houses being destroyed, with the plain at Orton under six feet of running water. By eight in the evening the flood was 17 feet up the 1804 Fochabers bridge: shortly past midnight an entire span cracked and fell. 'The shriek that spread along both banks of the river, when the bridge fell, was loud and agonising.' Two men., Anderson and Cuthbert, were swept away: Anderson's mother staring 'with a phrenzied air on the frightful chasm.'

Further downstream, Bogmoor houses had over five feet of water running through them. The flood had come so unexpectedly in the middle of the night that one man awoke to find ' the water rushing into the bed': he and his wife escaped just in time, the house being swept away behind them. At Garmouth, 15 houses were destroyed, the Spey here being reckoned a mile wide. Men waded through the streets, carrying out women, children and the elderly. Lauder tells of 'the surprise and terror of their countenances partially betrayed by the momentary appearance of some accidental light, as they appeared and vanished like spectres.' The 1997 flooding was bad enough, but...

53.   Round Blue Hill   *(Walk)*

Embracing Craigellachie, Aberlour and Dufftown, this 10-mile circuit is fine for a long summer day, and mostly straightforward. Park at Craigellachie to join the southbound Speyside Way under the A941. First, visit the 1814 bridge with its castellated stone turrets, its Welsh-made single cast-iron span the work of Thomas Telford (1757-1834). Workaholic son of a Dumfriesshire shepherd, he built so many roads, bridges, churches and harbours (plus the Caledonian Canal) that it's safe to assume there were six of him. From it look down: during the 1829 Flood the water roared barely under your feet.

From here, with the A95 above and the river below, the Way follows the old Strathspey railway track through a tunnel, the Macallan distillery complex prominent above the Spey's west bank. After a mile cross a broad haugh into Aberlour - we return soon. At the old railway station, now a tea-room by Alice Littler Park, turn left to the Square. Cross the A95 and continue east up Queen's Road. Past Fleming Cottage Hospital, bear right up Chapel Terrace, then steep left up Allachie

Drive, climbing out of Aberlour to fine views over the Spey and north to Ben Aigan.

Higher up the brae follow the edge of the Wood of Allachie. Where after a mile and a half the surfaced road becomes a track, it joins another uphill track by Gownie (287424), a ruin behind a belt of trees to the left. Here turn right, Ben Rinnes (**55**) prominent three miles to the south. At a locked forestry gate after 400 yards keep straight on past a gated left turn and an information board outlining routes through the wood ahead. Ignoring subsequent waymarked forks, follow this curving track due east over the hilltop saddle, then up a firebreak to a gate at the wood's eastern edge (302418), wide open views beyond.

With the half-bald Knock of Buchromb to the left

(north), and the Fiddich valley below, a short-cut back to Craigellachie may (I haven't tried it) be found by following the forest edge north then descending to Midtown of Buchromb (314432). There cross and briefly follow the A941 north-west before descending to the spur route of the Speyside Way (see below). This cuts off about three miles.

For Dufftown, keep straight over the moor to a low top. Taking to the heather if the gorse-thick track gets too difficult, continue east past a gate at the next forestry strip. With Dufftown visible below, bear right, following the forest fringe down to Burnhead. Here a track descends to the edge of Dufftown and enters Hill Street. Past the police station this joins Balvenie St. (Craigellachie A941). Turn left past Glenfiddich Distillery (Whisky Trail: see **106** for Dufftown).

A long half-mile of pavement leads to the Speyside Way carpark by Convalmore Distillery. Again via old railway track, this Speyside Way spur follows the Fiddich four miles to Craigellachie via the wooded river-gorge. Quarry dust packed into the railway ballast offers firm walking. Herons, dippers, warblers, and other birds thrive amid shrub-dense woods with the river dark below. This section is lovely, especially where the track crosses the Fiddich under a screen of huge beech and firs.

Now, to Aberlour, and a fine little walk to Linn Falls on the Lour Burn.

54. Aberlour's Linn Falls   *(History, Walk)*

Founded in 1812 by Charles Grant of Wester Elchies, today Charlestown of Aberlour (pop. 920; its full name almost as long as its broad main street) is noted for its spacious scale, pretty gardens, and the Alice Littler Speyside park - all of which won it the title of Scotland's 'best kept large village' not long ago. Its river-side site, under wooded slopes with Blue Hill and Ben Rinnes nearby, may have helped. Attracting anglers, tourists and walkers, with a distillery (owned by Pernod), Walker's shortbread factory and a well-known private school, this is a quiet place, despite the A95. It's hard to imagine drama here. But in the Muckle Spate houses, trees and people were swept away. 'Nae wonder than our teeth are chittering,' one witness told chronicler Thomas Dick Lauder.

Again, one winter night in 1879, the recently-rebuilt distillery burned down, the villagers rushing from their beds to roll out the threatened barrels. And there are darker tales. One despotic laird sat on a stone amid the Spey to try witches. If when thrown into the river they managed to swim ashore, they were innocent. This rever-sal of the usual process of trial-by-ordeal, whereby drowning meant innocence and floating proved guilt, was no consolation to non-swimmers.

Aberlour lies on the Lour Burn, its water used over a millennium ago by St. Drostan (or Dunstan: later Archbishop of Canterbury) to baptise local chiefs. Allegedly the nephew of St Columba, his well lies under a stone in the distillery grounds, by the burn. It's also said the Lour once had a kelpie (see **92**) that demand-ed human sacrifices. This gory tradition survived into modern times, less bloodily, as a distillery custom; the first cask of each new distillation being offered to the burn. It's said a new distillery manager, impatient with this wasteful habit, stopped it then, fishing the Spey, collapsed and suddenly died. The kelpie had taken revenge! Today the Lour suggests no such darkness, and not far up it are the pretty Linn Falls, a local beauty spot.

From the Square, pass the tea-room in the old railway station and cross the park to the riverside path - part of the Speyside Way. Follow it south past the footbridge a few hundred yards to where the Lour joins the Spey. Turn left up the burn past the cemetery to the old hump-backed bridge by the A95. Cross over and take the path signposted to Linn Falls, on the east bank of the burn and opposite the distillery. The path is clear, with a fine stand of Douglas Fir *en route*. In about half-a-mile it reaches a picnic area in a shady glade under the falls - an ideal place to dream of kelpies and saints.

Continuing above the falls to the left, a path ascends the wood back to Aberlour. At a parking space above the village look over rooftops and river before returning (the way obvious) past the hospital back to the Square.

55.   Ben Rinnes   *(Routes, Walk)*

South of Aberlour between Ballindalloch and Dufftown the long blue ridge of Ben Rinnes (2755ft., 840m) is visible from much of coastal Moray. In height and distance between the Cairngorms and Ben Aigan, on a clear day its broken granite tors stand out for miles. The view from its summit plateau can be superb, while the weird formation of the tors (called *scurran*, from the Gaelic *sgurr*, 'sharp peak') make them worth a visit. For Munro-baggers it's a stroll, but the last thousand feet on the direct path from the east will tax the unfit.

From Aberlour there are three approaches. First, 200 yards past the distillery the minor Edinvillie road turns sharp left from the A95 brae climbing south of the village. Second, round the bend atop the brae is the Glenallachie/Edinvillie turn east (256416). Third and most direct, a mile further on at a minor crossroads (247409), a road breaks east to Ben Rinnes and Edinvillie, soon (just before Edinvillie Primary School) reaching a right turn to Ben Rinnes Distillery. The longer, gentler track up Ben Rinnes via Baby's Hill starts from the distillery (259357).

Continuing east above the Lour this road is joined by first one then another lane from Edinvillie, a burnside hamlet (note the CAUTION FREE RANGE CHILDREN signs at either end). With the northeast scarp of Ben Rinnes looming closer over rough ground and moor, it continues to the Tomintoul-Dufftown B9009. Just before the junction, it squeezes through the Glack Harnes, a narrow bare pass between Round Hill (411m) and Meikle Conval (571m). Here, five miles south of Aberlour, begins the direct route up Ben Rinnes, via Round Hill and Roy's Hill (535m). Past a gated moorland track and halfway down the narrow pass, with parking space by a second gated track (282359), a board by the gate posted by the 'Friends of Ben Rinnes' (01340-820286) shows the way up.

(From Dufftown (**106**), follow the B9009 south almost four miles and turn right up the Edinvillie road half a mile to park as above.)

The zigzag track up Round Hill is steep but easy. Briefly level, it steepens again to Roy's Hill's rounded, boggy top, with fine views south to the Cairngorms. But above is the final 1000-foot slog over bare heath and broken rock to the summit, Scurran of Lochterlandoch. It looks close, looming like a medieval castle, yet the slope is steep, with many false brows. So take it easy. You're near when the wind starts beating. West over the broad triangular summit plateau is Scurran of Morinsh, ahead and below to the left. More intriguing, ahead to the right, is Scurran of Well. Cross heath and hopefully-dry peat-hag to this odd rock formation - like a vitrified fort, its layered stacks of rock split apart into alleys suggest some vast roofless courtyard.

Tracking north to the edge where the scurran overlooks the glen, a steep path descends west over watershed burns to the broad brow of Baby's Hill, and on to the Ben Rinnes Distillery two miles away. Also, far below, a track skirts the base of the ben, returning east to where you started. Descending, the urge is to leave the path too soon, crossing rough ground to join the track quickly. Ignore this urge. Follow the Baby's Hill path until the line of descent is comfortable, or risk floundering through heather-hidden potholes. On reaching the boggy, meandering track, keep to it. Cutting over the open ground between it and the visible road invites at least a soaking. In time the track reaches the road 400 yards west of where you parked, some six miles ago.

Feel you've earned a dram?

56.   Carron to Cardhu   *(Route, Distillery)*

Whisky Trail distilleries lie all about - Glenfiddich (**106**); Glenlivet a few miles south via the B9009 (**104**); Glen Grant in Rothes (**49**); Glenfarclas five miles south of Aberlour under Ben Rinnes (**58**); Cardhu by Knockando on the Spey's northwest bank. Only Strathisla (**111**) in Keith is at any great distance. Via the southbound A95, the closest is Glenfarclas, and we go that way soon, but first a look at Carron, Archiestown and Knockando, which means that Cardhu is our destination.

From Ben Rinnes return to the A95 and turn south (left) 400 yards to the Carron turn (right: 245405). Descend past the Daluaine and Imperial distilleries and over the Spey to the hamlet of Carron, three miles west of Aberlour, and sited in what Alfred Barnard called 'one of the most beautiful little glens in Scotland.' Here, via the railway track from Aberlour, the Speyside Way also crosses the river, continuing south four miles past Knockando and Blacksboat to cross the river again near Ballindalloch (**58**) .

Climbing the brae onward from Carron, a right then a left turn leads two miles to the moor of Ballintomb and to the B9102 at Archiestown, founded *c.*1760 by Sir Archibald Grant of Monymusk. With wide views over the Spey to the Convals and Ben Rinnes, from this remote village (pop. 160) the B9102 runs west past another Carron turn three miles to Cardhu (192431: 01340-810204), above the road just before Knockando.

Hugging a slope above the Spey, the distillery here at Cardow, ('black rock': the place as distinct from the whisky) is among the oldest, and was rebuilt in 1884-85. Highland cattle browse in a field behind: swans glide on a pond reflecting the kiln-house pagoda. There is a walk past Knockando Church, where three old Pictish stones are set in the kirkyard wall. Sadly this 1757 kirk was fire-gutted in 1991. With Tamdhu Distillery also nearby, Knockando *(cnocan-dubh*, 'little black hill') itself is a hamlet at the junction of the B9102 with the road from Dallas (**20**).

Converted from two 19th-century kilns and an old malt deposit building, in the visitor centre waxwork tableaux dramatise Cardhu's history. Taking out a 19-year lease on Cardow Farm on Whitsunday 1811, in 1816 John Cumming of nearby Wester Elchies was thrice convicted for illegal distilling, but let off with nominal fines. His wife Helen, who weekly carried the brew barefoot over the 12-mile Mannoch Hill track to Elgin for sale, did her best to hide the farm's true trade. One night warned just in time of two excisemen approaching, she hid the distilling apparatus, got out bread-making gear, and dusted her hands with flour. 'Come awa' ben,' she told the Preventers, 'I'm just baking.' Settling them down to eat, she went out to hoist a red warning flag over the barn.

It's also said the fairy folk aided Cardhu. One night Helen was busy distilling when a tiny man, poorly-clad and cold, knocked at the door., She invited him in, asking: 'Where are ye from?' He said: 'Sheean o' Mannoch' - the nearby fairy knowe. She gave him a bowl of Cardhu. He drained it, threw the bowl on the fire and declared: 'Brew wifie, brew, for you and yours will never want!' - a prediction later amply fulfilled.

57.   Knockando to Grantown   *(Route, Walk)*

From Knockando, the B9102 scenic route follows the Spey's west bank 16 miles southwest to Grantown, either close by the river or weaving through woodland above. Yet finding walks along this stretch is problematic. Below the road are Scotland's costliest salmon-beats; above it estate tracks climb through commercial forestry or private woodland to bare Monadhliath stalking and shooting moors. Locked gates and notices discourage public access, which is a pity, as from the first ridges of these wastes between Strathspey and the Great Glen there are fine views east over the Spey to Ben Rinnes (see photo next page).

Leaving Knockando, the road climbs over open heath past Roy's Hill (516m); a bare low brow with an ugly track gouged up it. Soon after this it descends past a left turn (B9138) over the Spey to Marypark, this route intersecting the Speyside Way by the old riverside railway station at Blacksboat. With dense forest rising right and a standing stone in the field just beyond the Blacksboat turn, the B9102 continues through pretty woodland under scree slopes before crossing the Gheallaidh Burn. Following the riverbank then climbing again, the road passes

Tulchan, once part of the vast Seafield estate. Herre there are stone gateways with 19th-century carriage lamps, prominent STRICTLY PRIVATE signs, and warnings of pheasants on the road.

Past a turn left to a concrete bridge over the Spey to Advie the road climbs a heathery, wooded slope then, now well above the Spey, continues through rolling, wooded, bungalowed land past Lettoch and Dalriach towards Grantown. At Tomvaich (066304), on flat ground amid scattered woods, a road breaks sharply back right (north) to Auchnagallan and Cottartown. From here a circular five-mile back-road walk (or drive) is possible. Park at the wide junction or at a right fork half-a-mile up this back road. With a half-forested hill to the right, a transmitter mast atop it, start up the right fork, north over flat reedy pasture. A gradual one-mile climb leads past Ballinlagg to a roadside steading (058334) below Knock of Auchnahannet, where a track climbing past Glenmore Loch leaves this back road. Below bare slopes and above a wide marsh the road now descends over a birch-clad burn to climb west past another moorland track, then south down to a junction (047336). A right turn wriggles southwest two miles to the Grantown-Nairn A939; the left turn (southeast) completes the circuit, the road running straight back to where you parked, with views east to the Cromdale Hills, forestry to the right, the reedy flat waste to the left.

There is nothing special here – it's just another forgotten place, off the track and without legend or history, and therefore ideal if you want to go where nobody else goes.

As for Grantown, three miles further south, we'll get there soon.

58.   Ballindalloch & Cromdale   (*Route, History*)

First, though, the main A95 down the Spey's east bank is not be despised either. Any way you go, you miss something. Fortunately, bridges connect these routes at Backsboat, Advie and Cromdale, allowing back-and-forth experiment.

Continuing south: past the Ben Rinnes/Carron turns the A95 climbs to bare land, after three miles passing Glenfarclas (212383: 01807-500245). Owned since 1836 by the Grants and among the last independent distilleries, snugly bleak below Ben Rinnes, this is another worthwhile visit. With a teetotal co-driver, you can have fun hereabouts!

Sweeping through Marypark past the B9138 turn over the Spey to Blacksboat and the B9102, the A95 approaches Ballindalloch, first passing the old Inveravon church (183376). Descend a steep short road (signposted Inveraven) to this white-harled kirk on its mound near the confluence of Avon and Spey. Here, besides the Macpherson-Grant mausoleum (1829), three Pictish symbol stones are cemented into the kirk's southeast wall. A place of worship since the 13th century, the kirk was built in 1806 and renovated in 1876. A prophecy that someday it will: 'gang down the Spey' fu' of folks' testifies to ancient belief in the destructive power of the Spey's spring floods (**52**).

Next, west of the road amid lush wood is the entry to Ballindalloch Castle (185365: 01807-500205: open daily Easter-September). Long the seat of Macpherson-Grants and dating from the mid-16th century, this grand country house occupies the wide haugh where the rivers meet. It's said efforts to built it on more defensible heights above were beaten by a supernatural force hurling the stones down to the river. So the laird sat up one night and heard the wind roar: 'Build on the cow-haugh', which is exactly what he did.

A mile on, by a war memorial at a sharp downhill bend, the pretty Strathavon B9008 departs to Glenlivet and Tomintoul. Under a mile up it at the Auldich lane (192349) the Tomintoul spur of the Speyside Way (having climbed from Cragganmore: see below), takes off up over Cairnacay (1605 ft.) to Glenlivet and Cairn Daimh (**104**).

Descending past Ballindalloch Castle's turreted gatehouse, the A95 crosses the Avon. Just after this on the left a lane departs four miles along and above the Avon's west bank past the restored 17th-century tower-house of Kilnmaichlie. This wooded, winding route dead-ends at Chapelton steading, a Neolithic ring-cairn in a field close by.

Just after this on the right the brief B9137 descends to Cragganmore Distillery past the old Ballindalloch railway station. Here, via a 19th-century iron girder bridge, the Speyside Way arrives from Carron (**56**) and leaves the river for two miles of tarmac, including a stretch of main road, before reaching the Auldich lane, as above.

Another mile on the A95 leaves Moray, entering Highland Region before passing Tormore Distillery. Opened in 1958, it was the 20th century's first new

Highland malt distillery. Next, at the war memorial (123341) above Advie, a minor road cuts sharply downhill and over the Spey to join the B9102 south of Tulchan. By the riverside soon after this, at Milton (105321) a minor road on the left loops high up the western flank of the Cromdale hills then descends to Cromdale – another interesting detour. Separating Strathavon and Strathspey, the ridge is the regional boundary.

A hamlet or small village, Cromdale ('Crooked Plain') was an early church settlement and Spey ferry-point, with a courthouse, jail, and hanging hill long before Grantown was founded. Here on 1 May 1690, not a year after Killiecrankie, where John Graham of Claverhouse, 'Bonnie Dundee' died at the height of their

victorious charge, Highlanders supporting the deposed James VII were routed by King William's forces under General Mackay - another gory mess. Here a third bridge (Boat of Cromdale: see photo and next walk) crosses the Spey to join the B9102 a mile before the latter enters Grantown.

Beyond Cromdale continuing along the Spey's wooded east bank three miles to more open ground, the A95 meets first the Bridge of Brown/Tomintoul A939 (043263) then the B970 (**97**) south to Nethybridge and Coylumbridge. Here too is the Spey Valley Smokehouse (01479-873078) where you can learn all about fish smoking.

Immediately after this the A95 crosses the Spey to a bypass roundabout and continues south to Aviemore (**66**); the road ahead entering Grantown-on-Spey.

59.   Grantown-on-Spey: Gateway Country   *(History, Walks)*

Nestling by the Spey amid pine, fir and silver beech, Grantown (pop. 3260) marks a hidden border between Upper and Lower Strathspey. To the west the Monadhliaths stretch towards the Great Glen: bog and crag without field or forest. From the southwest, the Spey flows from its wild remote source (**78**) past

Newtonmore, Kingussie, Aviemore and Boat of Garten: villages servicing tourism and winter sports. So too does Grantown. Yet Grantown has a solid elegance special to itself.

Existing before 1533, Old Grantown (Castletown of Freuchie) lay southwest of Castle Grant, seat of the chiefs of that clan (see **87**) since, in the 13th century, Sir John Grant was gifted lands earlier held by the Comyns. The castle (not open) is said to date from *c.*1200, though you'd never know it. An unhappy 18th-century redesign - even the Adams had their off-days - produced what Queen Victoria rightly called 'a very plain-looking house, like a factory.' During the '45 the Jacobites occupied this gaunt pile, enjoying the wine-cellar, and later Burns guested here. If he met the lecherous ghost of Lady Barbara (Barbie), walled up alive for her sins, he fails to mention it.

In 1694, after the Battle of Cromdale, by royal order a market cross was erected in hope that a new settlement would become the area's main burgh; but only in the 1760s did a new grid-planned town develop southwest of the castle. Founded by Sir Ludovic Grant, its chief mentor was his son, 'The Good Sir James'. After the '45 Sir Ludovic ('The Bad Sir Ludovic'?) had betrayed 84 men of Glenurquhart and Glenmoriston: maybe his son felt he had to make amends. Also founding Milton and Lewiston by Drumnadrochit on Loch Ness, Sir James, attempting to resist the emigration fever created by the Clearances, carefully supervised the town's growth. Soon a centre of linen manufacture and the area's main market town, by 1863, with the arrival of the railway and popular tourism, Grantown rivalled Inverness as the county's second burgh.

Well-planned, its Square unequalled for spacious elegance, Grantown caters to the holiday trade while avoiding the pizzeria-style of some other centres. Staid and quiet? Maybe, but no worse for it. With a seasonal information office (01479-872773) in the High Street, several local walks suggest Grantown's character. Here are two:

(**1**) At the southeast side of the Square a sign (FOREST WALKS & RIVER SPEY 1200 YARDS) directs you down Forest Street past the golf course to a forest track, once the military road. This, a carpark at the start, leads southeast under stately trees to the Spey. Sticking to the main trail, on reaching the riverside road turn left a half-mile past bungalows to Old Speybridge (040264: closed to traffic). Just before the bridge, also on the left, begins a rough road west to Anagach.

This winds through woodland and pasture on a shelf above (and hidden from) the Spey. Past Mid and Easter Anagach a woodland gate leads to a clearing and croft atop the riverbank at Craigroy (055273). Here, a gated path descends to the river, following it two miles north to the road and girder bridge at Boat of Cromdale (065289).

For a shorter return route, from Craigroy follow the main track on, curving left (west) into the wood. Stay left at the first main fork to a woodland crossing; here keeping left or straight ahead for various ways back to town.

For the longer riverside route, on reaching Boat of Cromdale climb the road west away from the bridge, looping up towards forestry and the B9102. (By the bridge there is a shortcut up the bank on the left, hard to spot.) With woodland now both sides take a track on the left (062291) to Nether Port. This winds pleasantly south under Scots Pine 400 yards past Nether Port cottage (061287). Keep left down to open ground and a wooden bridge over a burn. With views of the Cromdales over open flats cross the burn and a cattlegrid, not far, to a track on the right (locked gate and stile) into thick forestry.

Through the plantation this track curls down past an iron gate, a burn in the clearing to the right. A red waymarker directs you ahead on a track through open pinewood and hillocky glades to a forest Y-fork with a bench. Keep left and, at the next fork, right. Still following the red waymarker on an increasingly tedious, logged-out stretch, at a third main junction keep right, in time reaching a gate at the edge of the golf course. Cross the golf course back to town, or follow the forest fringe to the carpark.

(2) Another walk from the Square leads west, past the caravan site and under the old railway track up a zigzag minor road to the steading at Dreggie (023287). Here, with broad views, the road forks into two unsurfaced tracks. Follow the left fork past a copse and grassy track onto bare heath, the bald top of Beinn Mhor (1545 ft.) above Glen Beg a mile west. Turn south (left) on meeting a moor-top track. Pleasant going, but all too soon the track descends into the regulation sitka spruce. Yet it's an easy swing down through the wood, past the first left turn and a double junction onto the old railway track. Take the track west, back to where you started by the caravan site, or continue along it another half-mile to the A939 from Forres and Lochindorb (9). Further on, it winds past Castle Grant. There are some grand views and secluded forest dells *en route*.

And now these grand views lead us on, further up the Spey…

Above Grantown

4

Upper Strathspey – West

Aviemore, Kingussie & Newtonmore to Garva Bridge

60.   Introduction: 'The Drowned Land'

From Rothes to Grantown the strath of the Spey is mostly narrow, hemmed by hills and moor with little level ground. Yet beyond Grantown the land changes dramatically. Of a sudden, with the Cairngorms looming, on the eastern bank flat riverside haughs expand. Widest by Nethybridge (**97**), narrowing as the high hills crowd in, between Aviemore and Kingussie these haughs are often flooded as the Spey winds through Loch Insh and the Insh Marshes (**69**). Thus the name given to this beautiful, wild, unpredictable region as a whole – Badenoch, the 'drowned land' or 'drowned place'.

Badenoch embraces 300 square miles, running from Slochd ('Pit': 840252) near the summit of the pass crested by the Inverness-Perth A9 16 miles southeast of Inverness and four miles west of Carrbridge, to the Perth-Inverness county boundary at Drumochter ('ridge of the high ground': 631760), where A9 and railway together rise up and over a high bare pass by two evocatively-named hills – the Boar of Badenoch and the Sow of Atholl. Of those 300 square miles, two-thirds consist of bare land over 2000 feet high.

To the southeast, set back from the Spey behind a screen of flanking forests - Abernethy, Rothiemurchus, Inshriach - and foothills, the high, deeply cleft Grampian plateau dominates the landscape, amid it four of Britain's five highest mountains – Ben Macdhui (4296ft., 1309m), Braeriach (4248 ft., 1296m), Cairn Toul (4241 ft., 1294m), and Cairngorm ('blue hill': 4084 ft., 1245m).

With craggy bare slopes ascending almost directly above the Spey's west bank, the equally vast if lower, less scenic wilderness of the Monadhliaths ('grey mountains') attracts fewer folk. Amid endless miles of outcrop and bog stretching west to the Great Glen, the highest top of the unsung Monadhliaths is Cairn Mairg (3093 ft.). Yet it's in the southwestern range of these hills, not far from Garva Bridge and the Corrieyairick Pass (**78**) that the Spey starts life.

The chief Badenoch communities – Aviemore, Kingussie and Newtonmore - hug these slopes on the river's west bank. The railway and main A9 likewise follow the Spey much of the way, from Aviemore to Newtonmore, after which road and rail break south up Glen Truim and the river bears west past Laggan towards its source.

This section follows the Spey's west bank southwest to Garva Bridge and the entry to the Corrieyairick Pass. The following section returns northeast via the less populous but more popular and scenic land east of the Spey. With many sites and routes in either section geographically adjacent on opposite banks, cross-references are given as appropriate.

61.   Grantown to Boat of Garten   *(Route)*

From Grantown two main Speyside routes continue southwest. On the east bank, over the river on the Elgin A95 and first right after a few hundred yards, the B970 departs through Nethybridge to Coylumbridge where, meeting the Glenmore road (**91**), it turns right towards Aviemore, then at Inverdruie breaks left to continue via Feshiebridge (**86**) and Ruthven Barracks (**82**) before crossing the Spey to end at Kingussie (**72**) - a route explored, south to north, in the next section.

Joined at the bypass roundabout south of Grantown, the west bank A95 passes Craggan (restaurant one side, fishery and golf course the other), then after two miles a right turn (A938: see next chapter) to Dulnain Bridge and Carrbridge. With wide views of the Cairngorms over the floodplain, the A95 continues past a return loop from Dulnain Bridge round a high bend to a long straight below Curr Wood. At the crest of this bend a minor road (995227) descends left past ruined Broomhill railway station, crossing the Spey over a wooden bridge. It continues past a sign-posted riverside walk a mile to Nethybridge and the B970.

Amid forest on the right halfway down the long A95 straight is the Skye of Curr Heather Centre (01479-851359). With craft-shop and restaurant, here conifers, alpines, shrubs and a vast range of heathers are on display and for sale all year.

Not far on, left of the road by the river, a chambered cairn and standing stones nearby, is Tullochgorum (969214). Here, it's said, when long ago the old mansion was destroyed, the *gruagach* (female household spirit) also departed. Known as *Mag Molach* ('hairy paw'), this benign sprite sometimes appeared as a small boy with a candle to help Tullochgorum's drink-taken master home over the midnight moor: see **92**). Here too, though Tulloch (**94**) near Nethybridge is another claimant, may be the site of dire events behind the composition of the *Reel o' Tulloch*. The laird's raven-haired daughter Isobel loved Iain Dubh Gear ('short dark Iain'), one of the outlawed Macgregors, but her folk wanted her to marry a Robertson. With seven henchmen her brother Alan ambushed Iain who, fighting them off, shot Alan dead, then in elation composed and danced the reel. Yet this is a Highland love story, and must end tragically. Now on the run and caught crossing the Spey at Blacksboat (**57**) he was summarily executed. His head was shown to Isobel in the cell where she lay awaiting the birth of his child: dying of heartbreak she was buried at Kincardine (**94**), where a plain slab marks her grave.

The A95 continues to Drumuillie and the first of two turns to Boat of Garten (**65**), then at Kinveachy (912188) joins the Carrbridge-Aviemore B9153 below the Perth-Inverness railway and A9 trunk route. So, before Boat of Garten, first we visit Dulnain Bridge and Carrbridge, both on the River Dulnain, the only Spey tributary to rise west, high up Beinn Breac in the Monadhliaths.

62.   The Devils of Duthil   *(Route, History, Folklore)*

Two miles south of Grantown take the A938 to Dulnain Bridge (pop. 160); a wooded hamlet at a junction by the River Dulnain. A left turn here over the rapid, peaty river by an old stone bridge returns to the A95, or detours past the long roadside hamlet of Skye of Curr, also to the A95. Keep straight on along the north bank past a hotel on the right, Muckrach Lodge (1860), near it Muckrach Castle, long ruined, now restored. Here in the 16th century Patrick Grant of Freuchie built a castellated mansion before his father Sir John settled him at Rothiemurchus, where he ousted the Shaw Mackintoshes (see **87**).

With rising heath on the right and scrubby riverside ground to the left, after a half-mile a minor road (978250) turns left over the Dulnain to Balnaan: the south bank route to Carrbridge and our next walk. Easily missed, with a right turn in between up to Achnahannet, a few yards on a second left turn also joins the Balnaan road. First, though, the continuing A938 to Carrbridge via Duthil, a hamlet two miles further on.

In the graveyard of the whitewashed, now-unused 1826 church at Duthil is the imposing Grant Mausoleum, traditional burial place of Grant chiefs from 1585 till 1913. Once known as *Gleann a Chearnaich*, 'Glen of Heroes', due to the many warriors born and bred hereabouts, Duthil has many tales. It's said some of the kirk timbers came from Tom Bitlac Castle, a moated fort long ago built on a glacial moraine by Boat of Garten and named after the doughty 15th-century Bigla or Matilda, daughter of a local Comyn lord. Chatelaine of the fort, it's said she often came to worship at Duthil, *en route* hiding the castle keys in a broken stone called *Clach an Tuill Bitlac*, 'Bigla's Stone of the Hole'.

A curse from *c*.1700 concerns a rash minister who, when a son was born to the irreligious Grants of Dalrachney, remarked that yet another demon was added to the tribe. Seeking revenge, the Dalrachney patriarch laid on a baptismal banquet after which the minister, drunk, had to be carried to bed. Awakening, he found his host's dairymaid naked beside him. Public glee at this well-plotted scandal made his position impossible: he fled the parish but, as he did, swore that Duthil would have no ordained minister for seven generations. It's said that for the next two centuries the parish knew no peace. There was talk of witchcraft and the evil eye. As late as 1902 a Duthil woman allegedly remarked: 'Plenty of people have the evil eye and hurt both cattle and people with it.'

Of many old cairns hereabouts, among the biggest is one above Dochlaggie in the Deishar (928202: chamberless). Another, near the old house at Inverlaidnan (862214: **64**), has a stone paving round it and contains a cist that, when excavated, held human remains. The biggest is *Tom Taigh an Leigh* ('Knoll of the Doctor's House'), the tale being that unwed parents had to add a stone for each illegitimate child they had...

Past Duthil the B9007 breaks north over the moors past Lochindorb (**9**) to Forres and Nairn; a route not to miss. Beyond this junction the wooded A938 continues past holiday chalets to Carrbridge, also accessible via the Balnaan road south of the river.

63.   Round the Big Moss   *(Route, Walk)*

This six-mile circuit can also be walked from Carrbridge: if so, just adapt the description. Restful level going, rarely entirely enclosed by forestry, it's boggy in parts but offers no orienteering problems. Keep right and you can't go wrong.

As described, from the A938 a mile west of Dulnain Bridge turn south over the river on the minor road past Balnaan. With the Cairngorms impressive ahead to the south and the Monadhliaths crowding the west, drive southwest over rough, rising pasture, the banked river wriggling over the plain below. Ignoring left turns, continue straight for a mile then, with a low forested hill ahead, right-angle west another mile. Park where a track breaks left (south) to a gate, a silver birch copse one side, open fields the other (947237). Just beyond the gate and visible from the road is a derelict white cottage, beehives by it.

At a Y-fork beyond the cottage and a second gate, bear right (southwest) through silver birch and rowan woodland, open fields one side. This grassy track meanders gradually upward, conifer-dense Creag Garten to the left above reedy, mossy open ground. At the next fork (left up into forestry), keep right through the silver birch by the edge of the wood and above a flat heath to a gate into the forestry.

Past the gate, with Carrbridge glimpsed two miles ahead, stay southwest. At the next forestry Y-fork keep right (the left turn climbs Creag an Fhithich, Raven's Rock, then descends to Drumuillie and Boat of Garten). Entering denser forestry before returning almost to the plantation's edge, the broad track again veers left into deep wood, rising between Creag an Fhithich and Docharn's Craig. Here (926214) cut right down the short wooded bank and over a fence to the southern edge of Feith Mhor ('Big Moss').

Follow the forest fringe west then northwest over boggy ground: don't cut right too soon. Ignoring a wet path north over the moor, continue through a grove of mature Scots Pine, now tending northwest. With the tall steel-blue silo at Auchterblair prominent a mile north over the moor, and fenced cattle-pasture to the right, keep to the forest fringe where it bends north, over drier heath. Via sheep-paths and a footbridge over a burn near the forest, bear north then northeast via the heathery bank above the burn to a gate by the plantation. Here take care: the stile is rotten.

A second gate leads to Auchterblair (021227) and the back road, Carrbridge and the B9153 a mile to the west. Follow the road east two miles over flat riverside pasture past occasional hardwood copses back to where you started.

From Carrbridge start this walk up Carr Road opposite the village hall, between the old bridge and Landmark Visitor Centre (see below), then take it on from Auchterblair. This adds two miles to the circuit.

64.   Carrbridge to Inverlaidnan   *(Walk)*

At the junction of the A938 and the B9153 (the old A9) to Aviemore, the tourist village of Carrbridge (pop. 510) is named after the high-arched span over the Dulnain just west of the main street. Costing £100 when built in 1717, it followed local petition that burial parties bound for Duthil churchyard might safely cross the river, this after two men had drowned. Taking six months to build, it lost its parapets to 1829's Muckle Spate (**52**).

At the village's south end the Landmark Visitor Centre (907223: 01463-841613) lies amid 30 acres of native pine. Opened in 1970, rebuilt after burning down in 1973, it offers a treetop walk, forest trails and picnic areas, restaurant, gift-shop and audio-visual displays of Highland history. In summer the tree-shaded carpark is usually packed.

A seven-mile circular walk upriver and back the far side begins in the village or (my choice) a half-mile west of it. From the junction take the A938 west almost to the 30-mile limit. Park in a layby opposite a minor road on the left to Dalrachney. Follow this road past hostels above riverside pasture and a footbridge. From under the railway bridge this track climbs to the main A9. The view either way is clear, but cross only with great care.

On the far side a surfaced road to Lynphail passes Dalrachney steading then bends north over a burn. A wooden footbridge leads to a clear green track west through rough pasture, north of the river. Climb the edge of a heather moor where dead trees make spooky shapes. Approaching forestry, ford a burn to a high stile over a deer-fence (883224). The heathery, sandy track beyond climbs steadily through thick forestry. From a shallow top it descends through more open woodland, bare Monadhliath hilltops now visible to the west.

At a fork, leave the main track. Cut left down the forested slope towards the river below. Past a deer-fence the muddy track approaches a ruin near Sluggan Bridge (869221: see above), a fine single stone arch. Gated off and once part of yet another Wade road (**79**), over it a track leads southeast to the Dalnahaitnach-Carrbridge return route (see below), so shortening the walk if desired.

Here on the north bank the main track turns northwest into forestry. Leaving it, follow the riverbank west of the bridge over rough pasture under juniper bushes and crags. Where the river bends, climb the open heather slope to a lovely wooded area above a shingled flood-plain. Pick a way along this open bank with its natural woodland and grassy slopes to a boggy gully. Here turn south to a fenceline then, under electricity pylons by a ditch, bear right past a wooden gate and ruin to the track by Inverlaidnan (862215).

Take this track south to a wooden bridge over the Dulnain, sandy wooded scarps the far side. Climb up to (865210) a minor road west from Carrbridge to Dalnahaitnach a mile further southeast (see **67**). Turn left, north, towards Carrbridge, keeping to the road, with wide views west from the heather heath. After a mile the road enters forestry and (875214) intersects the Wade track from Sluggan Bridge. (Via high stile over deer fence the latter runs on south a mile to a left turn northeast. This extension offers a boots-off fording of the Allt Lorgy, also views north from the flank of Carn Lethendry.)

Continuing past a high stile at the return of this loop (893223), the road runs east through open land, the A9 now visible ahead. Pass a gypsy-style caravan then a sawmill to the Carrbridge 30-mile limit. Under the A9 and past a right turn to the railway station, on the left Urquhart's Brae leads downhill and right to the Ellan footbridge, Gurkha-built in 1992. On the river's north bank, turn left up a path 20 yards to a stile over a barbed-wire fence. Climb the bank over another fence, and bear right to where you parked.

Next, via the A95 to Drumuillie, or by taking the B9153 three woodland miles south from Carrbridge to the A95 junction then turning left, to Boat of Garten.

65.   Boat of Garten & the Kinveachy Giant   *(Routes, Folklore, Walk)*

On the A95 just beyond Drumuillie a minor left turn (944200) runs half a mile to a sign: 'Welcome to Boat of Garten, the Osprey Village'. This refers to the RSPB nature reserve and osprey hide two miles east, over the Spey by Loch Garten in Abernethy Forest (**95**).

Dating from the railway's arrival in 1863, Boat of Garten (pop. 615) gets its name from a chain-operated river-ferry, replaced by the present bridge at the end of the 19th century. Built to an L-plan on the Spey's west bank, its church dedicated to St Columba, this neat village, its Boat Hotel and Edwardian villas built to accommodate railway tourism, is one terminus of the Strathspey Steam Railway (01479-810725), Aviemore being the other. From the station (restoration begun in 1972) by the hotel, old steam-drawn trains run five times daily June-September, most days in April, May and October, with specials over the Christmas-New Year period. Privately run by volunteers, an extension of the railway north to Grantown-on-Spey is planned.

By the riverbridge and right of the road a signposted 'Riverside Walk' follows the Spey for a mile south, through mixed woodland and fields past the golf course. Bear right just before the white house at Wester Dalvoult to a junction under a steep slope. Bear left then right over the railway line through Scots pine to Kinchurdy Road, and turn right back into the village and the Boat Hotel.

Also by the Boat Hotel, the road right-angles west past a neat green and council housing, leaving the village to rejoin the A95. Soon, with the Perth-Inverness railway line and A9 running parallel atop a wooded bank ahead, under Kinveachy Lodge the A95 takes up the B9153 from Carrbridge.

Kinveachy Forest, it's said, was once home to an evil giant who hid his heart by nearby Beinn Ghuilbin (896177), under a stone called the Bonnet Stone. The tale is that the only way to kill the giant was for a man to lay his bonnet on this stone, then perform a rite that killed the heart. But whenever the watchful heart saw a bonneted man approach, it hid under another stone, and so the giant survived. In fact there are many Bonnet Stones in the Highlands, perhaps referring to the numerous Neolithic cairns and remains – after all, standing stones were once called *fir chreig*, 'false men' and, like the giant's heart, had the power to 'walk' or 'dance', especially after fall of night...

From Kinveachy, below A9 and railway the A95 turns south past Loch Vaa and Avielochan, between them at the foot of Beinn Ghuilbin and above the A9 a ruined first-century stone fort. Two ring cairns (at 897135, by Aviemore; and at 908155, by the railway a mile south of Avielochan); and a chambered cairn (909167, northeast bank of Avielochan) also testify to ancient human activity in the Spey Valley.

With a short link road to the A9 after another mile, the A95 continues into Aviemore, and as Grampian Road runs the length of this busy tourist centre.

66.   Aviemore: A Railway Town   (Visit, History)

Aviemore (*Agaidh Mor*, 'big gap': pop. 2430) wasn't always about fast food joints and tartan tourist shops. Before the Perth-Forres railway arrived in 1863, there was little here but an inn, condemned by one traveller in 1786 as 'very indifferently kept'. And in 1839 Lord Cockburn remarked sardonically: 'There are only two things wanted to make Aviemore one of the grandest places in Scotland. They are wood and a house.'

All that changed with the railway, especially with the later opening of the direct route to Inverness. The village (the Victorian station with its elegant footbridge and platform canopies now restored: photo next page) became an important junction. 'As one steps from the train at Aviemore after a long night journey from the South,' declared an enthusiast, 'one's travel-tiredness is instantly dispelled by the wonderful air of Upper Speyside.'

Yet until the 1960s what is now Badenoch's largest community was just a small village with a hotel or two. Then, via the growth of winter sports and highland tourism, when the Aviemore Centre opened in 1966 everything changed.

Discos, an ice-rink, hotels, shops and restaurants sprouted as if overnight, bringing not only an influx of tourists but an increase in local population and businesses: by no means all to the bad. Yet with the brutal concrete incongruity of the Centre and high-rise hotels dominating the older village, this is no architectural mecca. Chalets and new B&B-dominated estates encircle older stone-built houses as if besieging them. Fortunately, this planning failure is recognised: a proposed redevelopment will hopefully improve matters.

In any case, Aviemore is less about looks than location. Some 30 miles southeast of Inverness and bypassed by the A9, it offers a natural centre for visitors exploring this spectacular region. With the Spey one side and Craigellachie's crag above, here we're close to some of Scotland's most-visited sites – Loch an Eilean (**88**), Loch Garten (**95**), Glen Feshie (**85**) and, of course, the Cairngorms. From Aviemore the road through Coylumbridge and past Loch Morlich (**91**) leads to the Cairngorm ski-lift, this terminating at the Ptarmigan Restaurant: at 3540 ft. Britain's highest eatery. And early in 1999 a funicular railway up Cairngorm was approved: conservationists protest, but most local folk want it, the economy being largely reliant on tourism.

There is plenty of visitor accommodation: the tourist information office (01479-810363) south of the railway station on Grampian Road deals with bookings and offers information about the wide variety of outdoor activities available; nearby and also on Grampian Road is Aviemore Youth Hostel (01479-810345).

67.   Aviemore: Craigellachie & Cairn Creag Ghleannain   *(Walks)*

Immediately above and west of Aviemore over the A9 is Craigellachie, locally known as The Watch Hill (see **51** for other derivations). Once a gathering-point from which Clan Grant got its war-cry, this is now in part a National Nature Reserve, a 'nature trail' climbing its crag. To walk it, park at the tourist office and follow a path behind the youth hostel; or near the railway station turn west off Grampian Road to the Aviemore Centre. At the first junction bear left on the loop road, then left again. Head west towards the A9 and round the lochan below it to bear right under the pedestrian underpass. After this a steep, in places stepped path climbs above Loch Balladern (immediately west of and under the A9) through mature birch woodland to the crags above. The waymarked route circles a reservoir under the cliffs and then returns.

Another, much longer hill-track this side of the Spey - several walks nearby on the east bank are described later- starts a mile south of Aviemore by the bridge (882107) near Lynwilg House, this immediately north of where the A9 and B9152 run side-by-side and almost opposite the short link-road between them. Drive south from Aviemore on the B9152 to the link-road, with care turn right over the A9, then turn left on what was once the main road to park by the little bridge.

Start up the Alltnacriche private road, locally known as the Burma Road. Follow it over a cattlegrid up the wooded glen above the burn. Where it forks, bear right past a large house, Alltnacriche. With a fence to the left the track climbs steadily through trees to open moorland, the burn (now Allt Dubh) below to the left.

Crossing two bridges while climbing to a broad bare ridge, an hour or so brings you up to a cairn (847127) then over the ridge to a second cairn. Here (844131), with splendid views north, the track divides. The continuing route to the right descends northwest via a broad heathery glen bisected by Allt Ghiuthais to bridge the Dulnain near Dalnahaitnach (**64**) before turning northeast to Carrbridge.

Though the track is a public right of way, like so many others it crosses a private estate, and I hear that diverging from it, especially during the shooting and stalking seasons, is not a good idea. Shown on the OS map is an alternative return route south over the heather flanks of Geal-charn Mor (836123) down to Ballinluig Farm (864103). I've seen this route described in a recent guidebook but, given the above, and as I haven't walked it myself, maybe on this one return as you came.

Oh, and the advice is also that you keep your dog leashed.

68.   Loch Alvie & Loch Insh via Kincraig   *(Route, History)*

Departing south from Aviemore, the first road on the left crosses the Spey to Inverdruie, Coylumbridge, Glenmore and Cairngorm: from Inverdruie the B970 turns south past Loch an Eilean to Glen Feshie – all explored later. For now we take the B9152 (the old main road) past Loch Alvie to Kincraig and Kingussie. The A9 and railway run parallel or close by much of the way.

Before Loch Alvie first you see, prominent atop wooded Tor Alvie, a 90-foot-high column in memory of George 5th Duke of Gordon, 'The Cock of the North' (d.1836), the region's last great feudal overlord. His mother, the elegant Duchess Jane, got local lads to join the Gordon Highlanders by offering a kiss and a shilling (**45**). When she died, six black horses drew her hearse all the way from London. Buried at nearby Kinrara, which she loved, her monument is on low ground south of the Tor by the Spey.

The wooded road winds past pretty Loch Alvie and the white-harled Kirk of Alvie (864093). To visit, on rounding a bend by a cottage look right for the turn to the kirk manse (B&B). Both kirk and loch are named after St. Ailbhe, as an infant allegedly abandoned on a hillside. Like Romulus and Remus suckled by a she-wolf, adopted by Lochlan son of Laidir and taken to Ireland, later he became a Christian. It's said he visited Rome before settling here, his cell being associated with St Columba, while the first kirk – among the first Celtic Christian foundations in Scotland? - was dedicated to the ubiquitous St. Drostan (**54**).

When in 1880 the old kirk was renovated, 150 skeletons were found under the floor, lain head to head. The Rev. James Anderson reburied them in the kirkyard under a red granite stone with the inscription:

BURIED HERE
ARE
REMAINS OF 150 HUMAN BODIES

FOUND OCTOBER 1880
BENEATH THE FLOOR OF THIS
CHURCH
WHO THEY WERE
WHEN THEY LIVED
HOW THEY DIED
TRADITION NOTES NOT
THEIR BONES ARE DUST
THEIR GOOD SWORDS RUST
THEIR SOULS ARE
WITH THE SAINTS WE TRUST

Their death in battle is suggested by a legend that the loch is haunted by a *bean-nighe* ('washerwoman') – a webbed-foot hag who squatted by ford or water-side washing the bloody clouts of those about to die violently (see **92**).

Three miles on over the Moor of Alvie, with the A9 still close by, the B9152 reaches Kincraig (pop. 420). Here the Spey exits Loch Insh, lovely with its wooded islets and mountain backdrop, and home of Bewick and Whooper swans. Opposite the village war memorial a left turn descends under the railway, crossing the Spey by a one-lane wooden bridge (in her Highland Journal for 1860, Queen Victoria called the previous ferry 'a rude affair'). Beyond it, amid old Scots Pine on Tom an Eoin ('Knoll of the Swans') above the loch, is another old church – Insh (836054). Dedicated to St. Adamnan, the 7th-century biographer of Columba, it may date back to the Culdees (*cili deus*: early Celtic Christians of druid background). Renovated in the 1960s, and with a fine Iona Cross in the main window, this kirk has one of Scotland's 'flying bells'. It's said that, if removed, it will always return, and that, when once stolen to Perth, it kept tolling 'Tom an Eoin, Tom an Eoin' so endlessly that its abductors gave up and restored it to its proper home.

By the loch not much further up this road is Loch Insh Watersports Centre (01540-651272). As at Loch Morlich (**91**), this is a local mecca for watersports enthusiasts, and the Boathouse Restaurant also seems to be popular.

69. Dunachton & the Insh Marshes   (Route, History)

Beyond Kincraig, the B9152 parallels railway and A9 past Dunachton Lodge (821047), this above the southwest shore of Loch Insh. Once owned by the MacNivens, a Clan Chattan sept, Dunachton occupies the site of a castle built *c*.1500 by William Mackintosh after he married the MacNiven heiress, Isobel, who not much later drowned 'accidentally'. In 1690 the castle was burned down by Macdonald of Keppoch as part of his attack on Clan Chattan lands. Only the back wing survived to shelter the family.

It's said that near Dunachton (named after the Gaelic *dun*, 'fort') the Pictish king Nechtan (706-732) defeated a would-be usurper, 'King Harald'. South of the

Lodge is An Suidhe ('The Seat': 813072), a crag from which Harald watched the battle. Slain, he was buried on Creag Righ Tharailt ('King Harald's Crag': 791052). Below Dunachton in a hollow between the roads is a ruined chapel built c.1380 and dedicated to St. Drostan. Not much further on, below the railway, the loch gives way to the Insh Marshes. Occupying the flood-plain of the Spey and Scotland's largest inland marsh, here during the 1829 flood (**52**) the river roared a mile wide, and most winters this area between Kincraig and Kingussie turns into one vast loch. Though cattle once grazed and hay was cut here, efforts to drain these wetlands – vast embankments and broad drainage channels are clearly visible - have never succeeded, which may be as well. Now an RSPB nature reserve with almost 200 bird species resident or visiting, here each October up to 200 Whooper swans from Iceland arrive to winter. For information about the observation hides on the south side of the marsh ring 01540-661518.

This natural paradise is overlooked by the Highland Wildlife Park (805040: 01540-651270). From the B9152 turn right under the A9 (810037), and uphill to drive through birchwood and grassland where wolf, bear, boar, bison, lynx, reindeer and wild horses roam. Pets are not allowed in, but free kennels are available.

A mile on, to the right of the road up a private drive two miles before Kingussie, is an elegant Adam mansion house. Balavil (Belleville: 972023), was built on the site of the old castle of Raitts for James Macpherson (1723-96), known as 'Ossian' Macpherson for his central role in the 18th century's most notorious literary scandal...

70.   Macpherson's Ossian   *(Biography)*

Published in Edinburgh in 1760 just 15 years after the '45, *Fragments of Ancient Poetry, Collected in the Highlands of Scotland, and Translated from the Gaelic or Erse Languages* was followed in 1761 by *Fingal, an Ancient Epic in Six Books, Composed by Ossian, Son of Fingal*; and in 1763 by a third volume, *Temora*. Instant hits throughout Europe, in London hostile critics denounced these epics as fake. Few read them now, but controversy endures in academic circles.

So, who was James Macpherson?

A local farmer's son and college drop-out, in 1759 this village teacher impressed author John Home by quoting Gaelic verse from memory, and by offering written verse he said he'd collected in the Highlands. With the first 16 translated pieces published as *The Fragments*, some thought him a fantasist, but others encouraged his claim that he could find and translate an 'heroic poem' relating the Celtic hero Fingal's epic wars.

At first he refused the challenge. To make the epic credible meant reversing accepted history to claim that its protagonists Fingal and Ossian were originally Scots, only later adopted by the Irish as Fionn mac Cumhal and Oisin. He'd have to portray them as Caledonians invading Ulster c.AD200. So the first poem had to describe the Scots Fingal aiding the Irish against Norsemen 600 years before the earliest-known Norse invasions. Tricky. But (did the £60 subscription help?), he travelled, writing down oral poetry, translating old manuscripts, and back in Edinburgh said he'd found: 'a pretty complete poem, truly epic, concerning Fingal, and of an antiquity easily ascertainable.'

Fingal's purple prose ('His armour rattled in thunder, and the lightning of his eyes was terrible') was a hit everywhere but England. And not all Scots believed Macpherson. Philosopher David Hume denounced: 'a palpable and impudent forgery.' Challenged to produce Gaelic originals (hard, if oral: you can't cart old bards about like books), Macpherson submitted manuscripts, saying he'd print them if subscribers came forward. None did. Then, in *Journey to the Western Isles of Scotland* (1773), Dr. Samuel Johnson derided him, claiming there were not 500 lines in Gaelic over a century old. Macpherson, who was a big man, demanded a duel. This came to nothing. Macpherson was no fool. Turning to politics, in 1780 he became an MP - for Camelford in Cornwall: barely hibernian. Later he retired rich to Badenoch to build Balavil. Offered the confiscated lands of his Jacobite relative, Macpherson of Cluny (**77**), he sensibly refused them. The final irony came when he died. Granted burial in Westminster Abbey - odd, for a so-called militant Gael - he ended up entombed beside Johnson. Maybe their ghosts still argue.

In 1805 the Highland Society of Scotland reported that the Fingal/Ossian legend was ancient; and that, as admitted in his preface to *Fingal* Macpherson *had* embroidered, but on old oral material. The 1862 publication of *The Book of the Dean of Lismore* suggested his use of this 16th-century collection of early Gaelic poetry. Though basing only four passages on *Lismore*, which he'd thought too modern, this was the text he'd submitted as evidence. Though not, as he'd claimed, from the 3rd century (the earliest Scots Gaelic text is thought to be the 9th-10th century *Book of Deer*), it now looks like he reworked old tradition which, unwritten before he wrote it down, cannot be proved as such, either way.

A faker? Maybe. Imaginative? Certainly. Yet contemporary fans of Ossian included Goethe, Napoleon, and the great London visionary William Blake (1757-1827: 'Jerusalem', 'Tyger, Tyger' etc.). Fraud or not, Macpherson didn't do badly for himself – and, with the Scottish Tourist Board now setting up 'Project Ossian', a giant, globally-accessible database of information about Scottish tourist products - it looks like Johnson will be spinning in his grave for quite some time yet...

71.   The Cave of Raitts   *(History)*

At Lynchat west of Balavil on a ridge above the road is the Cave of Raitts (777019), alias the Robbers Cave, or *An Uamh Mhor* ('The Big Cave'). Horseshoe-shaped, 70 feet long by eight wide and seven high, 'Raitts' may be from the Gaelic *rath*, here implying an underground house, or house inside a hill; as in fairy raths.

Examining it in 1835 the philosopher Sir David Brewster found an underground Iron Age site well-used since. With a rusted lock amid old debris, once-flagstoned sides and ceiling, the side walls were of big stones perhaps taken from a

Neolithic circle, the 'Standing Stanys de Rathe de Kyngucy' (Kingussie). Within this particular circle in 1380 the Wolf of Badenoch (**10**) had argued his claim to local church lands with Bishop Burr of Moray. Burr, afraid of committing himself to an oath he'd later regret, had refused to enter the circle. Pagan beliefs died hard.

Here, or under a nearby farmhouse, 18 MacNivens once hid from Macpherson revenge. In Glentruim in the 14th century Macpherson cattle strayed over the shallow Spey from Cluny to the southern, NacNiven side at Breakachy (**81**). Angered by the potent intrusion of the Macphersons from Lochaber after Bruce ejected the Comyns from Badenoch, the MacNivens seized the cattle. Macpherson of Cluny (**77**) sent his daughter to beg them back. MacNiven returned them with her petticoats cut off and the bull's tongue cut out. This led to a Macpherson night assault on the MacNivens. By dawn only 18 MacNiven men lived - the fate of the women is unrecorded. Hiding in the Cave of Raitts, or under the farmhouse floor of Raitts, for some years they survived. But, one version has it, Alasdair Cainnteach (the Wordy) Macpherson suspected their hideout. Growing a long beard, he came to the farm disguised as a beggar. The women denied him entry but, pretending illness, he got their sympathy. Seeming to sleep, he saw them open a trapdoor to feed the fugitives. Leaving early, he returned with a war-party. The last MacNivens were beheaded on a tree-stump by the door of the cave/farmhouse.

Later known as a mostly amicable and sturdy folk, in time the Macphersons allied themselves with the Grants of Rothiemurchus (**87**), prospering in Badenoch and abroad, as Newtonmore's Clan Macpherson Museum (**75**) makes clear.

72.   Kingussie: 'Capital of Badenoch'   *(Visit, History)*

Nearing Kingussie ('head of the pinewood'; pronounced King-eusie: pop. 1440), the B9152 cuts under the A9 and again changes its number, becoming the A86 as it enters and runs up the Capital of Badenoch's long main street.

Quiet compared with Aviemore, as such this solid grey town is barely 200 years old. Yet as long ago as 565 a chapel here was dedicated to St. Columba; and on its site the old parish church, *Eaglais nan Colum Cille* (rebuilt 1624) became the focus of the community, with Kingussie the kirktown for the ancient Castle of Ruthven (**82**). In the kirkyard a stone commemorating the saint is said to have been 'planted by himself', and also commemorated is a Captain Clark whose grandson, Sir John A Macdonald, became Canada's first Prime Minister. And of course there are many Macpherson headstones, the settlement being created a parish *c*.1200 under Muriach the Parson who, when his brother died childless, became head of Clan Chattan and got papal permission to marry a daughter of the Thane of Cawdor. She bore him five sons, who all became known as Macpherson, 'Son of the Parson'; thus the name of the clan.

Surviving the Wolf's argument with Bishop Burr and gaining a Charter of Barony in 1451, Kingussie remained a backwater until 1799, when the 4th Duke of Gordon advertised: 'for tradesmen, manufacturers and shop keepers' to settle in the new village he built near the old church. Noted after 1786 for its fine schooling, the weaving and spinning industry encouraged by the Duke declined, but the railway's arrival led to an influx of tourists and sportsmen eager to shoot grouse, large villas being built as holiday homes on the pinewood slopes above the Spey. With tourism waning, after 1945 new trades developed, today including craft enterprises and a bone china factory on the industrial estate. And on Duke Street is the Highland Folk Museum (01540-661307). Established on Iona in 1934 by Dr Isobel Grant, who assembled the collection herself, it was moved to Laggan (**76**), and in 1944 found its present home. Now, with its Turf House, the Lewis Black House and the Clack Mill, it offers a fine collection of items vital to daily life in times past – and there are griddle-baked scones and pancakes!

On a grassy mound east of the Spey is the ruin of Ruthven Barracks, built in 1719 and blown up by the Jacobites in 1746. Later we visit to hear of the curse put on the Ruthven ferryman (**82**), then walk to Glen Tromie and back (**83**), but now and on this side of the river next is an equally-fine five-mile hill-and-loch circuit.

73.   Kingussie: Creag Bheag & Loch Gynack   *(Folklore, Walk)*

From the village centre start up Gynack Road by the Duke of Gordon Hotel and opposite the Ruthven road, then turn left into Ardvonie carpark (free). West of the carpark and the small park adjacent, climb to Tait's Brae. Cross to West Terrace and continue past wooded villas and bungalows to a turning-circle and drive at the end of the road: no parking here.

The drive climbs to two modern houses. Past the first on the left a grassy track climbs to a gate. Bear right up the forest fence through birch and juniper on a

rough track. With open moor rising left, the path levels off to a fork. Bear left, parallel to the old dyke, and climb steadily (soggily?) to Creag Bheag's rocky ridge (745017: 487m), with its tors, cairns and fine views – east over the Spey to the Cairngorms, north deep into the Monadhliaths, and west to Creag Dhubh (see **77**) above Newtonmore.

On the open top head southwest over the ridge to see Loch Gynack in its bare glen below, Creag Mhor's crags opposite. From here return as you came or descend the gentler western flank as you can to Loch Gynack's southwest shore and a wet path. Turn right along the lochside through boggy scrub woodland, Pitmain Lodge (748029) ahead over the water. At the loch's east end the path climbs right to a deer-fence and gate. There is no high stile: you have to sprawl over the gate. Continue east up a heathery rise through a young plantation to the top edge of the golf course (754023). Again a deer-fence, again no stile, but a hole torn through the fence by the corner lets you through.

Now on the golf course near a derelict cottage and lone pine, descend past the sixth tee, skirt the fifth green, and bear left (south). A path descends, right, through silver birch to the next green. Continue south along the wooded righthand edge of the fairway, watching for mishit drives. Skirt the first green via a fenceline path through silver birch to the caravan park atop Gynack Road (755016). Descend above Allt Mor's fine cascades a wooded half-mile past St Vincent's Hospital and so back to the carpark.

Loch Gynack is said to be haunted by Satan, this because Kingussie folk forgot when Sodom and Gomorrah were destroyed. Also fairies lived here with their fairy dogs; a breed improved if crossed with mortal canines. Once, a poor crofter decided to drown himself, hoping someone might pity his family. About to wade into the loch, he met a fairy woman. She said all would be well if, in a year, he returned to give her whatever or whoever first met him when he got home. Believing an orphaned lamb tethered by the door would be first, he went home. His wife and children rushed out, but his dog reached him first. A year later, his life much better, sadly he came to meet the fey lady, offering all he had if only he could keep his faithful dog. Denied, he demanded she take back her gifts but, even as she reminded him that this meant his life, the dog crawled to her. 'Meet me in a year,' she said, then vanished with the dog. A year later he returned, and there she was, with his old dog and a fine pup she gave him. It became the best working dog in the area, and its descendants, like all fairy dogs, had silver eyes and could see the wind.

74.   The Black Officer of Balachroan   *(History, Folklore)*

Above the B9152 out of Kingussie, for nearly a century Pitmain (745005) was the area's main inn, being opened in 1765 by John Maclean, his successor in 1811 being described as 'a good-natured man and very fond of boasting of his intimacy with the nobility.' Here the Dukes of Gordon hosted the area, the occasion being the dinner and ball after the annual cattle sale, the Pitmain Tryst. Little remains of the inn save part of the steading and a line of trees marking the boundary of a garden once-famed for 'its abundance of fruit'.

Less generous was the owner of Balachroan (733004) a mile west of Pitmain - Captain John Macpherson (1724-1800), known as 'Black John', or 'The Black Officer of Balachroan'. Born in Glentruim (**81**), as Badenoch's recruiting officer he tricked many young men into the army. At market he'd get them drunk then slip them the Shilling. If they took it, or caught it when he tossed it, they were marched away, few to return.

Retiring a captain and marrying late, he'd settled to farm Balachroan. A keen hunter, this 'improving' farmer soon had Badenoch's best crops and fattest cattle. Tales spread that he was a '*deisciobul an Diabhol*' who'd outwitted Auld Nick. It's said his first wish was that his crops be the envy of all. For this the Devil demanded their roots as his due. So John sowed corn and gave Satan the worthless roots. Accused of cheating, he said next year he'd take the roots, giving Satan the crops. Planting tatties, he gave the furious Devil the useless haulm. For his third wish he asked for the best cattle ever seen. In return Satan demanded all the beasts in the corner nearest the steading. Destroying the steading, as at Gordonstoun (**34**), Black John built a circular yard. Soon it held the finest herd of cattle ever seen but, when the Devil returned, there was no corner to claim.

So when at New Year 1800 the old man died violently in Glen Tromie (**83**) in the 'Catastrophe of Gaick', many said the Devil had finally got his own back.

As tenant of Gaick Forest, John often hunted from a stone-walled, heather-roofed bothy. A year before he'd organised a Chrismas hunt, but nobody turned up. Raging that he had a meeting and 'must be in Gaick tonight', with two dogs and a friend he set up Glen Tromie, reaching the bothy near midnight. Later, as he was drinking, the dogs began to howl. At a knock on the door he slipped out, but before it shut the other man saw a dark figure, then heard angry voices, one shrill like a billygoat. He heard John promise to return in a year with more men. Old John returned inside, shaking. 'He was a guest so angered by no company that he's going home,' he said. 'Has he far to go?' the friend asked. 'Yes,' said John, 'but he has a fast, strong horse.'

Finding no hoofprints outside next day, his friend told everyone how Satan had again met Black John. When a year later John arranged another hunt, all invited tried to refuse. Even so, on Monday 30 December 1799 he left for Gaick with four men. Another eight arrived late at the rendezvous, Aultlearic, home of his companion the year before, but found Iain Ban, the man's son, there to guide them. The youth even had new brogues for the hunt – yet, near Nuidebeg, these shoes oddly fell apart, leaving him barefoot (see **10**). Agreed that this was a warning, all returned home.

With the hunting party expected back by Friday to prepare for the old Christmas on Monday, January 6th, on New Year's Day a violent snowstorm blew up. By Friday it was over, but with no sign of the hunters a child at Nuide was questioned to divine the cause of their absence.

'When will they return?' he was asked. 'Never, never!' he replied.

So it proved. Those clearing a way up the snow-buried glen found the bothy demolished by an avalanche, parts of the roof a mile away. All five men were dead. Three, including John, lay in their heather beds, a fourth crouched as if removing his shoes when caught. The body of the fifth, Duncan Macfarlane, was found in snow 300 yards away two months later. The bad reputation of *Gaidhig dhubh nam feadan fiar* ('Black Gaick of the twisted ravines') was assured. Even today weird reports persist – phantom ghillies with ghostly ponies have been seen in this dreich pass.

Yet, though hated by some, many of his equals had viewed John warmly. Eulogies to his life and sudden death in active old age were penned; a memorial erected on the bothy-site in 1902 bears the names of the five dead. Later an elegy in Gaelic by Duncan MacKay, a bard of the time, was etched into a stainless steel plaque now bolted to the foot of the memorial stone by the owners of Gaick Forest.

75. Above Newtonmore: the Red Well   (History, Walk)

The Gaelic name for Newtonmore, *Bail Ur an t'Sleibh* (pop. 1175) means – the New Town on the Moor. Developed early in the 19th century three miles west of Kingussie on the road to the 1765 New Spey Bridge, Queen Victoria found it 'a very long poor-looking village,' and was not amused. Long a site where cattle were gathered after being driven over the Corrieyairack Pass (**78**) from Loch Ness and before being sold at Pitmain, it was here Glenbanchor folk came when cleared out for sheep, leaving them little to do but play shinty, for which sport today the village is locally famed. Once the battle-training exercise of Celtic warriors, it's played 12-a-side with sticks called 'camans'. These resemble hockey-sticks, but this wild game makes hockey look as placid as bowls.

Bypassed by the A9 which here runs south of the Spey, the village is one long main street until, by Main's Hotel at the west end, the road forks. The A86 crosses the River Calder and heads west to Loch Laggan, Spean Bridge and Fort William, while the B9150 passes the Clan Macpherson Museum before crossing the Spey to join the A9.

Opened in 1952 and the first to be devoted to a single clan, the museum is a must for anyone interested in local history and folklore. Among many items on display is the broken fiddle of the freebooter James Macpherson, executed in Banff in 1700, and source of the ever-popular 'Macpherson's Rant' (see **106**).

A six-mile moorland circuit starts from Newtonmore., or from above the village. Climbing 700 feet, and wet in parts, it offers grand views of the Monadhliath and Badenoch Hills, plus wild-life in abundance – even hares and grouse, now rare.

From the A86 (Kingussie end: 724995), turn right up narrow Strone Road half-a-mile to the moor. A left-hand bend by a ruin soon leads to a second, also by a ruin. Park on the verge. A gated track past the ruin reaches a second gate; a sign asking walkers to respect the stalking season and keep to the tracks. Beyond it, a new plantation to the left, the track forks. The right fork fords Allt na Feithe Buidhe ('Burn of the Yellow Moss'), a plank footbridge by it. Keep left, climbing steadily, Creag Dhubh (756m) prominent southwest, Glen Banchor below it, and bare Monadhliath brows ahead dominated by the ridges of Carn A' Chailleach (930m). The white buildings ahead are waterworks.

The track curls left and down over the boggy burn via wooden slats (716007). Past a left turn just beyond this crossing keep north on the main track, first tending right towards a plantation flanking Creag Mhor (604m) above Loch Gynack (**73**), then swinging left, northwest, towards a small glen. Past a wooden gate in a fenceline, join the burn (707017) where it exits the glen. The wide track north climbs the burn's east bank to a waterfall, by it the rusty remains of the Green Bothy. With fine views south, soon over the burn you see the Red Well, more accurately named than the Green Bothy. Here too by the track is a rock with an arrow and the initials JD. Turn back.

I'd read of a soggy track back to Newtonmore gained by fording the burn at the mouth of the glen. However, amid a downpour the foaming spate dissuaded me. Rather than return as I came, I followed the burn south via sheep-tracks over the heath. Before long, where the burn meets the flats to vanish into a soaking moss, I was floundering. Finally reaching low dry blaeberry heights amid the sodden moor, I came across three pyramidical cairns, expertly built and in a triangle, its base some 200 yards, smaller cairns to the east and northeast. What are these? A half-mile west of the main track, they offer mystery amid the mire. Yet I suggest that, on this walk, if the burn proves unfordable, save yourself trouble and return as you came.

76.   Newtonmore to Laggan   (*Route, History*)

From Newtonmore the A86 follows the Spey southwest under rocky Creag Dhubh past Cluny Castle and Balgowan eight miles to Laggan.

Leaving Newtonmore, north of the A86 where it crosses the River Calder and near the Falls of Calder (701994) is Banchor Cemetery (705989), site of an early chapel dedicated to St. Bride or Bridget of Kildare. Born to the Christian slave of a pagan bard, the historical St Bride (*c*.452-524) traditionally founded a community open to both sexes. Yet her feast on 1 February falls a day before the old pagan Candlemas, and her legend (she is born at sunrise, her house blazes with light, fire shoots from her brow when she takes the veil); is that of Brigit, fire-goddess of the mythic Tuatha de Danaan and daughter of their king, the Dagda, his ever-full cauldron a precursor of the Holy Grail. As this older Brigit ('The High One') was the Muse of Gaelic poets, and as Robert Louis Stevenson (see **77**) gained inspiration for his novel Catriona here, maybe she had blessed him.

The direction sign to the cemetery is in Gaelic: *An Rathad Daingnichtele le lagh Gu Cladh Bhrighde*, 'The Roadway Established by Law to St Bride's Graveyard', referring to a famous 1876 court case re-establishing a public right of way which had been obstructed by a new steading at Banchor Farm.

Two miles on and just past Bialudbeg (692973) where the first local township was cleared for sheep in 1797, amid a wide infertile plain the Spey takes up the River Truim (687963). At nearby Invernahavon in 1386, a raiding-party of Lochaber Camerons faced local Davidsons, Macintoshes and Macphersons. Refused their traditional position on the right wing, the latter withdrew over the Spey to watch the battle from a knoll north of the confluence. With the Davidsons overwhelmed, the desperate Mackintosh chief had his bard recite a satire to Cluny Macpherson's face, calling him a coward while claiming that Lochiel, not MacIntosh, had sent him. The ruse worked: now in their turn the Camerons were slaughtered. Ten years later, with the dispute still unsettled King Robert III ordered 30 men from each side to meet on the North Inch at Perth and fight to the death. In this infamous battle only one Cameron survived; of the victors, eleven lived, including their leader, Shaw Macintosh, granted the lands of Rothiemurchus (**87**) for his bravery.

Next, passing two lochans together known as Lochan Ovie and said still to hide French gold sent to finance the '45, thick-wooded slopes above the A86 flank the steep rock of Creag Dhubh (756m). Challenging Newtonmore Highland Games runners who each August race from the village to the summit and back, high up it is Cluny's Cave, one of Cluny Macpherson's hideouts (see next chapter). Creag Dubh is seen best from the Catlodge-Glen Truim road (**81**) high up the south side of the Spey, as is Cluny Castle (645945: not open). Hidden from the road in its wooded policies, only its lodge gates by the hamlet of Balgowan hint at its presence. In compensation, looking ahead and left and over the Spey, atop wooded Creag Ruadh you can see the prominent monument to 'Old' Cluny, chief of Clan

Macpherson during much of the 19th century.

And now, reaching the hamlet of Laggan by its bridge over the Spey, and before continuing west to Garva Bridge and the start of the Corrieyairick Pass, the tale of Cluny Macpherson's exploits after the '45...

77. Cluny: Cave, Cage, & Curse *(History)*

In *Kidnapped* (1886), R L Stevenson drew on the exploits of Ewan Macpherson (1706-64), who after Culloden had his estates seized and his new castle at Cluny burned down. Colonel of the Badenoch men during the '45 and spokesman of the Jacobite war council at Derby, after Culloden he oversaw the Highlanders' retreat. For the next nine years he lived on the run, never betrayed despite the £1000 on his head. Said to be of: 'low stature, very square, and a dark brown complection', and of 'extreme good sense', he was: 'beloved by his clan'. Mainly he hid in 'Cluny's Cave' (*Uamh Chluanidh*) high up Creag Dubh. At 670960 (approx), from this hard-to-reach redoubt he'd secretly visit his wife in the small house Cumberland left her. He had other hideouts, one underground by the Spey, another in the old house at Dalchully (595936: **78**) west of Cluny Castle under Dun da Lamh. It's said once troops commanded by a Munro surrounded this house: Cluny rushing out to hold Munro's horse while the soldiers looked for him, Munro tipping the grubby 'servant' before riding off. Most famous hideout of all, and as visited by David Balfour in *Kidnapped*, was a cave above Loch Ericht on Ben Alder.

This, Cluny's Cage or Prince Charlie's Cave, the OS map shows as sited above Alder Cottage north of the loch's southwest end. Harder to reach and with wider views is a site up the Alder Burn by the Peregrine's Rock, high on the ben's west side. Browne in *History of the Highlands* (1838) says it was: 'situated in the face of a very rough, high and rocky mountain...within a small thick bush of wood.' With trees laid to level the floor, a tree growing from the hillside was the centre-beam of the roof. Stevenson writes: 'The whole house had something of an egg shape; and it half hung, half stood in that steep, hillside thicket, like a wasp's nest in a green hawthorn.' With moss-covered, wattled walls, a projection of the cliff was the fireplace, smoke from it sufficiently rock-coloured to evade detection. It had an upper and a lower room, and its guests spent long hours playing cards while look-outs at greater and lesser distances watched for the redcoats.

Before fleeing to France Prince Charlie stayed here six days. First arriving at a hut at Mellanmuir with Lochiel, he was feasted on mutton, 'twenty Scotch pints' of whisky, dried beef sausages, a bacon ham, and butter and cheese. Eating minced collops from a saucepan ('the only fire-vessel they had'), he drained drams and declared: 'Now, gentlemen, I live like a prince.' Moved on for two nights to 'an extremely bad and smoky hut', he went next to the Cage, leaving it on 13 September 1746 for his final trek to Loch nan Uamh in Lochaber, where the frigate *L'Heureux* awaited him.

Nine years later, being 'in great straits', he wrote commanding Cluny to join him in Paris with whatever money Cluny could get. He never thought of the greater straits of those he'd abandoned. Yet in June 1755 the loyal Cluny escaped to France and, joined by his wife in 1757, died in exile at Dunkirk in 1764. Returning to Badenoch, his widow died a year later. No happy ending there, either.

As for the Curse of Cluny, *c.*1532 an Ulster chieftain visited Badenoch to wed Cluny Macpherson's eldest daughter, with him the warrior Cathalan, who fell for the bride's younger sister. Plotting an elopement, later that year he returned secretly from Ireland. The pair fled west up the Corrieyairick Pass, but her exhaustion made them stop the night in a cave on Creag a' Chathalan (Cathalan's Rock). Old Cluny, learning of the elopement, sent clansmen after them, demanding that they return with the Irishman's heart, or else. With snow falling, the lovers' path from the cave was traced; Cathallan was murdered. Too late, after the men returned with his daughter and Cathallan's heart, Cluny opened the Ulsterman's wallet and, from the papers in it, realised the dead man had been of noble birth, and fit for his grieving daughter. In remorse he erected a stone over Cathalan's grave – a stone said still to stand, though now well-weathered.

Out of Macpherson hands since the 1930s, for a decade in the late 19th century the present Cluny Castle annually hosted Andrew Carnegie, the Scots-American millionaire. Those disliking his flying the Stars and Stripes above the castle were mollified by his generosity. Previously, Queen Victoria had considered it for her Highland residence before choosing Balmoral. 'Royal Deeside' was so nearly 'Royal Badenoch'!

78.   Laggan to Garva Bridge   *(Route, History)*

Once associated with the Witch of Laggan, who had the odd ability to turn herself into a cat, this one-store hamlet (pop. 160) by a bridge over the Spey is where Wade's military road breaks west from the A86 six miles to Garva Bridge and on to the start of the Corrieyairick Pass.

Also in Laggan lived Mrs Grant, wife of the minister who built the parish church in 1785. Widowed with eight children, her *Letters from the Mountains* (1806) made her as much a celebrity as her literary namesake, Elizabeth Grant of Rothiemurchus (**87**). An earlier minister (the church then a heather-thatched building higher up the Spey) was Duncan Macpherson, a formidable man locally called the 'Ministeir Mor'. Living at Dalchully over the river, when it was in spate he often preached across it to his congregation on the far side; while to get the young men into church he agreed with them that, if they attended, he'd let them play shinty before and after the service.

The old military road follows the Spey's north bank past Blairgie (606946), a farm occupied 200 years ago by Sergeant John Macpherson, in whose arms General Wolfe died at the Battle of Quebec in 1759. Two miles beyond it, amid flat pasture under stony bare hills, south of the river is Dalchully House, where Cluny

Macpherson sometimes hid after the '45. Here too, during the '45, General Johnny Cope did his famous 'About-Turn', deciding not to pursue Prince Charlie's men up the Corrieyairick.

At a point where an old trail breaks north up Glen Markie, the road crosses the river by the Spey Dam under Dun da Lamh ('fort of the two hands': 583929). Named for its situation 600 feet up a steep, densely-wooded spur of the Black Craig, this fine Iron Age fort is unlike many others of the same era in that its dry stone walls show no signs of vitrification (see **109**). Up to nine feet high and 23 feet wide, they enclose an area the size of a football pitch. With a steep fall on all sides, it is best approached along the ridge from the southwest.

The stretch of water behind the Spey Dam is sometimes called Loch Shirra after the glen to the southwest. For fishing permits and boat hire apply at Laggan Store: you're asked to drive slowly during the lambing season. Well-embanked above soggy waterside flats and crossing a deep-cut canal just before Glenshero Lodge, the Spey itself running parallel immediately to the north, the road cuts through forestry to broad, empty land by Garvamore (528943). The lonely steading here was once a 'stance' on the drove route over the Corrieyairick; and, as such, vitally important when the military road was built.

Under a mile on is two-arched Garva Bridge, signs by the carpark noting that the road ahead is closed, and advising hillwalkers to call the local head stalker (01528-544222). The Spey here is little more than a big burn flowing through broken rocks – impressive, but a toddler compared with its downstream maturity.

The continuing road climbs rocky heath past forestry to end after three miles at a wooden bridge by Melgarve. By the start of the stony track departing into the hills ahead a notice warns *Danger: high altitude pass, extreme weather possible, vehicular passage not advised.* Also noted are unsafe bridges ahead, and a 1998 voluntary agreement with 4x4 enthusiasts not to use the track during a period of survey by Historic Scotland.

Here the little Spey, meandering not far south, is close to its birth in Loch Spey. As for the track ahead, it leads to the 2519ft. pass from the Upper Spey to the Great Glen. Known as the Corrieyairick, it is also known as the greatest achievement of the 18th-century military road-builder, General George Wade.

79.   Wade's Military Roads   *(History)*

It's hard to avoid the roads built by General Wade (1673-1748) and his successors, notably Major William Caulfeild - yes, Caulf*ei*ld is how it's spelt. Throughout the Central Highlands these roads and bridges were built to link Hanoverian military outposts established after the first two Jacobite uprisings (1689, 1715). Made to aid the movement of troops, baggage and gun-trains through wild, formerly roadless terrain, they are named after Wade. In fact he oversaw about 250 miles of road and 40 bridges; his successor Caulfeild 1000 miles of road and 800 bridges. Yet Wade masterminded the network, and created the major routes. These include the roads from Inverness to Dunkeld, Inverness to Fort Augustus, and the spectacular route over the Corrieyairick.

Descending to the south end of Loch Ness at Fort Augustus, this 28-mile route is his masterpiece, with 13 (some say only 11) hair-raising hairpin-bends over the top of the pass. Walk it (I haven't) to work out how many hairpins there are. A phantom piper and other fearsome spectres are said to haunt the route – some perhaps the ghosts of soldiers who had too many drams at Garvamore before starting over the pass. With 18 stone bridges, the work was completed between the beginning of April and the end of October 1731. 500 soldiers worked a 10-hour day with no days off. When this huge task was finished, Wade gave: 'each detachment an ox-feast and liquor; six oxen were roasted whole; one at the head of each party. The joy was great...' – is *that* a surprise!

Planning and surveying these routes himself, Wade preferred fords to costly bridges (though not stinting when it came to the Tay Bridge at Aberfeldy) and, where possible, like the Romans, drove straight. The road-building soldiers got double-time, save on days when bad weather made work impossible, and they didn't get paid at all...

Grandson of a man whose Irish lands had in Cromwell's time been granted in lieu of pay, Wade had risen steadily through the ranks of the British Army. A proven soldier in the field, later an MP and intelligence agent, his time came when in 1724 the wily Simon 11th Lord Lovat self-seekingly sought to raise Highland Companies to control Jacobitism. But nobody trusted the 'Old Fox', he'd already switched sides too often. Warned against him, King George I sent Wade north to: 'conduce to the quiet of his Majestry's faithful subjects.' Later stripping Lovat of his company on suspicion of pocketing pay due to his men, Wade, now Commander-in-Chief North Britain, developed the strategy that made his name.

Arriving in Inverness in 1725, first he tried to drive a road south via Essich, but found it too circuitous. In 1732, he tried again, getting as far as Foyers along Loch Ness-side before the geography defeated him. At one section by Inverfarigaig - the Black Rock - over 2000 yards of conglomerate precipice dropping sheer into the loch had to be blasted. The miners dangled by ropes from the top while drilling charge-holes. Yet at Foyers he had to abandon the lochside and pursue the high road south through Stratherrick, that route now the B862.

Leaving Scotland in 1740 he became a privy councillor in 1742 and a year later was promoted to field-marshal. Dying in London with a fortune of £100,000 (he held shares in the lead and strontium mines at Strontian), he was buried in Westminster Abbey. Yet he lived long enough to see his work aid the final crushing of Highland society after the 1745 revolt.

In the 'British' National Anthem (in a verse now diplomatically ignored), the hope is expressed that Wade will: 'like a torrent rush, rebellious Scots to crush', and: 'confound their politics, frustrate their knavish tricks.'

If you mean to walk the Corrieyairack, be prepared. Meanwhile the rest of us return to Laggan, to explore the route from Laggan Bridge via Catlodge to Glen Truim. Having explored the Spey's west bank, next we return downriver on the east bank via Glen Tromie, Glen Feshie, Rothiemurchus, Glen More and the Abernethy Forest. After that it's on to Tomintoul and up through old Banffshire.

*Garva Bridge (see **78**)*

5

Upper Strathspey – East

Glen Tromie, Glen Feshie, Rothiemurchus & Abernethy

80.   Introduction: Mountain, Forest & Glen

Though superficially similar (bare high ground) to the Monadhliath wilderness west of the Spey, in many ways the region east of it could not be less alike. The west bank from Kingussie to Aviemore and beyond has little flat ground, but on the east bank there are wide haughs. The western slopes, save for a few plantations, are largely barren until north of Aviemore, but the east bank is densely clad in forestry or natural woodland from Bridge of Tromie to beyond Nethybridge – the Inshriach, Rothiemurchus, and Abernethy Forests, all thriving in the lee of the Cairngorms. From the west only one main tributary enters the Spey (the Dulnain, near Grantown), but from the east, one after the other, the Truim, Tromie, Feshie, Druie, Nethy and Avon pour into the Spey.

Likewise the glens and straths carrying these streams are grander than any to the west, several with long-distance high-ground tracks to regions south and east – Glen Tromie to Dalnacardoch via Gaick and to Blair Atholl via Minigaig Pass; Glen Feshie to Blair Atholl via Glen Tilt and to Braemar via Glen Geldie; the Lairig Ghru to Braemar; and Strath Nethy also to Braemar via Glen Derry. And while only a few lochans dot the unsung Monadhliaths, in and about the Cairngorms Loch an Eilean, Loch Einich, Loch Morlich, Loch Garten, Loch Avon and others are celebrated for their beauty.

The result? The Cairngorms swarm with visitors, walkers, climbers and skiers, and this very popularity is cause for concern. Formed over 500 million years ago and Britain's largest area of arctic mountain landscape, the foothills of this vast granitic massif host some of the widest, least disturbed areas of native forest left in the land. Yet it and its flora and fauna are increasingly threatened by social and economic pressures of a sort also found in the Lake District, the Peak District and Snowdonia. You need only visit Rothiemurchus (**87**) on a summer day to realise we're all part of the problem - one much-used track-junction below the Lairig Ghru is called 'Piccadilly' (**91**). So if you seek solitude, you may not find it here, at least in summer.

This section touches only briefly on the higher ground – many other guides deal with the tops and long-distance trails – but remember, the hills can be dangerous. If intending a long hike, take all due precautions. Let someone know where you're going and when you mean to be back. The Cairngorms demand respect.

81.   Glentruim to Drumochter   *(Route, History)*

For the east bank route, from Laggan cross the Spey on the A86, which from here runs southwest past Loch Laggan to Spean Bridge, then immediately turn left on the A889 (614937: Dalwhinnie 7, Perth 64).

Under the monument to 'Old' Cluny (**76**), this Wade road climbs a mile east to Catlodge (634919) and Calum Piobhar's cairn, erected in 1960 in memory of Malcolm Macpherson (d.1898), once piper to Cluny Macpherson, and in his day widely reckoned the finest player of pibroch in the Highlands. The gateposts of the lodge are guarded by stone wildcats, as in the Macpherson crest and motto: *'Touch not the cat bot a glove'*, meaning 'Touch not the cat with exposed claws' or 'Touch not the cat without a glove.'

Here, where the A889 bends south, climbing then descending through Dalwhinnie to the A9, turn east above the Spey on a minor road to Glentruim ('Valley of the Elder'), soon passing Breakachy, ('speckled field': 638928), site of the MacNiven feud with the Macphersons (**71**) and later the home of Corporal Samuel Macpherson. Leading the Black Watch Mutiny of 1743, when 112 men of the regiment tried to march home to Scotland from London, along with a Shaw of Rothiemurchus and a Macpherson of Laggan he was arrested and executed at the Tower of London

With Cluny Castle visible the far side of the broad, flat-pastured glen, the road winds on opposite Creag Dubh and Cluny's Cave. Three miles east of Breakachy and just west of Mains of Glentruim (680944), a fenced enclosure with a fine view upriver features a cairn erected in 1996 to commemorate Cluny Macpherson (**77**). Next the road descends over the River Truim and the Perth-Inverness railway to join the A9 two miles north of the cascading Falls of Truim (680922): there is a carpark by the A9.

The Truim rises on An Torc in Drumochter, 2500 feet high on the old Perthshire-Inverness boundary. Known as the 'Boar of Badenoch', with its sister the 'Sow of Atholl' this bare conical hill dominates the east side of the pass and (like Ben Macdhui: see **92**) is said to be haunted, by the giant 'Spectre of the Boar'.

With the railway and the A9 alongside (the route engineered 1728-30, yet again by Wade) the river runs north 15 miles past Dalwhinnie to meet the Spey at Invertruim, site of the 1386 battle (**76**).

At the head of Loch Ericht, Dalwhinnie, 'the meeting dell', is the last community (pop. 100) before Blair Atholl and Pitlochry in Perthshire. With a hotel, distillery (visitor centre: 01528-522208), and little else, here occurred another bloody affray. Agreeing to meet Murray of Atholl unarmed with two companions each to decide a boundary dispute, but warned by a seer that Atholl meant to kill him, Lochiel hid 200 men nearby. Finding Atholl unarmed with two followers as agreed, he decided to hang the false seer. But as they talked Atholl's cloak kept slipping until, replacing it again, he did so with it turned inside out. Jumping up, Lochiel saw the heads of men approaching stealthily. 'What's this?' he demanded. 'Atholl sheep come to eat Lochaber grass,' Atholl answered. Waving his bonnet, Lochiel replied as his men charged: 'And here are Lochaber dogs come to worry Atholl sheep.' Few of Atholl's men lived. Their burial mounds could be seen near the railway bridge until 1980, when the field was ploughed and forested.

It's said that between Drumochter and Dalwhinnie the medieval wizard Michael Scot was attacked by a huge white worm. His friends fled, but he slew the beast which, cut in three pieces, they carried to the inn at Dalwhinnie. Offering free lodging in return for the middle portion, the landlord had his wife make dragon-soup. Tasting a drop of it, Michael instantly knew not only the language of birds and beasts, but also that the landlord would kill him for stealing the worm's power, and so with his friends he fled. This reminds of the Welsh tale in which young Gwion, set by the goddess Cerridwen to stir a bubbling pot of dragon-broth, is likewise enlightened when a drop flies out and burns his thumb, which he sucks. Shapeshifting into hare, fish, bird then grain of corn, he flees the furious hag, but she catches and swallows him. Nine months later he is reborn to her as the Dark Age poet Taliesin. Odd, how these tales mutate and survive.

82.   Ruthven: Barracks & Ferry   *(History, Folklore)*

Joining the A9 in Glentruim at 692952, turn left and north. Passing the 'Gateway to the Highlands' information centre at Ralia, after two miles take the B9150 left, over the river to Newtonmore (the A9 continues past Nuide and Ruthven to cross the Spey by Kingussie). From Newtonmore return to Kingussie via the A86 and, opposite the Duke of Gordon Hotel turn right on the B970 (Ruthven Barracks 1 mile).

Again crossing the Spey, turn up a brae to the ruin of Ruthven Barracks (765997), prominent on its grassy part-artificial mound. Long before the barracks was built in 1719 only to be blown up by the Jacobites in 1746, this site commanded a main Spey crossing, the first known castle here being built in the 13th century by the Comyns of Badenoch. In *c.*1405 the Wolf of Badenoch died at Ruthven (see **10** for the spooky legend), and after 1452 the Gordon Earls of Huntly held the castle, here in 1546 imprisoning Cameron of Lochiel and MacDonald of Keppoch. Mary

Queen of Scots and the Marquis of Montrose both visited, but in 1689 the Jacobites torched the castle. So the barracks was built, and in 1745 defended against 300 Highlanders by 12 men led by a Sergeant Molloy. Insisting that he was: '...too old a soldier to surrender a garrison of such strength without bloody noses,' he held out, losing only one man. Yet in February 1746 the barracks was taken and fired, and after Culloden it was here Prince Charlie's followers held their final rendezvous before melting away into the hills and history.

    As for the river-crossing, before the first bridge was built the only way between Ruthven and Kingussie was via ferry, the boathouse being on the Kingussie side, as was the church. The fare was a penny but one Communion Sunday long ago the river was in spate. Seeing his chance, the greedy ferryman charged sixpence. Many poor folk from the Ruthven side couldn't afford this and had to return home, including an old woman who hadn't missed a communion in half a century. Noting her absence, the minister at Kingussie sent an elder to find out if she was all right. Finding her ill and hearing how the ferryman had denied her a crossing, back in Kingussie he went to the man's house and cursed him: 'You will be deprived of your living, your house and your land, and be sure of this: you will die an unnatural death and your body will be devoured by beasts.'
    Soon after a bridge was built and the ferryman lost his job. Finding work at a meal mill in Kingussie, one day he was sent to close the mill sluice. This involved crossing a narrow plank from the mill loft. Under the plank was a pigsty. When he failed to return, the miller investigated, and found the man's body being eaten by the pigs. He'd fallen from the plank: the frightened beasts had attacked and killed him...

83.   Ruthven to Glen Tromie   *(Walk)*

This varied six-mile circuit (extensions possible) is best not done, as I did it, on an autumn day of fierce blast and driving rain. Or maybe it is – if it's the right kind of stormy day when, once you're soaked, the sun comes out brilliantly, hurling double rainbows against the hills, making the land more beautiful than if there had been no wild blast at all.

Two miles south of Ruthven, birch-clad Glen Tromie is less-known than neighbouring Glen Feshie (**85**) and the Cairngorm heights beyond. Associated with the 'Catastrophe of Gaick' (**74**), the glen and its rapid little river run some 20 miles north from Loch an t-Seilich ('of the willows') by Gaick Lodge. The public footpath (see below) south to Perthshire is shown as the only such route on maps of 1689 and 1725 before Wade's 1728-30 road over the Drumochter Pass made it redundant.

From the barracks carpark climb a grassy roadside bank a few yards west to two gates into adjacent fields. Cross the stile by the wooden gate (Scottish Rights of Way Society). Follow the fence south to a second gate. Here the track forks. Bear right, then curve left through a gap between grassy knolls under pylons to a fenced ruin (762988). Continue past it some 20 yards through a stone dyke to a tall stile by a deer-fence gate.

Over the stile drop south a few yards to where a tributary joins the Burn of Ruthven. Cross the burn then, just to the left on rising ground (east of south) pick up a faint, grassy track. Soon obvious, this at first aims at a radio mast atop bare heathery Beinn Buidhe (769985: 369m), then bends up and right, round the hill. Over the boggy sink and burn below to the right (west) is equally-bare Creag Druim Gheallogaidh (425m).

With views back over Kingussie to Creag Bheag (**73**), keeping the mast above left bear south round Beinn Buidhe over a wet moorland sink, then climb to an empty fenced crest. About 100 yards before the fence, keep left at a fork (771974). The track to the right reaches Glen Tromie two miles further south, where a ford (tricky in spate) over the river gains the public footpath south to Dalnacardoch via the Black or Gaick Pass.

Past a broken gate in the fence and cairns at the open crest the left fork descends to the Woods of Glentromie – mature silver birch here and on the glen's steep opposite slope. Over a high stile (deer fence), the path drops through ferny woodland, cutting left (east) above Glentromie Lodge (776967) by a sign requesting privacy for residents.

Over another stile near the bottom follow the deer-fence left to a surfaced road by a cottage and a white, gated bridge over the river (779968). The road opposite, a public right of way, runs northeast two miles to Bridge of Tromie and a left turn onto the B970 two miles back to Ruthven – less attractive than the following, shorter option.

Just before the white bridge, two grassy tracks break left along the river's west bank to meet under a derelict cottage/kennels. The track continues by the river through clearings and birch copses before curving up and away, north then north-west. Leaving woodland for flat open heather moor, it meets the B970 at 781996, near a track the other side of the road to Invertromie Farm, once home of Big Farquhar, the Invertromie Giant - see Affleck Gray's *Legends of the Cairngorms* for the tale of his war with the Red Comyn of Ruthven and Black Donald of Glentromie. Here, turn left one mile back to Ruthven via the B970.

84.   Insh Marshes to Glen Feshie   *(Routes)*

From Ruthven the B970 runs northeast through broken wooded land, *en route* passing Insh Marshes Nature Reserve carpark (775998: see **69**). With the steep scarps east of and above Glen Feshie visible over intervening moortop, Glen Tromie in between is hidden as the road drops to cross Tromie Bridge (789995). Here begins the public footpath to Blair Atholl via Minigaig Pass and to Dalnacardoch via the Black or Gaick Pass. Also close by, unseen from the road, is a hamlet, Drumguish (795997), from which a five-mile track departs southeast to Glen Feshie via moortop and forestry. Crossing a ramshackle bridge over Allt Chomhraig, it passes the ruin at Baileguish (824981), crosses Allt na Caoileag then, past a building visible ahead, returns to forestry before descending to the west-bank Glen Feshie track near Stonetoper (see **86**).

Two miles northeast of the dead-end road to Drumguish the B970 passes through Insh – a hamlet (phone-box, no store) amid mixed woodland, juniper and heather heath above the Insh marshes. In two more miles, with Loch Insh (**68**) close to the north, on the right by Insh House (835038) a minor road starts south through Inshriach Forest past the Uath Lochans leads to Balnascriten in Glen Feshie. There a locked gate ends public access by car, though walkers can continue up the glen and beyond.

This is one way to start walking Glen Feshie, though not the best.

Past this right turn, for Feshiebridge and the next walk round Lower Glen Feshie and the Uath Lochans keep straight on past Milehouse. Ignoring the next two left turns past Loch Insh to Kincraig, stay on the B970, which bends east downhill through forest to a carpark by Feshiebridge, the Feshie here charging dramatically over boulders through a narrow gorge on its way to meet the Spey just north of Kincraig.

85.   Lower Glen Feshie & Uath Lochans   *(Walk)*

Flanking the main Cairngorm massif and formed by eroding glaciers during the last ice age, this impressive U-shaped glen starts near Loch Insh and runs miles south to high bleak moor, carrying a public right of way towards Glen Tilt in Perthshire and east to Braemar via Glen Geldie. Though popular and.often crowded, this fine glen has so far avoided the fate Wade was first to consider; of having a highway driven through it to connect the Dee and the Spey. Even so, its ecology is under threat, its old pine forest failing to regenerate due in part to red deer which, bred to be stalked, strip new growth.

For a circular seven-mile walk via the Uath Lochans and the viewpoint atop Creag Far-leitire, from Feshiebridge carpark follow yellow/orange waymarkers a few yards south to a path (signposted to Glen Feshie and Glen Tilt) under a cottage by the bridge, which survived the 1829 flood (**52**).

Above the cascading river, with the first great scarp (Creag Mhigeachaidh: 742m) ahead to the left, the track climbs into dense forestry. If you see a glider, it's from the landing strip over the river. Reaching open ground beyond a gate in a stone dyke, at a grassy fork bear left down to the flood plain. Continue south over grassy flats past scattered birch under a wooded ridge. Under an old quarry, with the river still hidden to the left, a second gate leads to another fork. Here, with a white farmhouse (Ballintean: 846019) visible ahead, keep left over a burn, past white-painted posts through scrubwood pasture. Soon a metal gate leads to the river's broad shingle-bank, rich in sand and flood-debris.

With fenced pasture to the right follow the riverbank towards Ballintean and its riding stables, taking a path bearing right from the eroded bank almost to the buildings. Scottish Rights of Way Society signs send you left, under the garden, then right past the converted steading, then left again up a stony track – i.e., a zigzag. Under a bungalow continue south on the grassy track through silver birch 400 yards to a junction, and just beyond it join the road (844015) from Insh House to Balnascriten.

Turn right, north, half a mile up this forest road to the signposted left turn for the Uath Lochans (833022). For a shorter circuit, continue along the road to Balnespick (see below). But if so, you'll miss the lochans and the Big View. Under tall trees with a carpark and boards describing local flora, fauna and routes up and about the crag ahead, the lochans are lovely. The waymarked track climbs past the crag into forest, curling right (east). Where the viewless slope gets dull, a minor path (red arrow) climbs right from the main track - the return route and quickest way to the viewpoint.

Continuing up the main trail, at the next junction turn right up to the fine viewpoint (830030). It overlooks forest slopes north up Strathspey past Loch Insh and the Duke of Gordon memorial (**68**), and east over Glen Feshie to the bare heights beyond. The continuing path follows the pine-rooted cliff-edge before descending above the lochans via the red-arrow trail to the main track.

Back at the road, turn left half-a-mile over a cattlegrid. Just above Balnespick steading (837037), turn right on a fine drystane-dyked track north to Feshiebridge; forest one side, broad Speyside views the other. Reaching the B970 after a mile, turn right, downhill, to the carpark.

86.   Upper Glen Feshie   *(Walk)*

From Feshiebridge the B970 climbs a wooded brae east of the river past a right turn. This leads five miles up Glen Feshie past Lagganlia, a gliding club, and a hostel to end at Achlean (853975) - the best place to park for this walk to the upper glen.

For the alternative west bank route, from Insh House drive past the Uath Lochans three miles to a locked gate by Balnascriten (841999). Before this gate park by a bridge over Allt Fhearnasdail (where a hill-track breaks southeast). Follow the road past the gate into viewless forestry above the river. After a mile a fork (847947) breaks west to Drumguish (**84**) and Kingussie; Braemar (26 miles) and Blair Atholl (33) also indicated. In another half-mile leave the forest by a white cottage at Stonetoper (849971), noting the request to stay off the hills between August 1 and October 20. With Achlean over the river and views opening, the track continues south along the grassy slope, the river below and bare moor rising to hills beyond. Soon a track cuts down to a footbridge (851965).

If starting from Achlean, so avoiding the dull forestry trek both out and back, cross heath south to this bridge and join the west bank road. With vast Coire Garbhlach ('the rough corrie') steeply indenting the glen's east wall, and the views grand, the road descends to the river below mature Scots Pine. Past a track climbing the slope and by a wide, shingled riverbend is Carnachuan (845938), a half-mile north of Glenfeshie Lodge.

At Carnachuan, by a memorial to soldiers training here during the last war, signs indicate the way on to Braemar and Blair Atholl. A ricketty wooden footbridge crosses the river, here running through shingle. You are warned CROSS AT

OWN RISK. On the far side (the scenery ahead splendid) is a three-way path junction amid heather and juniper scrub. Bearing left on a grassy track past scattered old Scots Pine, return north up the river's west bank. The path climbs through scrappy forestry and mossy glades to deeper forest. A fork may confuse, but anyway the plantation ends 200 yards north of it. Bear right up the bank of Allt Garbhlach, which high up Coire Garbhlach at approx. 878947 plunges in a 300 foot fall. Cross this rapid, rocky burn with care, then continue north over the open moor past or over the first footbridge, and so back to whichever starting-point.

A fine outing! No wonder Queen Victoria visited twice, in 1860 and 1861; Sir Edwin 'Monarch of the Glen' Landseer also spent time here, roaming higher up the glen than this walk takes us. Landseer's Falls on the the Allt na Leuma , a triple leap of over 160 feet (886894), are so-named because the painter had a hut nearby. In addition, east of and above Achlean are the Falls of Badan Mosach (858971) – cascades amid the trees plunging about 150 feet; this near the Foxhunters' Path to the head of Loch Einich (**90**)..

87. Rothiemurchus & the Grants *(Route, History)*

From Feshiebridge the B970 runs northeast via forest and heather moor past the hamlet of Dalnavert and Inshriach Alpine Nurseries (01540-651287), and near Inshriach House (873074) enters Rothiemurchus Estate – a region of mountains, lochs, glens and remnants of the once-great Caledonian Forest. Running north from Braeriach and Loch Einich to Loch Pityoulish (**94**); east from Loch an Eilean and Aviemore to Loch Morlich and the Lairig Ghru (**91**), the estate caters for mountain and woodland walking, bird-watching, watersports, fishing and falconry, and annually draws thousands of visitors.

Held for over 400 years by the Grants of Rothiemurchus, its name may mean (*Rath Mhor Ghiuthais*) 'Plain of the Big Pines'. Once Comyn-owned, after Bannockburn in 1314 Robert the Bruce gave all Comyn land to Thomas Randolph, 1st Earl of Moray (**6**). Later the Wolf of Badenoch occupied the old Comyn castles at Lochindorb, Ruthven and Loch an Eilean (**88**), but in 1452 James II gifted the region as a whole to the 1st Earl of Huntly (**45**): it remained Gordon land for the next 400 years.

Also potent were the Shaw Macintoshes, who first leased Rothiemurchus in 1236. Ferquhand the 5th chief was slain by Comyns, who seized the lands. Exiled to Perthshire, Ferquhand's son Angus returned and took revenge, burying the Comyns he slew near Calart Hill at *Lag nan Chuimeanach* ('Hollow of the Comyns': **94**) by Loch Pityoulish: the mounds survive. Back at Rothiemurchus, Angus murdered Dallas, his mother's second husband, then gave his mother the severed head. Cursing him, she roused hue and cry. Outlawed, he fled, and when he died Rothiemurchus reverted to the crown.

Settled here *c.*1580 by his father Sir John Grant of Freuchie, 'gin he would win it from the Shaws', Patrick Grant moved from Muckrach (**62**) to the Dell of

Rothiemurchus (by Inverdruie, over the river from Aviemore), then to the Doune (Gaelic *dun*, 'fort': 887100) a mile or so south. This takeover involved the departure not only of the Shaws but their family goblin, the *Bodach an Duin* (see **92**), who went to guard the grave of the last Shaw chief of Rothiemurchus, though not too successfully. Buried in Rothiemurchus kirkyard (886093, unused since 1929), Grants dug up and propped his body against his widow's door at Dalnavert. Again buried and again removed to Dalnavert, a third time the Shaws buried it, this time under the Laird's seat in the church, where the Grants at last let it be. Also in this kirkyard, under a flat gravestone with five stones on it, lie the remains of Farquhar Shaw, victor of the terrible combat at Perth in 1396 (**76**). The stones, resembling cheeses and probably from The Doune, are said to be dangerous to move. A footman of the Duke of Bedford who threw one into the Spey died within a week; more recently, two men who moved the stones died within the year. So take care!

A later Grant laird, also Patrick but called MacAlpine, was a friend of Rob Roy Macgregor (1671-1734). When The Mackintosh provocatively built a mill just inside his own boundary meaning to divert Grant water to run it, Grant appealed to Rob Roy. Called on to demolish the mill, Mackintosh mustered his men, but Rob Roy arrived with 150 Macgregors. The mill was burned, Rob Roy warning Macintosh to stop bothering the Grants, or else. Left in peace, MacAlpine, who remarried aged 78, died in 1743.

As for the Doune, long unused but now restored, it had a haunted bedroom which attracted a guest eager to spend the night in it. Soon, for no clear reason, he was petrified. A gust of wind blowing out the paraffin lamp, he fled for the door, hit his head on it, and fell unconscious. Later he learned how, some 200 years earlier, the laird's deranged son had been locked in that room. Breaking out, on the stairs he'd met and strangled a servant-girl, then thrown himself down the stairs, fatally.

Here in the early 19th century Elizabeth Grant, daughter of the laird, wrote her witty, stylish *Memoirs of a Highland Lady* - a valuable insight into that era. She tells of Black Sandy Grant who, with the old laird's son involved with a housekeeper who'd borne him three children, was called on for a solution. Disguised, he waylaid the woman and cut off one of her ears. Removing himself to Grantown, he got in a fight with a drover, left the man for dead, and fled to America. End of story? Not quite. His son, born in Ohio in 1822, commanded the Union armies during the American Civil War, and in 1868 became President of the USA. His name? General Ulysses S Grant.

As for the ousted Shaws, they too made a transatlantic mark. Emigrating to Canada, Helen Shaw of Dalnavert was the mother of Canada's first Prime Minister, Sir John Macdonald (1815-91). Odd, that two families so long at war over Rothiemurchus each produced a leader, not just of neighbouring estates, but of neighbouring countries...

88.   Round Loch an Eilean   (History, Walk)

From the B970 a mile south of Inverdruie and near the Doune driveway a minor road (891097) breaks east a mile to Loch an Eilean, a famed beauty-spot. At the entry to this road a carved stone pillar commemorates Dr James Martineau (d.1900). Brother of Victorian novelist Harriet Martineau and a leader of the Unitarian Movement, he set up a local school of drawing and carving, and when he died his students carved this memorial.

With visitor centre and 'nature trail' Loch an Eilean is often overcrowded in summer. Nor do you want to start a walk from the carpark, where a fee is asked.

For a six-mile circuit, continue up the B970 to Inverdruie. At the junction with the Aviemore/Coylumbridge road turn right, past Rothiemurchus Visitor Centre (01479-810858), not far, to a right turn (903108) to Tullochgrue/Blackpark. In half-a-mile park at a Y-fork by a white cottage (905099). Start left to Tullochgrue, where after the '45 Lady Jean Gordon, wife of MacAlpine's son James Grant, sheltered Lord Lewie Gordon. Nearby is the Lady's Well, where MacAlpine got the only water he'd drink. Past Lower Tullochgrue the road climbs pasture up to derelict Upper Tullochgrue. Over a cattlegrid onto heather moor with fine views east over Rothiemurchus Forest to the Lairig Ghru, it ends at a gate just before Whitewell (915086). There is a carpark here too, from which a footpath descends east to Rothiemurchus Forest to meet the trail from Coylumbridge to Glen Einich (**90**). From this point there are two options.

Either bear west (right) over heather heath, not far, to a wood. Over a deer-fence gate a downhill track leaves the wood past a white cottage (Achnagoichan: 914082). With views ahead to conical Carn Eilrig (742m) between the heads of the

Lairig Ghru and Glen Einich, this track bears left. Before re-entering forestry a path descends to a moorland track. This Y-forks 100 yards before a gate. Bear right, then right again, now on the main track west from the Cairngorm Club footbridge over the Druie (926078).

Probably simpler, from Whitewell descend to the Coylumbridge-Glen Einich track. Follow it south past a right turn to Achnagoichan, then join the east-bound track as above. This is the old *Rathad nam Mearlach* ('Thieves' Road') once used by cattle-reivers. Crossing two burns amid heather moor dotted with juniper and Scots Pine, in a wide airy mile it reaches a wooded junction (906077) above Loch an Eilean.

For the short route up the loch's east shore (signposted to Aviemore) turn right; otherwise keep left round the loch's wooded southern verge. In a mile, two tracks depart south (left) round either side of Loch Gamhna to Feshiebridge. Continue round Loch an Eilean's inlets via the main trail, or try less-used paths over rougher ground nearer the lochside. After a mile, west of the loch by a cottage, the main track enters a clearing, a rocky promontory below and, offshore, the ruined, overgrown castle on its islet (898079).

Originally a crannog, or artificial isle, with wicker huts on crude platforms, the first stone castle was Comyn-built. Here the Wolf growled, and here *c.*1525, when Lachlan Macintosh of Dunachton was murdered, his clansmen besieged the castle and chained the killers until 1531. Found guilty, the ringleader Malcolm Macintosh was beheaded and quartered, his two Davidson companions being tortured then hanged and quartered, their heads spiked on poles.

Here too in 1651 James Grant of Rothiemurchus married Grace Macintosh, alias Giorsal Mhor ('Big Grace'). When defeated Jacobites under General Buchan besieged the castle after the Battle of Cromdale (1690: **58**), she cast the bullets that beat them back. After that the castle was abandoned. It's said an underwater causeway zigzags from castle to shore, but it remains undiscovered.

Also here *c.*1899 the last native osprey (**95**) was shot and its eggs snatched. Now once again ospreys fish at Loch an Eilean, a birdwatcher's paradise with rare species like crested tits, crossbills and tree creepers.

Soon after the castle the main track reaches the loch's northern strand by the carpark and picnic area. Gaining the road that leads out past the Martineau monument to the B970, after 50 yards turn right up a climbing track (897087) past open fields and through woodland back to Blackpark. With breaks, this varied walk should take about four hours.

89.   The Felling of Rothiemurchus Forest   *(History)*

Circa 8300BC the end of the last Ice Age left bare land surrounded by rising seas. By 7000BC, the sea 75 feet lower than now, the Irish land-link was lost as sparse birch, pine and hazel forests invaded the tundra. Wolf, brown bear, fox, blue hare, wildcat, deer and wild ox arrived, followed by Mesolithic hunter-gatherers *c.*7500BC at Crail in Fife, later at Rhum and other Hebridean or West Coast sites. By 6000BC the English Channel opened, making Britain an island. Temperatures jumped to 2°C (3.6°F) above present norms, bringing heavier rainfall. Soon most of Scotland grew a dense, closed forest; the tree-line (save in the northeast) over 3000 feet. More folk ventured north, by 4500BC starting to clear land, cultivate crops and domesticate animals, later building the great megalithic (big stone) monuments that still amaze us today, as at Callanish and Stenness.

With bad weather causing depopulation *c.*1500BC; almost a millennium later the first stone *duns* and hill-forts suggest hard times. Later the Romans clashed with Caledonii and other tribes of the north: after the Romans withdrew Anglo-Saxons and Gaels began to infiltrate the land. And so, *c.*AD570, it's said that the bard Myrrdin (Merlin), crazed by the death of his king Gwenddolau, retreated into the Forest of Celydon (Caledonian Forest) to live with the beasts.

A millennium later dense forest still covered Badenoch and Rothiemurchus. Though felling began by AD800, with Viking demand for wood plus the onset of the Little Ice Age *c.*1200 denuding the Outer Hebrides, the pine forests of the Central Highlands remained largely intact until after the 1715 Jacobite rebellion. Then, with some Highland chiefs willing to sell and other estates forfeit, English merchants began logging for ship-building, smelting, and to construct urban drainage and water systems.

In 1728 Sir James Grant sold 60,000 trees to the York Building Company for just £7,000; in 1783 the Duke of Gordon sold part of Glenmore Forest to William Osbourne of Kingston-on-Hull. After that the Hull Company made a fortune rafting timber down the Spey to Garmouth and Kingston-on-Spey, where clippers, Baltic traders and Royal Navy supply vessels were built during the good years (**41**).

Even as Highlanders were being evicted for sheep the forests were cut, until *c.*1850 imported timber reduced the value of native pine. Local men got good money – and more. Before dawn on a cutting day fellers, draggers and loggers got a gill of neat whisky ladled out from wooden casks holding a firkin (about 40 pints, nearly 20 litres). At midday they got the same again, also bannocks and cheese, and again as night fell.

At first sawed into planks where felled, later whole logs were run to the Spey or neighbouring lochans via upstream tributaries - the Luinneag from Loch Morlich, the Beanaidh from Loch Einich, and the Milton Burn from Loch an Eilean. At the outfall of these lochs were dams with heavy sluice-gates. Opened, these loosed a torrent into which the loggers poled stacked logs, hooking or riding them, some to Inverdruie mills, some to the Spey, with garrons (heavy draught-horses) used for land-haulage. These 'runs' were big events, crowds applauding those riding or 'clipping' the logs – a dangerous affair. The threat of drowning or crushing was ever-present; log-jams could take days to clear.

On reaching the Spey the logs were taken over by Ballindalloch (**58**) 'floaters' – rafting-specialists, their chief known as Admiral of the Spey. With logs bound together into cigar-shaped rafts, in their ox-hide currachs they guided their cargo 50 miles to Garmouth. Skilled floaters made the journey in 12 hours then, currach on back, returned to Rothiemurchus by night, on foot – so it's said. Back in a smoky bothy on heather beds they'd sleep in wet plaids, usually well fou.

One floater, 18-year-old Duncan Grant of Tulchan, is said to have carried his currach 600 miles to London to race other small craft on the Thames; this after the Chief of Grant, visiting London, bet an English friend that: 'I have on the Spey a subject who, in a boat of bullock's hide, could outstrip the fastest of your craft.' Winning the race, Duncan gave the gold coins showered on him to his chief, asking that they go to the Lady of Grant to help the Rothiemurchus poor. Then he walked back home, maybe returning in time for the Floaters' Ball, held every Christmas at the Rothiemurchus Home Farm.

With trade dwindling, in 1860 much surviving Rothiemurchus timber was cut into sleepers for the Highland Railway, opened in 1863. Today, with natural regeneration in some areas, and extensive planting in Glenmore and Abernethy Forest, hopefully the will to protect these ancient woodlands will prevail.

90.   Loch Einich   *(Walk)*

At Dell of Rothiemurchus turn left for Aviemore (**66**); right past Rothiemurchus Visitor Centre to Coylumbridge. Here, with the Glenmore/Cairngorm road continuing, opposite the B970 turn north nine miles to Nethybridge (**96**), the Glen Einich track starts south beyond a locked gate. Not far south, an old drove road branches left (917100) to the Cairngorm Club footbridge over the Druie and so to the Lairig Ghru (**91**).

Some 16 miles there and back, the Loch Einich trek may be shortened by starting from the carpark at Whitewell (**88**). Over heather moorland amid scattered pine it joins the energetic Am Beanaidh, a River Druie tributary running north from Loch Einich, and follows it up the glen. Problems may arise in wet weather, with several burns to be forded, Beanaidh Bheag (925029) being hard to cross in spate. Yet in good weather the walk to this wild, grand mountain loch is splendid. Part of the Cairngorm National Nature Reserve, and set in a vast U-shaped trough under the facing corries and buttresses of Braeriach and Sgoran Dubh Mor, Loch Einich is hugely impressive.

At the loch's northern end are the remains of the weir built to create the logging spates (**89**), while at the head of the glen, south of and high above the loch, the Falls of Coire Odhar (913974) consist of eight consecutive cascades plunging, in all, nearly a thousand feet (298 metres). With the view over the loch from the head of the falls breathtaking, the shortest route to this point is via the Foxhunters' Path from Achlean in Glen Feshie (**86**), not via the long hike up Glen Einich, which offers several other falls. These are found on the Beanaidh Bheag (see above) at Easan na Bruaich ('the little waterfall of the height': 924018), by it a path up Braeriach; in Coire Bogha Cloiche (923928: near a stalkers' path climbing from the foot of the loch); and, higher up this path, there is a twin fall at the head of Coire Dhondail (925979).

The height climbed on this trek is about 650 feet. Mountain bikes can be hired from Rothiemurchus Visitor Centre at Inverdruie.

91.   Loch Morlich to the Lairig Ghru   *(Walk)*

From Coylumbridge (*cruing leum*, 'narrow leap') a road runs four miles east to Loch Morlich and the Queen's Forest in Glenmore Forest Park, then south another two miles to the Cairngorm carpark and ski-lift to the Ptarmigan Restaurant (004048) near the summit.

Fringing Rothiemurchus estate, the Queen's Forest was so-named in 1935 to mark the Silver Jubilee of King George V and Queen Mary. Once a royal forest, later the hunting ground of the Stewarts of Kincardine, here since 1923 the Forestry Commission has planted some 4000 acres, much of it native pinewood, on slopes round Loch Morlich. Picturesque below Cairngorm, this shallow (but for a pit at the eastern end) near-circular loch hosts wind-driven water sports and picnic beaches served by carparks by the water and at Glenmore Forest Park Visitor Centre (01479-861220: 978098). Daily reindeer-viewing excursions depart from nearby Reindeer House (01479-861228); the National Outdoor Training Centre at Glenmore Lodge (987095) is also just east of the loch, which is two miles south of the entry to the notorious Lairig Ghru.

Visible from afar as a deep notch in the mountain wall the Lairig Ghru (*Lairig Cruaidh*, 'hard pass' or Lairig Gruamach, 'gloomy pass') bisects the Cairngorm plateau. Rising southeast to a 2733-ft. top at the regional boundary (974014) near the Pools of Dee then following the fledgling Dee, it carried the old drove trail to Braemar. It's said once young Rothiemurchus girls trudged through it to sell baskets of eggs they carried on their heads. Were there no hens in Braemar? Either way, it is no Sunday afternoon stroll, and should not be treated lightly. Every year folk come to grief in this dreich pass.

To approach it, park at Loch Morlich's northwest edge (957097) and start south by a bridge over the Luineag where it leaves the loch. At the first forest fork keep right past Lochan nam Geadas. Where further on the main track bears left to Rothiemurchus Lodge, turn right at the sign to Piccadilly/Lairig Ghru over a gate to heather and Scots Pine. At the Piccadilly track-junction (938076) it's straight on for the Cairngorm Club footbridge and Glen Einich or Loch an Eilean: here bear left, climbing high above Allt Druidh. Reaching pine-studded open moor with the pass ahead and the scenery awesome, follow the rough path a mile to a junction (948057) at the gaping mouth of the pass.

Here a left turn back to Rothiemurchus Lodge offers options. For a longer, wilder circuit, enter the pass; Castle Hill (728m) to the left; shapely Carn Eilrig (742m) to the right. In a mile, now hemmed by sheer rock walls and opposite a prominent knoll to the right, with the top of the pass still over two miles ahead a rough path (958037) breaks back northeast up Chalamain Gap, a boulder-strewn pass between Creag a' Chalamain (787m) and Creag an Leth-choin (Lurcher's Crag: 1053m). The reward for this hard stretch comes with the view at the top: down to the Linn of Dee and over to Ben Macdhui. From the cairn the path descends through peat bogs to cross a burn (974064). Here you can turn west up the burn, continuing over the rocky Eag a'Chait pass (965065) under Castle Hill before descending steeply to Rothiemurchus Lodge (953068: see below), or continue north to the mountain road at the edge of the forest (984074)).

For a shorter circuit, at the mouth of the Lairig Ghru turn left to Rothiemurchus Lodge, at first over rocky open hillside with fine views, but for the second half-mile over boggy ground. At the lodge turn left down the main track to Loch Morlich: follow it back or, before it enters the forest, break right over heather moor along the forestry edge via an intermittent path east into a pleasant glen. Descend into a boggy gully, then climb to a high stile and blaeberry heath dotted with Scots Pine. Push through a juniper thicket to a boggy glen; over a burn bear left to a gated forestry road (966076). Follow this northeast over logged ground to a junction (974084). Turning left here and at the next junction, bear east through the forest above Loch Morlich. Keep right at a third junction (964084) and down to the loch. Turn left through a gate onto a path north up the verge of the loch. On meeting the original outward track turn right, back to where you parked.

Another popular circuit from Loch Morlich climbs Meall a' Bhuachaille, Shepherd's Hill. But first…things that go bump in the night…

92.   Big Grey Men & Other Sprites   *(Folklore)*

Weirder beings than Michael Scot (**81**) or the Witch of Laggan (**78**) once roamed this land. It's said Loch Morlich was haunted by the terrible *Bodach Lamh Dheirg* ('Old Man of the Bloody Hand') – a spectral Highland warrior, one hand dripping with blood. To meet him meant instant challenge to mortal combat. Boldness paid off, but cowards died. Protecting wild beasts, he killed hunters who abandoned wounded animals. Eco-agencies may have replaced him today, but take care! If you abuse the land and the eco-police don't get you, maybe the bodach will!

The fearsome *eachuisge* (water-horse or kelpie) patrolled many waters, among them Lochindorb, Loch Pityoulish, Loch Garten and the Lour Burn. The Spey kelpie, An t-Each Ban, was white, but mostly it appeared as a wild-eyed black horse browsing by a ford, tempting weary travellers to mount in hope of a dry crossing then throwing them off to drown. Though supernatural, if caught in horse-shape it could be harnessed with a bridle blessed by the sign of the cross. Willox the Wizard of Glen Avon (**101**) claimed his grand-uncle Macgregor had done the opposite, seizing and cutting off the bridle of the Lochindorb kelpie, which became a raging fiend that pursued him to Dulnain Bridge.

Lochs Garten and Mallachie (**95**) were the home of a water-horse-cum-water-bull. With jet-black mane, broad back, huge head and glaring eyes it devoured lambs and young children. Tying a rope to a boulder by Loch Garten, a Nethybridge crofter once rowed out and sank a gaff baited with a lamb. That night a thunderstorm vied with the monster's roars. At dawn the old man found the boulder gone, dragged into the loch. But the water was calm and the beast never appeared again.

Loch Garten folk also had to put up with *Am Bodach Ghoirtean* ('The Old Man of Garten'), who nightly roamed the land howling of impending death. His fatal sister was the *bean-sidhe* (banshee, 'fairy-woman'; in places known as *cointeach*, 'keener'). A bloodless, boneless, snow-haired hag with huge hollow eyesockets, in tattered white rags she wailed outside the door of the dying. The best clans all had their own private banshee, while lesser folk made do with the raucous hoodie crow. The web-footed *bean-nighe* ('washerwoman') squatted by a ford, washing the bloody clouts of those about to die in battle. To let her see you before you saw her was fatal, though maybe only those about to die could see her at all. Green-kirtled, the likewise web-footed *fuath* sported yellow hair, a tail and mane, but had no nose; the shaggy and lecherous *urisk* haunted waterfalls; the long-haired *gruagach* liked milk; and we met the *cu sith*, fairy dog, at Loch Gynack (**73**). As for fairy cats, dog-sized and black save for a white patch on the breast, might they be relatives of the big black cats lately encountered from Advie to Kellas (**19**)?

Yet of all these weird sprites best-known and allegedly still active is the Big Grey Man (*Fear Liath Mor*) of Ben Macdhui, the highest Cairngorm peak.

At a Cairngorm Club meeting in 1925 Norman Collie – an Aberdeen man, Professor of Organic Chemistry at London University and a renowned climber – claimed never to have been so petrified as when alone on Ben Macdhui in 1891. Descending from the summit in dense fog: '…every few steps I took I heard a crunch, and then another crunch as if someone was walking after me but taking steps three or four the length of my own.' Stopping to listen, hearing it again but seeing nothing, terrified he fled, '…staggering blindly among the boulders for four or five miles nearly down to Rothiemurchus Forest.' He concluded that: '…there is something very queer about the top of Ben Macdhui and I will not go back there again by myself…'

With his tale causing a Nessie-style media furore, it emerged that a Dr. A M Kellas (who had died on the 1921-22 Everest Expedition) had earlier written to Collie, telling how once his brother and he had seen a giant figure approach from the summit cairn. It vanished into a corrie but, stricken by fear, they'd fled. Experienced on peaks throughout the world, neither Collie nor Kellas had met anything like it anywhere else. Both admitted their dread of Ben Macdhui only late in life when they had little to lose.

So what had scared them? Many subsequent tales of odd visions seen and ghostly voices or fairy music heard on this high plateau suggest the hallucinations of oxygen-starved Himalayan climbers, or shadows cast by a low sun against mist - but I wouldn't be too sure…

93. Up Meall a' Bhuachaille   *(Walk)*

Highest of the Kincardine hills flanking the Cairngorm massif, the steep, distinctively conical Meall a' Bhuachaille (Shepherd's Hill: 991116; 2654ft.) offers a grandstand view of Cairngorm corries over the Ryvoan Pass below. Best approached from the southwest, the six-mile circuit suggested here introduces longer-range routes.

Behind Glenmore Visitor Centre (978098: **91**) cross a burn (blue and orange markers) and climb a sandy forest path to a junction. Bear left (orange marker) to Allt Coire Chondlaich, following this burn over a footbridge and steeply to the top of the forest (983109). Now on open heath a path climbs, also steeply, to a saddle between Meall a' Bhuachaille and Creagan Gorm ('little blue hill': 978120), the slope encouraging stops to enjoy the mountain views opening up over Loch Morlich below.

With fine views north over Abernethy Forest and the summit of Meall a' Bhuachaille above to the right, from this saddle a clear track breaks west up Creagan Gorm then, the path now faint and wet, follows the ridge past intermediate tops to Craiggowrie (963135: 2250ft.). At an old fence just past Craiggowrie's summit a rough path descends west to the forest's northwestern edge. High above the Milton Burn follow a forest track southeast to the Badaguish Centre (956115). Just beyond Badaguish, for the direct return to Glenmore bear left (east) – the right fork, via a further left turn, descends to the northwest edge of Loch Morlich.

For Meall a' Buachaille, from the saddle climb the eroded track to the sheltering summit cairn's vast panorama. From Cairngorm the view runs west past Braeriach over Carn Eilrig and Loch Morlich to the Monadhliaths, and north over lower, rolling hills to the Moray coast. Now bearing northeast on an ugly track, descend left down a rough steep rocky path past a rock shaped like a stern bird of prey to Ryvoan Bothy (005115).

Just above a bare sink the bothy, once a farm, hugs a track north from Glenmore to Abernethy Forest, in two miles joining a trail above the River Nethy (see **96**).

Turning right (south) back to Glenmore, at 003111 above Loch a' Garbh Choire on the left the Strathnethy track is signposted to Braemar. Breaking east under Stac na h-Iolaire (2434ft.), on reaching the Nethy at Bynack Stable (021105) it forks – south up Strathnethy between Bynack peaks and Cairngorm slopes to Loch Avon, or southeast over the high bare Lairig an Laoigh ('Pass of the Calves'), once a drove trail. After five or so miles the latter reaches the Fords of Avon (042032), meeting the track west up Glen Avon from Inchrory (**101**) before continuing south through Glen Derry to Deeside.

From Ryvoan continuing southeast to Glenmore, a heathery pass leads to Lochan Uaine under Creag nan Gall's pine-rich scree slopes. The 'Green Lochan' is just that; an emerald amid the wilderness. At its south end, take the main track back to Glenmore, or (blue marker) cut right up a steep rocky path to a forestry track above the glen. Through a felled area then a plantation this track descends to Glenmore, Loch Morlich visible before a left turn brings you down past Reindeer House to the visitor centre where you parked.

A Forestry Commission pamphlet describing Glenmore Forest Park and its walks is available at the visitor centre.

94.   To Tulloch Moor & Loch Garten   *(Routes, History)*

From Coylumbridge the B970 runs north past Lochs Pityoulish and Garten nine miles to Nethybridge on its forest haugh east of the Spey, then continues four miles past Revack to the A95 by Grantown (**59**).

In detail: crossing the Druie at Coylumbridge the B970 soon leaves both forest and Rothiemurchus for open rolling land, and in a mile or so passes reedy, pine-fringed, kelpie-haunted Loch Pityoulish – lovely in the sun, maybe less so on a winter night. Just east of it, at *Lag nan Chuimeanach* ('Hollow of the Comyns'), grassy mounds mark the graves of Comyns decimated by Shaw Mackintoshes long ago (**87**). On the slope above (930129), a ruined Iron Age *dun* looks over the Spey to its twin above Loch Vaa (**65**).

Two miles further on, near Glencairn by a bend of the Spey, on a mound off the road is Kincardine church (938155). In parts 12th century, with a leper's 'peep' or narrow window (for those excluded to see inside) in the east wall, here 15th century Grants seeking revenge for their murdered chief and his son cornered the Comyns responsible. A burning arrow sent into the thatched roof fired the building: the Comyns were incinerated; the only one who got out was cut down. In the churchyard, with its filled-in Well of Tomhaldidh ('Mound of the Wolf'), is a stone to Sir Walter Stewart, grandson of Robert II and son of the Wolf of Badenoch (**10**), knighted for bravery at the Battle of Harlaw near Inverurie in 1411.

Just past Glencairn a minor road breaks right to Tulloch Moor. Anonymous amid silver birch, the turn up this lovely track (942163) is easily missed. With Abernethy Forest nearby, it gains an airy heath below Craiggowrie (**93**). Narrow and walkable, it rolls up and down, birch amid heather either side, hillside crofts off to the right, Loch Mallachie in its boggy sink to the left. In three miles it descends through mixed woodland to Tulloch (981164) – a few crofts and a phone-box. This hidden back road is a delight.

Forking left from it both before then at Tulloch, a back route to Nethybridge runs north through Abernethy Forest west of Tore Hill, past a left turn west half-a-mile to Loch Garten, home both of *bodach* (**92**) and osprey (see below). Soon the continuing Nethybridge route takes up another road from Tulloch, round the east side of Tore Hill.

Passing through Street of Kincardine a mile north of the Tulloch Moor turn, soon the B970 reaches a junction (950191), the left turn crossing the Spey to Boat of Garten (**65**). Here, by the sign 'Loch Garten 2', continue north on the B970 then right at the sign to Loch Garten, Tulloch, and Tulloch Moor. A mile down this woodland road an RSPB sign introduces Abernethy Forest Nature Reserve - 12,795 hectares (50 square miles) of forest, loch and mountain. In the old Highland sense 'forest' means 'deer forest', including open moor and mountain. So, with over 3300 hectares of Scots Pine, this reserve's topmost boundary is the peak of Ben Macdhui.

On the right, leading to Lochs Garten and Mallachie, is the Forest Walks carpark, with the Loch Garten Osprey Centre straight ahead.

95.   Loch Garten: Ospreys & Others   (*Wildlife, Walks*)

From the Forest Walks carpark (just off-road: 971183) waymarked trails depart south. The simplest loops past Loch Garten to Loch Mallachie and back. Longer routes bear west of Loch Mallachie then north through forestry before returning.

The OS map shows, west of Loch Mallachie, a path bearing south out of the forest to the Tulloch Moor road. Maybe I started too late in the day. From Loch Garten's reedy lagoons over a wooded neck to Loch Mallachie (see photo next page) is a fine short walk but then, off-track, Loch Mallachie's boggy verges bar direct access to the moor. Taking a bike-churned path northwest (966175) through the wood to a main forestry road (957178) and turning south over a burn, I looked for this path, but with light failing found no sign of it.

A much finer Abernethy Forest walk traverses old pine-wood above the Nethy two miles further east (**96**). Still, placid Loch Mallachie is worth a visit.

Half-a-mile beyond the Forest Walks a potholed carpark serves the Loch Garten Osprey Centre, its shop and well-equipped hide visited by almost two million people since this fish-eating sea-hawk (*Pandion haliaetus*), driven out a century ago (**88**), first returned to Scotland in the 1950s. Arriving from West Africa in April and leaving in August, its numbers have greatly increased since that first pair.

Growing to about 58cm in length, brown above and white below with a large brown patch running through the eye of the white, loosely-crested head, its hooked grey beak, powerful talons and sharply-angled wings make this fish-hawk a spectacular sight when on the hunt. Gliding and flapping above the water, on sighting a large fish near the surface it plummets feet-first, often submerging completely

before re-emerging with trout or pike gripped in spiny-scaled talons. Shaking its plumage to remove the water, it carries prey weighing up to 2kg back to its large nest, usually atop a pine. Built of sticks, this nest is added to year on year. The white, chocolate-blotched eggs are incubated mainly by the hen: once hatched it may be nine weeks before the young can fly.

It's hard to tell how many ospreys now breed in Scotland, as many folk aware of a pair keep quiet about it. The mood has changed since the days of men like Charles St. John (1809-56), who advocated extermination. Yet the public love-affair with predators like the osprey means that other species and their habitats suffer. The grouse, prey of protected raptors, nears extinction, in turn endangering the maintenance of open moor. There's no easy solution: in nature the knock-on effect, often unforeseen, is everything…

This RSPB reserve also hosts goosander, crested tit, siskin and Scottish crossbill, the latter unique to Scotland, its bill specially adapted to prise seeds from the cones of pine-trees. Early in autumn some 1500-2000 greylag geese from Iceland arrive here, staying till late March, though when Loch Garten freezes they move further south.

96. Through Abernethy Forest to Loch a' Chnuic *(Walk)*

With old pinewood, high moorland, a lonely loch and winding river-glen, this fine 10-mile circuit starts three miles southeast of Nethybridge, ('The Forest Village': pop. 670). From the ospreys turn north on the B970 three miles; or continue north-east to the Tulloch road, a left turn here meeting the B970 at Nethybridge. Past a store and over the narrow bridge at the village crossroads turn right, east towards the A939 and Tomintoul (**100**).

After a half-mile of wooded houses and chalets, at 'Causer' turn right onto the Lettoch/Lurg road. With Cairngorm views opening up, cross a burn at Lettoch and cattlegrids at Clachaig. Reaching a broad crofting moor, park on the left by the Bynackbeg track (035179). Here, just beyond a path the map shows starting by Ailanbeg, the tarmac ends with Lurg steading visible ahead.

Start south by a fence parallel to and left of electricity poles crossing the moor. Leaving these for a track through cattle pasture, aim at two peaks ahead, one notched – the Bynacks. Past a gate on heather moor bear left of the pinewood ahead. Over a low open rise join another track from the left. Down over a tawny burn (033164) amid scattered Scots Pine and up the far bank the track climbs past a gated deer-fence then forks.

Follow a rough track left through heather into fine old pinewood (see photo next page). Widening, this southbound track - mossy and pine-needled amid juniper and blaeberry, burn below, mountain views ahead – soon beguiles. Before long a track from below right joins it (030158) – the first option for a shorter hike: note it for possible later use (see below).

After a mile the track Y-forks, views ahead drawing you left up to a crossing track at the forest's edge (029142). This runs east (left) round Carn a' Chnuic past Loch a' Chnuic to the Braes of Abernethy – strictly there-and-back, yet its views south over pine-studded heath up Strathnethy and southwest to Shepherd's Hill (**93**) demand at least part of the mile-long detour to the loch. Miss it and you may never return!

Back at the junction (029142), return as you came (right fork) or, for more fine views, keep left (west) down through the wood, over a burn, then up through heathery woodland to a track-crossing (025145) above the glen of the Nethy. A right turn here runs above the river's east bank a mile north to 025161: there one turn climbs to the outbound track at 030158; the other bridges the river near the Forest Lodge (see below). This route avoids fording the river, but lacks the views from the high, open west bank.

For the latter, over the junction at 025145 descend the track ahead to the flood-plain, and ford the Nethy, here ankle-deep and safe save if in spate (022144). Over the ford bear first right then left up to a main track under the trees. A left turn south leads past Ryvoan Bothy to Glenmore (**93**): turn right, north, high above the river and its scarp, broad views to the Cromdales (**58**) soon opening up. At a crossing (018160) after a mile descend right past a gate over a road to a Forest Reserve information board. Continue straight at the sign *Sorry No Vehicles Beyond This Point*, i.e., northeast along the main track, past a white cottage to the left, the vast red wooden Forest Lodge to the right.

Out of the wood the track reaches a junction by a bridge (023164: see above). To avoid a ricketty footbridge ahead, cross the river here and climb past the junction (025161: above) to the higher junction at 030158, there turning left to return as you came.

Or turn left (north) a few yards to a rough right fork into riverbank pasture. Past where a burn joins the Nethy and below Lyngarrie (021168), where woodland begins a ricketty wooden footbridge with corrugated tin floor crosses the river. Undertake at your own risk. On the reedy east bank, bear diagonally over wet, ditched ground up a low heathery scarp to the electricity poles from the Lurg road to the Forest Lodge. Turn left, parallel to them, to a fence and the track back to where you parked. Simple!

97. Nethybridge to the Tomintoul Road (*Route*)

From Nethybridge, from which signposted Speyside walks depart, there are two options. First, to complete

the B970 route and the Speyside loop from Grantown (**59**) begun so many miles ago, from the village continue north past Nethybridge Hotel. With low wooded hills to the right, just past the Abernethy Golf Club course and a second Nethybridge-Tomintoul turn by the road on the left is white-harled Abernethy church. On a mound in the adjacent field the crumbling walls of Castle Roy (*ruadh*, 'red') still stand. Probably 13th century and never roofed, this Comyn stronghold overlooking the Spey plain was essentially defensive, with wooden lean-to huts once built up against the interior walls. As with Urquhart Castle by Loch Ness, it's said that a plague-infested treasure lies buried in or near the castle

Through pasture and woods the road winds north. On the right at the start of its final descent to the A95 is Revack Lodge (033254), part of the Revack estate which, with the neighbouring Dorback estate, was sold early in 1999. Over 28,000 acres combined, bestowed on Clan Grant by William and Mary, these estates were owned by the Grants for 300 years. In 1994 a 65-acre visitor centre opened here with orchid houses, play-areas and woodland walks: whether it continues as a going concern remains to be seen.

So meeting the main Grantown-Aberlour A95 by the Spey Valley Smokehouse (**58**), a left turn crosses the Spey into Grantown, under a mile away. The right turn runs a few hundred yards to a junction with the A939 to Tomintoul, 13 miles southeast over the moors past Bridge of Brown, and our next destination...but one.

98.   The Braes of Abernethy: Up Geal Charn   *Walk)*

I have two reasons for including this seven-mile walk up and about Geal Charn (091128: 2692ft.), a bare whaleback amid the Braes of Abernethy - a desolate region not connected with the biscuit invented by John Abernethy (1764-1831).

One is that I was conned up it amid a whiteout by a friend who, having done all the Munros, is now after all the Corbetts (2500-3000 feet). I thought we were out for a low-level stroll, but when at Dorback Lodge (079169) he pulled out crampons and ice-axes, too late I realised what was afoot. I've forgiven you, George...well, almost.

The second reason is that this area is widely ignored in favour of better-known, more romantic places and heights. Why come here with Speyside and the Cairngorms so close? Yet folk do. After we'd clambered over the first snowy rise into the emptiness, from a high brow ahead descended a rapid, intense figure, so absorbed in his wilderness dream that, though passing us not 20 yards away, he acknowledged us not at all as he padded on. Perhaps he was a ghost from another time, or maybe we were ghosts to him...

From Nethybridge take the Tomintoul back road east three miles to a forest-edged moorland junction (047197). Turn right three miles on a very minor road past wooded crofts to park left in an abandoned quarry just before the gated Dorback track. Or, from the Grantown-Tomintoul A939 (another old military road) turn south at 066215 to the junction (047197, as above), then turn left.

On the broad track past the empty lodge (where several long-distance hill tracks converge) and its kennels, fork right at the first junction then keep ahead past another track departing right before the second gate after the kennels. Following the north bank of Allt Mor southeast up into the bare hills, the track is visible far ahead. Continue past a left turn up Tom na Fianaig (096157), then past a sink below to the right from which Allt na Gamhuinn (see below) joins Allt Mor. Crossing several burns, with bare slopes closing in both sides, after over two miles at approx. 107136 leave the track to descend right over Allt Mor. Start southwest up the bare flank opposite, aiming always at the higher brow ahead and above. And avoid whiteouts.

Having failed to do this, I can't tell you much about this trackless route. There's an initial crest, then a sink (amid which the Wandering Wayfarer passed us), then a further steady climb southwest up to the long bare top of Geal Charn. A westward turn curves over this flat top to a cairn (091126), where the weather did us a favour, cloud lifting enough to show the wild bleak snow-shrouded hills all about. Impressive.

Descending northwest to Allt nan Gamhuinn, near some pines cross this burn in its boggy dell (091144), so gaining a north-running track which, parallel to and a half-mile west of the main track above Allt Mor, soon rounds a bare-browed hill. Now, with views north over Dorback, the track forks right down to the abandoned steading at Upper Dell (083163). Beyond this point, either bear left over marshland south of the burn to a ford (077165), over it turning right through a gate and uphill by a fence to where you parked; or, just northeast of the steading, ford the burn to gain the outward track at 087164, returning as you began.

Now, via Bridge of Brown's hospitable tea-rooms on the steep slope entering that part of Moray still called Banffshire by its natives, to Tomintoul...and old Banffshire.

The Cairngorms and Lairig Ghru from near Coylumbridge

6

Old Banffshire

Tomintoul, Dufftown & Keith to Buckie & Cullen

99.   Introduction: Old Banffshire

Scan any old map and on it you'll see, flanked by Moray, Inverness and Aberdeen, the old County of Banff. To the southwest beginning atop Ben Macdhui, its western boundary ran north via Cairngorm, the Water of Caiplich and the Cromdales to Orton. Thereafter it broke north-east to the Moray Firth between Spey Bay and Portgordon; this because the Dukes of Gordon (45) didn't want their lands either side of Speymouth in two counties.

From here bearing east via Buckie, Cullen, Banff and Macduff, at the Tore of Troup it turned southwest to the Deveron, following it west of Turriff past Forgue to Rothiemay, then coursing the Isla almost to Keith. Continuing south over the Dufftown-Huntly road through Haugh of Glass to cross the Cabrach via the Buck, it swung southwest along the Ladder Hills. Running east of Tomintoul to the Don's headwaters above Inchrory in Glenavon, finally it turned west over Ben Avon and so back to Ben Macdhui.

Today much of the old county is now part of Moray District. From just east of Cullen (120) the boundary runs south over the Knock (113) to the Deveron, then follows the old boundary as above. Old Banffshire east of this boundary is now part of Banff and Buchan. Yet, even if administratively sliced up like a pizza, Banffshire retains its own identity.

Never as douce as Moray or Aberdeen, the old county was rich in roguery. The derring-do of outlaw James Macpherson (106), Glenlivet's hidden stills (104), the coastal smuggling 200 years ago when folk from laird to cottar dealt in contraband (117) – plenty went on, mostly hidden. Banffshire was once also Scotland's main refuge for persecuted Catholics, with a Catholic seminary at Scalan in the Braes of Glenlivet (102), and the Catholic Dukes of Gordon at Fochabers protected half Scotland's Dissenters (44).

So, first to Tomintoul, then via Glenlivet and Dufftown to Auchindoun Castle in the Cabrach and north up the Deveron to Haugh of Glass. Strathisla Distillery in Keith refuels us, then it's east along the coast via Buckie to Cullen and the summit of the Bin of Cullen, where this journey ends. As for the rest of old Banffshire, that awaits another tour.

First, Tomintoul (*tom an t-sabhail*, 'hillside of the barn'), an airy high village on an open slope above the beautiful River Avon...

100.   Tomintoul: 'Lord Williams' & the Queen's View   *(History, Walk)*

Terminus of the Speyside Way from Ballindalloch (58) via Glenlivet, Tomintoul (pop. 320) is bisected by the A939 running east from near Grantown and on towards Braemar via the Lecht and Corgarff Castle, both with their unruly ghosts (102, 107).

From Bridge of Brown (98) the A939 climbs a steep brae to White Bridge carpark (133209), start of a four-mile circular walk past Kylnadrochit Lodge (149198) in Strathavon – this detailed in a Glenlivet Estate pamphlet available from

Tomintoul's information centre: see below. Continuing, the road descends to the Avon, the wooded drive by the bridge on the right leading to Kylnadrochit. Over the bridge the B9136 breaks left (north) down Strathavon, first passing an old Wade bridge, then crossing the Conglass *en route* to Drumin and Bridgend of Glenlivet (**105**) – as pretty a route as any in the area.

Soon the A939 reaches Tomintoul's long main street, then its wide and draughty Square, ranged about by three hotels and a museum/information centre (01807-580225: Easter-October).

1150 feet high near the confluence of Ailnack and Avon, not long ago Tomintoul was a source of embarrassment to Scotland Yard, which in 1986 set up a covert fund for undercover operations. Given control of the fund, by 1990 accountant Tony Williams - buying up and renovating local properties as 'Lord Williams of Tomintoul' – had helped himself to £5 million. Getting careless, in May 1995 he began a new career, behind bars. Yet few Toulers ('towellers') disapproved of their roguish benefactor. He'd created 40 jobs and brought in the tourists, and after he was jailed the local brewery created a special beer, *The Laird of Tomintoul*, in his honour. For Tomintoul was never genteel. Founded in 1776 when the 4th Duke of Gordon decided to develop this 'bleak and barren moor', in 1797 an unimpressed contributor to the First Statistical Account declared: 'Tomintoul is inhabited by 37 families without a manufacture. All of them sell whisky and all of them drink it. When disengaged from this business, the women spin yarn, kiss their inamoratos, or dance to the discordant sounds of an old fiddle.' And in 1860 Queen Victoria noted in her diary that 'Tomintoul was the most tumble-down poor-looking place I ever saw.'

Yet she gave royal approval to Avonside, especially to the Queen's View. This, signposted as the 'Tomintoul Country Walk', is reached by walking or driving the road to Delnabo, departing right from the village's southeast end. Past the Highland Games Field and after half-a-mile the road forks left to a car-park (164173), then on to the Queen's View, where Victoria had a picnic. For a two-mile circular walk continue past this point on the Inchrory estate road above the Avon. Above Delavorar (167158), where the west bank road crosses the river to join the estate road, turn right over the Avon, its waters allegedly Scotland's clearest. Beyond the steading follow the tarmac road north through pleasant birch wood and over the Water of Ailnack by turreted Delnabo Lodge (160170), the Ailnack meeting the Avon nearby. Past Delnabo cross the Avon via the 1882 girder bridge and climb the brae to a fork. Turn right to the carpark, or left to Tomintoul.

The gorge carrying the Ailnack deepens upriver. Carved into the bare moors, with its hanging valleys this is one of Scotland's least-known scenic wonders.

101.   Tomintoul: the Ailnack Gorge & Beyond   *(Walk, Hill-Routes)*

For this eight-mile moorland walk, from Tomintoul or the Queen's View carpark (see above) cross the 1882 bridge over the Avon, then turn right up the tree-lined private drive past harled, restored 19th century Delnabo Lodge. Once there was a corn-mill here; here too in 1647 the Royalist 2nd Marquis of Huntly was caught by Cromwell's men and later executed in Edinburgh. Beyond a gate by the kennels the track forks. Keep straight on and up.

The sole access to the track above the gorge, other than by a hike from Bridge of Brown up Glen Brown round the west flank of Carn Meadhonach, is via the lodge drive. Though long in public use, public access was questioned a decade ago. It now seems to be accepted but, if in doubt, check locally, especially during the shooting/stalking seasons.

Under mature wood, with the gorge opening below the broad track climbs right to an open saddle, ground to the right as well as left briefly dropping away as the scale of the V-shaped gorge to the left (following the riverbed of this mini-Grand Canyon is ill-advised) becomes obvious. With juniper-rich hanging valleys and sudden edges, it was created amid the last Ice Age. Finding its former eastern exit down Glen Loin to Inchrory ice-blocked, the loch then in the vast Caiplich basin to the south forced a way down the Ailnack instead.

Somewhere amid these awesome slopes is a cave used by the 17th-century bandit Sheumas-an-Tuim ('James of the Hill') - James Grant of Carron. Despite years of murder and mayhem aimed mostly at the Grants of Ballindalloch (**58**), though captured in 1630 and jailed in Edinburgh Castle, he escaped, got a pardon, and died in his bed – scot-free.

The rough track follows the gorge southwest over open moor, wide views north to Ben Rinnes, south to Ben Avon. Where it ends, faint heather paths continue a mile through juniper scrub until, with the diminished gorge now accessible, a steep heathery bank drops to the Ca-du Ford (135136). Here the tumbling Ailnack

can be crossed, rock to rock, or waded – with care: the water's not deep, but the rocks are slippery. Picnic here, then return as you came, via the track past Delnabo.

Across the ford and above a steep gully the moor, in places boggy, flattens towards the north. Half a mile to the east a shallow cut between low bare slopes descends past a ruin (144135) to a track northeast along a silver birch slope past derelict Wester Gaulrig (157137). Nearby lived Grigor Willox MacGregor, alias Willox the Wizard, who told Sir Thomas Dick Lauder about the kelpie's bridle (**92**). Descending into Glen Avon the track bridges the Avon to gain the Inchrory estate road under Auchnahyle (165143). Delavorar is a mile to the north: Delnabo, the Queen's View and Tomintoul not far beyond.

From Auchnakyle the estate road, open to walkers, continues four miles south up the glen to Inchrory Lodge. Under the brows of Ben Avon, with security fences and helicopter pad it now resembles a James Bond movie set. Here the Avon turns west 14 miles up Glenavon past Fords of Avon (042032: **93**) and over the Lairig an Laoigh to Loch Avon below Cairngorm. A rough track follows the river: a mile west of Inchrory steep-sided Glen Loin breaks north then northwest to the Caiplich peat-hag. Soon after The Castle (123108) rears at the head of the Ailnack Gorge: this rock looks artificial, but isn't.

Also from Inchrory begins a four-mile trek southwest up the long ridge of Ben Avon (3843 feet, 1171m), then down past its broken tors through the Sneck Pass to Beinn a' Bhuird (Table Mountain: 3924 feet, 1196m).

A third route from Inchrory heads six miles east up a bare glen above the fledgling River Don past Delnadamph Lodge to Corgarff Castle (255087: **107**) by Cock Bridge on the A939 from Tomintoul. This (Tomintoul-Corgarff) is a two-car walk – one either end.

102. East to the Lecht, North to Tomnavoulin   *(Routes)*

At a junction just north of Tomintoul (174188) the A939 breaks southeast, following the River Conglass past Blairnamarrow ('Field of the Dead': 210154). A mile on is the ruined cottage where in 1920 Percy Toplis, the 'Monocled Mutineer', hid out. Shooting and wounding a farmer and policeman investigating the fire he'd lit, he fled by bike over the Lecht (2090 ft.). Britain's most wanted man, a few days later near Penrith he was ambushed and shot dead by police. He was just 23, and totally dislocated by his war experiences in Flanders.

Usually the first in Scotland to be snow-bound, the Lecht road was made in 1754 by men of the 33rd Regiment under Lord Charles Hay. He left a carved memorial at the Well of Lecht (235152) where, bending sharply south, the road climbs steep up to and past the ski-centre at the summit, entering Gordon District. Also close by this bend and the well is the old Iron Mine, built probably by the York Building Company in 1730. With a picnic spot nearby this square two-storey building has been restored by the District Council.

North from the junction at 174188, after c
the right to the 1844 Auchriachan Mill (182186)
then flanks the aptly-named Feith Musach ('Gl
commercially. After four miles, opposite the Pole
lated Bochel (491m) to the east, a right turn up th
den land where cattle-reivers, smugglers, illicit
hid out 200 years ago. One lane leads to the 19
Chapeltown (242208); up a track a mile further
(*sgalan*, 'shieling': 246194), a large farmhouse,
over a hundred Catholic priests were secr
Cumberland's troops, it was repaired, then in 1
opposite. Also at Scalan is the 1897 church of C
second on the site, financed by the Marquess of
Pluscarden (**17**).

A mile north of Knockandhu the B9
Tomnavoulin ('Mill on the Hill') and Tamnavulin-Glenlivet Distillery (note variant
spelling) – one of the few Glenlivet-named distilleries, other than *The* Glenlivet,
actually *in* Glenlivet. Starting production as recently as 1967, its Old Mill Visitor
Centre and Museum (Easter-October: tel. 01807-590285) is in an old carding mill
hugging a steep bank above the Livet – and this is where we start a 10 mile circuit
via the site of the Battle of Glenlivet (248295) fought in 1594 above the Allt a'
Choileachan - Burn of the Little Hillocks, or of the Grouse Cocks.

103.   The Battle of Glenlivet   *(History, Walk)*

South of Ben Rinnes (**55**), the short walk to this battlesite is via two forest miles
from the Dufftown B9009 just north of the Croft Inn at Shenval (215296). A longer
there-and-back forest route starts from a carpark at Allanreid (235249: below). Both
routes are dull.

This circuit, though with dull stretches, is more varied and offers options.
From the visitor centre and via a footbridge over the Livet, turn right up a bank to
the Tombae Road, past the twin-spired 1829 Church of the Incarnation. Curl east
round Cairn Muldonich (1857 ft.) above the Suie burn for a long mile. Over a cattlegrid a track forks left up to forestry flanking Cairn Muldonich. This is the way to
go – but first, just beyond this fork, is the Allanreid carpark, by a sweet riverside
haugh. Here a tablet commemorates one Margaret Brown, 'who loved this spot'. So
will you. It's a fine place to drowse.

(Also a six-mile circuit starts here, following the Livet southeast along the
north bank, then by the second footbridge crossing to the south. Swinging west over
the Blye Water via farmland and moor to the Braes of Glenlivet, the route returns
north under and west of The Bochel. At a fork past Glack a right turn leads to the
first footbridge over the Livet, and so back to Allanreid – again, see the Glenlivet
Estate pamphlet: I haven't walked it.).

Now to the battle. Past a forestry gate (237251) the uphill track follows Cairn Muldonich's east flank - two long miles of dreary spruce before, swinging left to brief open hilltop moor, broader vistas open. The track descends (watch for red deer on Carn a' Bhodaich up ahead and right) to the forested glen of Allt a' Choileachan. Soon amid mature pine it turns sharp to an open bend over a feeder-burn, the spur-track to the 1594 battlesite steep on the right (246291).

In this bloody affray, the Catholic earls Huntly and Erroll with 800 horse and 1200 infantry, most Gordons, routed 10,000 Highlanders under the Protestant Duke of Argyll. Ordered by James VI not to engage Huntly before the king's army joined him, the 18-year-old Argyll refused to negotiate, though the outnumbered Catholic rebels had field artillery. With his ragged army strung out over miles, Argyll's van-guard was surprised. 2000 men were in flight before he even got there. He fled too, leaving over 500 dead. Their victory did the Catholic cause no good. Enraged, James destroyed Huntly Castle (**45**) and Erroll's seat at Slains. As for the Highlanders, for the first time they fed the guns of modern war...

As now the Highlands feed the spruce. Returning to the main track, contin-ue west along a straight dark avenue under claw-like boughs. At a main junction after a mile (229293), Carn Tighearn climbing right, the continuing track runs on a mile to the B9009 by Shenval (see above). Instead, turn sharp left on a broad red track, down to and over Allt a' Choileachan. Climb hard right to more forestry, ignoring left turns. At 225282 a track on the right flanks Tom na Liach then descends open ground past Auchorachan to the Tombae road, a left turn returning you back to Tomnavulin in over a mile.

To stay higher longer, past this turn continue south and down over the tiny Burn of Nevie to a gate (224281). With broad views over Glenlivet, the track enters one last narrow Forestry belt then descends to Nevie and the B9008. Another option is to follow the edge of the forestry south atop the high pasture until you see the dis-tillery, keeping above a steep birch-fringed bank to the right. When Wester Claggan appears on the left, descend to the road (or take the farm-track). Turn right (north) back to where you started.

104. Above Glenlivet: Up Carn Daimh   *(History, Walk)*

Not just *uisgebeatha* but its remoteness made Glenlivet famous. Many folk first came to this hidden glen when on the run after the '45. Settling down as 'farmers' they began distilling. In 1824, with over 200 illicit stills in the area, George Smith (1792-1871) took out the licence that made The Glenlivet famous, so enraging his neighbours that, it's said, he slept with two hairtrigger pistols under his pillow. They were understandably angry: within two decades his success had put them all out of business. Briefly taking a distillery at Delnabo (**101**), in 1858 he and his son built a distillery on the present site at Minmore. With the railway's arrival at Ballindalloch (**58**) easing supply problems, by 1880 Glenlivet's name was imitated by so many other distilleries (some as far as Elgin, so making Glenlivet 'the longest glen in

Scotland') it was legally ruled that The Glenlivet was exactly that.

Some folk say The Glenlivet's secret lies in water drawn from Josie's Well, which the rain takes two years to reach. With the visitor centre (01542-783220) open mid-March-October, from Tomnavoulin you get there via Gallowhill (see below) or by continuing north up the B9008, turning left at Auchbreck a mile to Bridgend of Glenlivet, and left again to the distillery. (From Ballindalloch take the B9008 to Bridgend of Glenlivet and follow the signs. From Dufftown take the B9009 south to Auchbreck and turn right.)

From Minmore a fine seven-mile walk ascends Carn Daimh then returns via Tomnavoulin. Passing the ruin of Blairfindy Castle (built as a hunting seat in 1586 by the Earl of Huntly) over a field to the east, walk or drive uphill to a T-junction by Blairfindy Lodge (193285). Turn right and park 200 yards on by a cinder track, on its gate the Speyside Way marker.

Past a derelict the track climbs pasture by the forestry fenceline, then over a gate continues past grouse butts to open moor, views of Ben Rinnes (55) behind. Over a low saddle west of Carn Liath (1795 ft.) the dome of Carn Daimh (pron. *Dye*) appears ahead, the path easy but possibly wet. After an open mile with views west to the Cromdales, over a fence continue up along another forestry fenceline until, just short of the summit a signpost (182254) indicates a path on the left to Tomnavoulin – one way down.

From Carn Daimh (1866 ft., the magnificent view running north past Ben Rinnes to Morven in Caithness, east over the Bochel and Ladder Hills to Lochnagar, south to Ben Avon and Ben Macdhui) the Speyside Way continues south over the Feith Musach three miles to Tomintoul. For a longer circuit, rather than return to the Tomnavoulin signpost, descend southeast to the forest fenceline and follow it towards Cairn Ellick. Where (189240) the forestry edge turns east and downhill, follow it to a track. Turning left, descend north past abandoned Craighead (194248) over the Slough Burn, through a belt of trees and over Allt a' Choire by the plank bridge to Westertown (see below).

Or, taking the signposted path, descend east to Glenlivet, Cairn Muldonich beyond, Tomnavoulin soon in view. With Craighead below right, from the heather veer left over rough pasture to a gap in a forestry belt below. Bear right down a field to Westertown, then left on the burnside track to Tomnavoulin. Joining the B9008, turn left, then left again up the Gallowhill road (signposted Blairfindy Lodge). Climb past Gallowhill, Glenlivet Distillery below, and so back to wherever you parked.

105. Drumin Castle to Dufftown   *(Route)*

Past Blairfindy Lodge and the Carn Daimh turn the lane descends a wooded, north-facing brae to the Strathavon B9136 (**100**). A half-mile left of the junction is ruined Drumin Castle (185304), a 14th century tower once guarding the Speyside approach to the Lecht (**102**). Its strategic site on a bluff above the confluence of Livet and Avon encouraged the Wolf of Badenoch to commandeer it along with Ruthven, Loch an Eilean and Lochindorb.

The right turn on the B9136 crosses the Livet to join the B9008. Here a left turn leads three miles north above the Avon to the Speyside A95 above Ballindalloch (**58**), *en route* passing Craggan (186322), 300 yards south of which the flat Craggan Stones mark an open air preaching site used by dissenters during the 1843 Schism. To the right the B9008 curls through Bridgend of Glenlivet and past the distillery road to Auchbreck, where the B9009 turns north past Shenval (**103**) 10 miles via bleak Glen Rinnes to Dufftown.

This route characterises mid-Banffshire. Past dull forestry and scattered steadings, many derelict, it twists past ice-gouged hillocks to follow the Dullan Water under the bare brows of Thunderslap Hill (**108**) and Jock's Hill to the east; Ben Rinnes (**55**) looming above the modern slab of Allt a' Bhainne Distillery (1975: 276344) immediately to the west.

About two miles past the Edinvillie turn (289356) northwest up the narrow Glack Harnes pass between Ben Rinnes and bald, rounded Meikle Conval (1867 ft.), a track up Meikle Conval starts by a bridge (304373). A mile on under neighbouring Little Conval (1811 ft., with a ruined Iron Age fort), at 304364 a lane descends right, over the Dullan then sharp left along a wooded slope under Jock's Hill. Passing the Giant's Chair (see below), it enters Dufftown via Kirktown of Mortlach. For interest, try this approach.

As for the B9009, continuing past Dufftown golf course, in two miles it rounds a brow and descends into Dufftown via broad Conval Street.

145

106. Dufftown: Distilleries & the Giant's Seat   *(History, Walk)*

'Rome was built on seven hills; Dufftown was built on seven stills.' Founded in 1817 by James Duff, 4th Earl of Fife, on a slope above the confluence of Fiddich and Dullan, this raw town (pop. 1680) of wide streets is noted for ruined Balvenie Castle, its battlemented clock-tower, the old parish church at Mortlach, and its seven distilleries, especially Glenfiddich.

Founded by William Grant with equipment from Cardhu (**56**), production here began at Christmas 1887. Still owned by the Grants and open all year, from the Square this Whisky Trail distillery is found by taking Balvenie Street north (A941 to Craigellachie). Just past the 30-mile limit turn right to the visitor centre (01340-820373) and carpark.

Nearby off the same back-road to the Keith B9014 is Balvenie Castle (324406), a massive 13th century courtyard, walls mostly intact. Once a Comyn fort, in 1459 it was taken over by the Stewart Earls of Atholl, and in 1615 by the Innes family. Mary Queen of Scots stayed here in 1562; in 1644 it sheltered Montrose, and after Killiecrankie in 1689 victorious Jacobites occupied it. Abandoned following its final occupation by government troops after Culloden in 1746, it's open 1 April to 30 September (admission fee charged).

Dominating the Square and once the town jail, the elaborate 1839 Gothic Clock Tower now houses the tourist information centre (01340-820501: summer only) and a small museum. On it a wall-plaque commemorates local man George Stephen, founder and first president of the Canadian Pacific Railway. The clock, from Banff, is allegedly 'The clock that hung Macpherson' – the fiddler-brigand caught in Keith and executed in Banff in 1700, his enemy Lord Braco advancing the clock an hour to ensure he'd hang before a reprieve arrived. It's said that on the scaffold he played 'Macpherson's Rant', composed in his death-cell the night before. As the Burns version goes:

> *Sae rantingly, sae wantonly,*
> *Sae dauntingly, gaed he,*
> *He play'd a spring, and danc'd it round*
> *Below the gallows-tree*

Then he broke his fiddle over the hangman's head and jumped into eternity. That's the story, anyway. Is this clock really the original? As for the fiddle, it's now found in Newtonmore's Clan Macpherson Museum (**75**).

From the Square, Church Street descends a wooded brae to Mortlach Parish Church, open Easter-October. Allegedly founded AD566 by St. Moluag of Lismore, with a Pictish cross in the graveyard and another, the Elephant Stone, in the vestibule, this kirk was largely rebuilt in 1876 and 1931, but 13th century remnants survive. It's said that, having routed the Danes here in 1010, King Malcolm II extended it three spears' lengths in thanksgiving. An octagonal watch-house in the kirkyard was once used to guard against grave-robbers.

For a two-mile circular walk, from the church bear downhill and right through a gate to a bridge over the Dullan. On the far side keep right on the riverside path to a sign: *Giant's Chair Walk, 1 mile*. Continue past a weir opposite Dufftown-Glenlivet Distillery and south into the Dullan's ash-and-alder-fringed glen. Under steepening banks, the path doglegs past a second weir, climbing left over a tiny footbridge. Continue along the glen's wooded eastern slope amid foxglove and giant woodrush, a view of Meikle Conval opening up . Now fenced and stepped, the path crosses another footbridge by the aptly named Linen Apron Waterfall (324382), then descends to the Dullan. A short climb reaches the Giant's Chair, a rocky plinth overhanging the dark, moss-fringed river under the trees. A few yards on, to the right just before a substantial footbridge (383319) over the Dullan, is the Giant's Cradle, another odd, water-sculpted rock formation

Crossing the bridge, bear right through a field up a wooded bank to a swing gate onto a back road. Turn right up this road between open pastures back to Dufftown, open views of the Convals and hills north of Dufftown contrasting with the Dullan's depths just explored, and so back past Pittyvaich Distillery to Mortlach Church – a pleasant stroll.

Next, something starker – Auchindoun and the Cabrach.

107. Auchindoun Castle   *(History, Walk)*

From a bare hilltop southeast of Dufftown the ruin of Auchindoun Castle (348374) glowers over the A941 Cabrach route to Rhynie, its towerhouse rearing above obdurately buttresssed outer walls. Built to control the Cabrach, once a whisky-smuggling route, it stood just over a century before a Gordon-Mackintosh feud led to its destruction in 1592.

From Dufftown take the Huntly A920 half a mile east then turn right (south) up the A941. A mile up this road park by the Historic Scotland sign indicating Auchindoun up a stony track on the left. Between rough pasture and plantations past Upper Keithack the half-mile walk leads to Pictish earthworks. Atop these stand the ruin, sky visible through the gaping windows of its crumbling three-storey tower, the oddly-named Scalp (1509 ft.) providing a suitably dreich backdrop.

All but one of the outer gateways are bricked up, signs warning: DANGER LOOSE MASONRY PLEASE KEEP CLEAR. Yet the gate at the east entry is easily scaled, making the bricking up of the rest pointless, at least as a way of keeping people out.

A plaque at the South Gate tells how Auchindoun was built by Thomas Cochrane, Earl of Mar – a favourite of James III, he was hanged by the barons in 1482 - and taken over by the Gordons in 1535. It also tells how Sir Adam Gordon of Auchindoun perpetrated the most atrocious deed in the history of Mar - the burning to death of Margaret Campbell, wife of Forbes of Towie, and 27 of her family and servants at Corgarff in November 1571.

The sack of Corgarff (by Cock Bridge on the A939 Tomintoul-Braemar road: **102**) was thought so outrageous it led an unknown bard to pen the ballad, 'Edom O'Gordon'. It's said Adam - *'It fell about the Martinmas/When the wind blew shrill and cauld'-* attacked Corgraff with the Master of Forbes and his men elsewhere. Allegedly he came to Corgarff with lustful intent, but Margaret would not surrender. Infuriated, the villain bellowed:

'Gie up your house, ye fair lady
Gie up your house to me,
Or I will burn yoursel therein,
Bot and your babies three.'

Margaret still refused, Adam carried out his threat. Corgarff burned. All within died but, the ballad claims, for Margaret's 'dochter dear'. Lowered from the burning castle in a pair of sheets, Edom speared her to death. Only on turning over her body with his spear did he regret his deed, crying: *'You are the first that e'er I wished lived again.'*

Yet, as usual, 'history is the lie commonly agreed upon'. The event did occur, during the civil war between the supporters of Mary Queen of Scots and her son, the young James VI. In the northeast Catholic Gordons (see **45**) opposed Forbes, Frasers and Keiths. In 1571, with his brother the Earl of Huntly fighting in the south, Adam routed the Master of Forbes at Clatt. Forbes escaped, was reinforced, but in Aberdeen was again defeated and this time captured. Adam sent forces to occupy Forbes strongholds. A Captain Kerr came to Corgraff; he fired the castle. Adam Gordon was not present. Yet it was done in his name, balladry blames him, and he wasn't a lovable fellow. The later destruction of Auchindoun, leaving it in the dreich state you find it now, was at least poetic justice.

108.   Above Glen Fiddich   *(Walk)*

A mile south of Auchindoun amid bare hills the A941 winds down a wooded brae to cross the Fiddich at Bridgehough (341358). Here, by a roadside lodge on the river's west bank, with parking space, a gated estate road and adjacent steep drive provide the start and finish of an eight-mile circular walk. From Glen Fiddich it climbs past Thunderslap Hill to bare hilltop moor before returning via the steadings at Glencorrie and Smithstown.

There is one steep stretch, and the lonely top is exposed.

Begin on the estate road, signposted 'Glenfiddich Lodge Private'. Via the river's northwest bank and under mature pine forest the road up the narrow glen steadily climbs above the Fiddich then levels off. Follow it until, after two miles, Glenfiddich Lodge ahead, on the right a rough track (315304) starts up a steep heathery gully to an open moorland saddle between Thunderslap Hill (1709 ft.) and the more distant Laird's Seat (1500 ft).

This 'track' soon deteriorates. A better track runs parallel on the other side of the gully: it may be worth crossing to it. Near the crest the tracks converge; at the crest, with fine views over Glen Rinnes below of Ben Rinnes and the Convals, there is a crossing track, also a clear view north to the ruin at Mayo (315355), the walk's halfway point.

Ignoring the crossing, head straight on, now curling slightly down and right. Don't make our mistake: the track the OS map shows as breaking north at 307341 is mostly gone. Floundering over boggy flats to a sodden sunken way climbing towards Mayo was no fun. Keep left, west of bare Tom nan Eun, down towards Achbreck (299339). At a fork (300342) above Achbreck, bear right on a clear track along the northeast flank of the ridge above Glen Rinnes. This is longer and means more down-then-up, but beats a bog-bath.

With a deer fence one side and a young plantation the other, when just above the mostly-intact ruin at Mayo, the track curls west (left) towards the ridge's plant-ed crest. Soon a high stile over the deer fence (314355) leads to a grass track and a sudden fine view northeast down the green valley ahead, over Glencorrie steading to Auchindoun Castle.

Descend this banked track to sheep-pasture, then break diagonally right down the pasture to a gate, crossing a burn onto a track to the Glencorrie back-road; or keep to high ground until above Enoch steading (332373), then descend to the road. The only problem with the first option is that in wet weather the Glencorrie track is a cow-mire.

A mile up the back road (from Glencorrie you could short-cut east over a low ridge to Smithtown) and 200 yards past the Nether Enoch turn-off at 335372 a stony track breaks right (south). This rises gently between fields through the derelict steading at Smithtown, continuing left round a low brow to a cattle-pasture fence. Follow this down to a gate, one-strand barbed wire fences either side. Over it, bear left parallel to a silver birch avenue down a muddy field to a sunken lane,

Blackfolds House amid trees to the right. Over a gate this lane joins the Blackfolds drive. Descend this 300 yards to the A941 and your car.

This walk, taxing in parts but worthwhile, should take about four hours.

109.   To Keith via the Cabrach and Haugh of Glass   *(Route, Walk)*

Continuing south on the lonely Cabrach route, the road climbs through a narrow bare defile to a broad view beyond, in the distance the elegant Buck (2306 ft.) marking the District boundary. Continue down a long brae to Bridgend (374316). Here, seven miles from Dufftown, a minor road breaks north above the Deveron to Haugh of Glass: soon our route.

First, on towards Cabrach and Rhynie. Crossing the Black Water by its confluence with the Deveron the road climbs past the Grouse Inn (379305), famed for its huge variety of malts on optic. Up a narrow glen following then crossing the Deveron before leaving the river at Cabrach (a parish, not even a hamlet), the road runs on over bare moor past The Buck. Entering Gordon District, it descends past Tap O' Noth (1848ft., 485294) to Rhynie.

Though outside the area this tour covers, Tap O' Noth demands mention, for atop its bleak dome is one of Scotland's finest Iron Age vitrified forts. From a carpark by Brae of Scurdargue (484284), loop left over pasture and up the forestry edge to a track. Climbing the hill's west flank this traverses the south slope to the fort's east entrance. The size of a football pitch, the grassy interior lies within huge walls of tumbled slag, on the south and east sides vitrified – fused by intense heat into runs of lumpy, glassy stone. Tap O'Noth is a mystery, with a haunting atmosphere. What caused the vitrification? Nobody knows for sure, but possibly the walls were timber-laced, with wooden huts and firewood laid up against them, so that conflagrations (accidental or not) might well have produced sufficient heat. And one other thing about Tap O' Noth – the views from the top are spectacular.

Returning now to Bridgend, turning north up the minor road seven miles to Haugh of Glass it soon becomes clear that this little-known glen is beautiful. Passing Lower Cabrach Church and a primary school, the road steadily climbs the open glen's west flank, the Deveron far below, the opposite ridges impressive. It's mysterious and evocative, from another time. Past scattered hill-farms, many abandoned, from the crest a gradual descent passes Mill of Lynabain, pink-harled Beldorney Castle (423370), and a stone circle left of the road (425378). Reaching the river at Haugh of Glass, by a war memorial (424394) the road forks: left to a lane south up the Markie Water, right along the wooded riverbank past Blairmore School to the A920 from Dufftown to Huntly, or straight on a mile to the A920.

Keeping straight on (Keith 9), at the A920 turn left then, in a hundred yards, right on the back road to Drummuir via pasture, scrubwood and moor. Passing Mains of Blairmore (414431) with its Gothic porch and an old millhouse by the burn below the road, four miles north of Glass turn right on the B9115 to Keith (left to Drummuir: see below). A mile on at the next junction (416454), turn left at the old sign to Fife Keith (the B9115 continues to the Keith-Huntly A96). This left turn crosses high pasture then the Keith-Dufftown railway (an association to save it exists) to join the B9014 just south of Mill of Towie.

Here, turn right three miles north to Keith and Strathisla Distillery, both explored soon. First, though, from Dufftown to Drummuir and beyond.

110.   Above Drummuir   *(Route, Walk)*

The above route is a *very* roundabout way from Dufftown to Keith. The B9014, the direct route, 11 miles long, leaves Dufftown north past left turns either side of the Fiddich, the first running past Balvenie Castle and Glenfiddich Distillery to the Craigellachie A941, the second a back road high above the Fiddich via Kininvie to Maggieknockater (**51**).

Climbing a brae two miles to forestry hiding Loch Park below to the west, over a brow the road descends a north-facing slope, the baronial pile of Drummuir Castle (371441) in wooded grounds by the River Isla ahead to the left. Built in 1848 by Thomas Mackenzie for Admiral Archibald Duff, of the family owning Drummuir since 1621, in 1908 its owner Thomas Gordon Duff declared: 'It ought to be pulled down and a house suitable to the climate of the pocket of the owner built.' Yet it survives, being restored 1986-88. Now leased to the distillers J&B, its grounds host Loch Park Adventure Centre (01542-810334), offering outdoor activities and courses, also walks round the loch and castle garden.

From the bottom of the brae facing the castle the B9014 climbs under mature wood past Drummuir village before continuing via Mill of Towie to Keith (see above). Either from brae-bottom or village (from a lane between the school and the estate office), turn left downhill to a junction of the lanes. Crossing railway and Isla, which here is little more than a burn, turn left for Botriphine Parish Church (1820), its site dedicated to the 7th-century St. Fumac. A well nearby once held his wooden effigy, which was ritually washed every 3rd of May at St. Fumac's Fair.

Up Manse Brae past West Lodge and the Long Avenue to the elaborately-turreted castle the back road climbs north up and over wide open moor before descending to the Keith-Mulben A95 by Glentauchers Distillery. *En route*, on the moortop, it crosses two cattlegrids. From the first (372457), an ungated track breaks west past a plantation - the start of a fine six-mile circuit offering better, more continuous views than the map suggests, much of the forestry shown as cloaking Mount Pleasant (355485) having been felled.

From the cattlegrid, start west up the track through a new plantation past a fenceline and forestry on the left. The track descends then rises to a new belt of forestry, this to the right. Here, with ruined Glenheath below and views of Ben Rinnes and the Convals beyond, the track vanishes into pasture. At the top, where the forestry breaks left, keep straight on via a short dark fenced track between the trees to an overgrown north-south track (352454).

Turning right, with forestry both sides follow this soggy track 200 yards to a gate onto open moor, a young plantation on the left. Keep straight 400 yards on a rough heather track to mature wood ahead, the going boggy. Past a gate into this dark wood (by it an old carved stone, 'D' one side, 'A' the other), tracks diverge. Keep right, north, on the darkest track which, though soon opening out amid dying trees, becomes lumpy, boggy and deep-rutted as it runs north to meet, at the edge of the wood, a main forestry road (356464).

Here the walk improves. Turn right through a gate on the main track over an open moorland slope under the low rise of Knockan, fine views southwest up Speyside, west to Ben Aigan (**51**) over the A95, and north over the Moray Firth. Entering another mature plantation, more open than the map suggests, continue north along the logged western slope under Machattie's Cairn, the fringe of the wood ahead surreal with matchstick-like bare tall pines, many dead, others half-fallen supporting each other. Past this brief strip the track climbs to wider views by a junction (358454) with a main track climbing open ground from the A95 below. From here the track curls northeast then east round Mount Pleasant, the views especially fine northwest over the Moray plain to Covesea Lighthouse (**32**), east to The Balloch (**112**) above Keith and on to the Knock (**113**). Now bearing southeast, the track dips into a final half-mile stretch of dense dark wood, emerging onto the road by Gateside (367476), attractive with its red doors and black-pointed stonework.

Turning right, follow the road back towards Drummuir, the Hill of Towie off to the left past a ruined steading. Over a cattlegrid the airy road levels to wide views again, dipping then climbing this last mile, crossing the Burn of Towie back to where you parked.

111.   Keith & Strathisla: Scotch History   *(History, Visit)*

Sited where railway and main A96 cross the Isla, this agricultural town (pop. 4900) has more history than first looks suggest. Occupying the eastern riverbank from the old kirkyard to Milton, the old town dates back to *c.*700, when St Maelrubha evangelised the area. Long a cattle-mart, later a linen centre importing Dutch and Russian flax, it was gifted to Kinloss Abbey by William the Lion (1165-1214). By 1500 the 22nd Abbot Thomas Crystal oversaw Keith's *brasinas* (breweries); by 1545 an 'Ailhous' occupied the site of the Highlands' first legal distillery – Milton (1786), now Strathisla. Today Seagram-owned, its Chivas Regal water comes from the same *fons bullien* ('bubbling spring') as used by the bubbling monks.

Meanwhile Keith passed from the Diocese of Moray to the Ogilvies, its owners for over two centuries. One of that ilk was St. John Ogilvie (1580-1615), Scotland's first post-Reformation saint. Hanged for denying the anti-Catholic oath of loyalty to the crown, he was canonised in 1976. Later the brigand Macpherson (**106**) was caught here, and here too in 1746 the Jacobites won their last victory before Culloden dispersed them forever.

After 1750 Keith grew fast. The Ogilvie Earl of Findlater laid out New Keith; c.1759 the Earl of Fife built rival Newmill on a slope a mile to the north, its streets broad and central square expansive; and on the Isla's west bank after 1817 Fife Keith was built under the same patronage, its streets about Regent Square broader still.

From Drummuir (B9104), Mulben (A95) or Fochabers (A96) it's Fife Keith you enter first. Over the Isla and up past Seafield Avenue (the B9116 to Newmill via Strathisla Distillery), then past the Banff A95 turn opposite narrow Mid Street shops, the A96 swings south up Moss Street past Reidhaven Square. This vast square was built to accommodate the Summer Eve Fair, once the region's greatest animal trys. Held each September, it has been succeeded by the popular Keith Agricultural Show, which takes place each August.

Likewise popular with many folk is what's created under the elegant pagodas of Strathisla Distillery (01542-783044: visitor centre open February-30

November), worth visiting not just for the tour and a dram but the history too. For here in 1786 legal distilling began in the north.

A bottle of scotch costs under two pounds to produce. With tax 400% over cost, we can moan, and often do. But there's nothing new in this. For by the 18th century illicit Highland whisky was so preferred to the legal Lowland product that, in 1784, the Wash Act sought to create a Lowland monopoly by over-taxing northern production, also by declaring stills under 20 gallons capacity illicit. Any Highland distiller with sufficient capital to overcome these hurdles had then to be declared 'fit and proper to keep stills' by the Excise Board in Edinburgh, meaning by Lowlanders.

In 1786 George Taylor took out the first licence in the north. Monopolising local flax dressing, a business then in decline, he set up at Milton/Strathisla with a 40-gallon still. Sued for £500 for installing a second still, his local peers fined this public benefactor just £2/2/0 (£2.10). Later a recluse, he died falling from his horse.

With the Wash Act abolished, also in 1786, a standard duty was put on all Scottish distillers. An 1814 law banned stills under 500 gallons capacity; but in 1820 an Inland Revenue report stated that most of the whisky drunk in Scotland was still smuggled. This led to the law of 1823, Smith of Glenlivet (**104**) being the first keen beneficiary.

So, swingeing tax is nothing new. Nor, comparatively, does a dram cost you. In 1900 a bottle of Strathisla was 12.5p: a third of the then-average weekly wage. Think about it as you visit. Whisky Galore? You wish.

112.   Keith: Up Meikle Balloch   *(Walks)*

The forested whaleback of Meikle Balloch (473496: 1200 ft.) east of Keith offers various options, walk-wise - (**1**) up and down; (**2**) round and up, or (**3**) up, round and about through woods and fields below to the pretty Falls of Tarnash just south of Keith near the A96.

East of Reidhaven Square and the A96, Bridge Street becomes the Edindiach road, meandering two miles east past Dunnyduff Wood to the water treatment plant at Herricks. By the edge of Balloch Wood just beyond, the road swings right (462502). Parking by two forestry tracks starting left, take the higher track to the first junction in the wood. From this junction (**1**) and (**2**) proceed; the first option involving the stiffest climb, straight up the flank of the hill.

(**1**) Turn right 150 yards to a firebreak, its faint path marked by a blue-banded post, a clearing or turning circle just beyond. The straight slog up through dense spruce is dull, but the forestry thins, the now-rockier path climbing peaty banks to Meikle Balloch's broad, heathery top and fine panoramas. On a clear day Ben Wyvis shows far to the west; the Moray Firth widens beyond the Bin of Cullen (**122**), the Knock's bald dome is prominent to the east, and Huntly hills lead south to Ben Rinnes ridges. Now aiming at Ben Rinnes, cross the top to a southward track down into the trees (468486). Past a second hilltop clearing on the left continue down a mile past a quarry to a fork (464475). This fork is also involved in (**2**).

(**2**) Turn left onto the main track for an eight-mile clockwise circuit round the base of the hill and the forest edge, north then east. An open, scrappy stretch leads after two miles to a fork (477504), Little Balloch (912 ft.) ahead. Turn right (south) up and along Meikle Balloch's forested slope, straight on past a Y-fork then an open saddle between the two hills. Back in dense forestry descend to an open crossing. Keep right by the forest edge past a felled, devastated area. Ignoring left forks and back in dense forest, at a junction (473472) bear right again, curling northwest above the hidden Glen of Coachford to open slope. Just beyond a white-harled cottage below, and where mature forest begins again, is a fork (464475); the rough uphill track on the right the same as the one descended in (1). Climbing the track, once atop the hill you find the firebreak descent (467494) climbed in (1) by bearing left down to or along the forest fringe. A small white cairn 20 yards out from the trees marks the hidden path downhill. That's (2).

(3) From the fork at 464475 the main track bears northwest into the forest 50 yards to another fork, the right turn following the edge of Balloch Wood north back to Herricks where you parked. For a longer walk turn left to open ground above the Glen of Coachford. At a five-way junction (462474: a steading on the left) turn right (northwest), following the edge of the wood on the old military road to Keith. Past another track breaking right towards Herricks just before the wood ends, continue northwest through fields to Mains of Birkenburn (451485), visible ahead, at the farm turning left down a lane to Tarnash.

By a stone bridge over the Tarnash burn (442489: just short of the A96), descend concrete steps north through mixed woodland to the popular falls (433490). The burnside path continues to an open glade below Dunnyduff Wood. At a junction over the burn, if parked in Keith, bear left via the wooded bank above the A96 back to town. If at Herricks, turn right and north round the hillock above the burn to the Edindiach Road, turning right a mile back to your car.

For the short there-and-back way to Tarnash Falls, at the Keith 30-mile limit (Huntly side), bear left on a path along the wooded bank below housing and above the A96. After almost joining the A96 by a section of old road, the path bends left into the open glade under Dunnyduff Wood, where a right turn over a footbridge leads to the falls.

113.   Round Rothiemay & the Knock   *(Routes, Walk)*

From Meikle Balloch the District boundary follows the Isla to the Deveron past Rothiemay then north over the Knock to the sea. A hard wide rolling land with lit-tle wealth, many ruins, and few visitors, it's worth a circuit, not least in order to visit Rothiemay then climb the Knock.

From Keith the A96 runs south past the Tarnash turn and successive right turns to Drummuir, entering Gordon Distict amid open pasture, the Mill of Botary below by a road on the right to Boghead and Windyraw, names that say it all. The continuing A96 descends round a bend to a gully and a minor left turn to Cairnie and Ruthven (B9018: 482447). Through these hamlets this road runs five miles northeast over poor ground to the Huntly-Portsoy B9022 by the Isla. A left turn over the river quickly leads to the B9118 turn right to Milltown of Rothiemay (*rath a' mhaigh*; possibly 'fort on the plain'). Past the Isla-Deveron confluence the wooded road enters this hidden village, snug under hills by the river.

A right turn by the village war memorial descends past a castellated house, the post office/store, and the Forbes Arms Hotel by the Deveron. Here, under wood-

ed Fourman Hill, the road leaves Moray. The left turn climbs past council housing to the Keith-Aberchirder B9117: for Rothiemay Stone Circle (552487) turn right 400 yards. In a field to the right, its huge recumbent flanked either side by two large outliers, this is really a semi-circle. Not far on is the baronial gateway (1906) of now-vanished Rothiemay Castle. The continuing route to the Huntly-Banff A97 at Marnoch above the Deveron is lovely, and well worth the drive.

Climbing north from Rothiemay on the B9117 (Keith 7), at Rothiemay Crossroads the B9117 continues to Keith. The right turn north on the Portsoy B9022 crosses a bare, stony flatland dominated by the Knock (537552; 1412 ft.), its peaty heather dome annually raced there-and-back from nearby Cornhill. The main track up it is near the B9022 junction with the Banff-Keith A95 at Glenbarry. Turn right on the A95 past Glenbarry Inn 400 yards to a left turn by a cottage on a bend (to the right a stone dyke under beeches by a B&B). This metalled left turn runs west almost a mile through Swilebog steading up to a T-junction: park on the left by a pond. The path up the Knock starts from a gate a few yards right of the junction.

North, the Banff-Portsoy roads soon diverge: west, the Glenbarry-Keith A95 approaches hills south of the Isla flood-plain. Huge piles of boulders in roadside fields show how hard it was to clear this land. Past minor roads right to Sillyearn and Edingight west of the Knock the road picks up the B9117 from Rothiemay then, with the wooded Ballochs looming, a left turn south (497513) over the Isla past an abandoned hotel leads to Balloch Wood or, once over the Isla, left through pasture and forestry to Ruthven.

Still above the Isla flats, two miles short of Keith the B9018 to Cullen (**120**) breaks north past Berryhillock and Deskford – hamlets amid poor farmland. A mile further on the B9116 climbs right to Newmill, a left turn at the west end of its broad main street descending a wooded brae over the Isla and the railway into Keith.

114.   The Road to Buckie   *(Routes)*

At a wooded junction by the Chivas bonded warehouses west of and below Fife Keith the Fochabers/Elgin A96 bears right, over the railway; the B9016 north to the A98 Portgordon crossroads and Buckie leaving it after two miles. Also from this junction the A95 runs west to Mulben crossroads (354506) a mile past the Drummuir (**110**) turn by Glentauchers Distillery: at Mulben the A95 turns south to Craigellachie (**51**). The road continuing west (B9013) passes Auchroisk Distillery's awry sharp roofs then, before descending to the Spey at Boat O' Brig, the Bridgeton track below Ben Aigan (Speyside Way: **48**).

From Mulben the minor road north climbs past another vast Chivas bond into forestry before crossing the A96 (381555). This staggered left-to-right crossing over a fast semi-blind curve demands care. Again cresting forestry, the continuing road (an enigmatic hi-tech installation atop forested slopes opposite) runs down to the B9016, north from Keith and the A96 via Aultmore Distillery (402535).

With sea-views opening ahead, the B9016 descends the semi-wooded Braes of Enzie (once 'papistical country': **44**) to the coastal plain. Still on the slope (398596) above a Y-fork by cottages near the Z-bend over a burn, a right turn to Allaloth offers 'Oxhill Walk', a gravel carpark a few yards down serving this Crown Estate walkette, complete with hielan' coo an' calfie in a paddock. This back-road continues up past the old railway to hilltop forest running five miles east from Corsekell Moss and the Hill of Stonyslacks to Aultmore – a maze of dark tracks, and the lair of foxes and feral cats (see **19**).

The left turn from the Y-fork by the cottages crosses the A98 at Tynet by the 'Secret Church'(also **44**) and continues via Nether Dallachy to Spey Bay (**41**); the B9016 continues over a crossroads (right via Clochan and Preshome to Drybridge) to reach the A98 a mile south of Portgordon and the sea. Here, it's left past Tynet through Fochabers to Elgin; the right turn, east to Fraserburgh, bypasses Buckie, Findochty and Portknockie then bisects Cullen – fine if in a hurry, but less interesting than the coast road through the fisher-towns.

From this staggered crossing continue north past a maltings to Portgordon (A990). Founded in 1797 by the fourth Duke of Gordon (**45**), this drowsy village was once the area's biggest port. By 1874 its harbour, lately restored by the Gurkhas, could hold up to 350 ships. At a sea-front junction the left turn runs three miles past 'Beaufighter Road' and Upper Dallachy to the Spey Bay B9104 by Romancamp Gate (**43**). 'Beaufighter Road' (372632) runs north past a disused airfield and Nether Dallachy's bungalows to Spey Bay. Also from this sea-front junction the B990 bears east through Portgordon to Buckpool past the restored shoreline Gollachy Ice House, built in 1834 to freeze salmon caught in summertime.

Buckpool is one long main street of fishermen's houses, neat and solid, the outer stairs of some dating from when the first floor was used as net loft space. Past the restored harbour (1857) and the Yardie and Seatown (a preservation area) the road joins the A942, so entering Buckie proper, turning right up to the 'new town' round Cluny Square, or left down past the fish mart to Cluny Harbour.

115. Buckie: Fisher History and Beliefs   *(History, Folklore)*

Half by the sea and half on the bank above, Banffshire's largest town (pop 8,350), with Britain's only twin-spired Catholic church (St. Peter's; 1857), sprawls along three miles of coast from Buckpool to Portessie. Its southern edge hasn't yet reached the bypassing main A98, but rapid growth by the A942 to Buckie cross-roads (432642) suggests it won't be long.

Windswept and functional, Buckie was always a fisher-town. With the oldest station, Nether Buckie, dating back nearly 350 years, many fisher families have lived here or nearby almost as long. 200 years ago the Seatown was full of Cowies and Murrays, the latter from Helmsdale over the Firth. The Clarks, Farquhars and Gardens of Portessie were farmers who took up fishing early in the 19th century; the Fletts of Findochty came from Shetland and, *c.*1720, the Slaters from Orkney. With Buckie's many churches reflecting their varied denominations, some folk also belong to sects like the Closed Brethen.

Sponsored by John Gordon of Cluny in 1880, by 1913 the fleet of steam drifters working from Cluny Harbour was Scotland's biggest. Visit on a Saturday morning with the boats in, their masts and electronic gear like a forest against the outer sea wall, then visit the Buckie Drifter (April-October: 01542-834646) in Freuchny Road. Harbour tours, with visits to net-makers and boat-builders, may be booked at this heritage centre.

As for the meaning of the name Buckie, in 'Days of Yore' (1888, reprinted in 1997) George Hutcheson suggested the German *bucht*, 'bay'. In Chambers' Scots Dictionary (1911, 1968), a 'buckie' is, variously, a sea-snail or its shell: a child's rattle made of rushes; fruit of the wild rose, a smart blow or push; a mischievous boy, or a hare's backside. Before the new town was built 'up the brae' the Shore of Buckie was known for its whelks – in Old Scots, 'buckies'. Dwelly's Gaelic Dictionary offers *bocaid* (pron. bok-itch, a whelk). Given Buckie's export trade in shellfish, this seems as good an explanation as any.

Hutcheson's book is full of fisher beliefs. Some men claimed that, going out each day, they met a 'cockie-coo' (a *cu sith*, fairy dog? - see **92**) that stole their bonnets. This they accepted, but if when bound for sea anyone asked where they were going, they'd return home, or even get violent. To meet an 'ill-footed' man or beast en route to the boat meant bad luck. Rabbits, dogs and hares (into which witches were thought to shapeshift) were 'ill-fitted' and calamitous; while meeting a minister was also bad luck. To mention one at sea could be fatal, the sea-gods being pre-Christian, or maybe because ministers meant funerals. To speak the name of Ross was also taboo. A Buckie sceptic out in a Ross-built boat tried to get his Portknockie brother-in-law to say the dreaded name, asking who'd built the boat, and so on. Failing, cruelly he spoke it himself, horrifying the other man, despite which they got a good catch. And *c.*1810 a credulous Buckie fisherman, Bouffie, was tricked when Portgordon men put a rubbish-filled hare's skin on his boat. Seeing it and prophesying doom, he refused to sail. His crew, in on the joke, sailed without him, next day returning with a fine catch. Like the Portgordon man, he never lived it down.

To dye wool, doors and windows had to be shut to prevent an 'evil eye' looking in to spoil the work. On New Year's Day, no fire should be given out from the house. A sick man was given a cog of water, a shilling dropped in it. If, the water drunk, the coin stuck to the bottom, he'd live. If not, he'd die. Lamps were never burned on the side of the house where lines were baited. Leaving a ladle in the kailpot with the lid on was unlucky. New-wed girls were circled by their mothers, who held a burning fir-stick with a hole in it, to drive off fairies out to steal a new-born child,

Strange beliefs? Maybe not, considering the dangers of the sea.

116. Shoreline Rocks: Findochty to Portessie   *(Walk)*

East of Buckie shipyards and Portessie's long shoreline main street the A942 climbs past Strathlene Golf Course a mile to Findochty (pop. 1020: locally *Finnechty*), a steep-faced, neat little fisher village dating from 1440. In 1568 the Ord family acquired the land, later building the now-ruined castle below the road west of the village, and in 1716 contracting Fraserburgh men to fish from the cliff-hemmed harbour. Now home to pleasure craft alone, a white kirk (1863) prominent on a crag above, the harbour makes a good start to a short but invigorating shoreline walk to Portessie, returning via the castle.

Entering the village, turn left down Schoolhill, then left again at the camp/caravan sign. Parking, start west past the caravans under the low cliff and golf course. Over a footbridge spanning a rocky sea-inlet, a grassy bank above tidal rocks leads to a fork. Here it's up to the golf course or down to the cove ahead, the latter route a rocky scramble above the breakers to a shingle beach. A short stretch is under water at high tide.

Past a cave, offshore cormorants hanging out their wings, a grassy path climbs a low headland to a fork, again left to the golf course, right for Portessie via jagged rocks and tidal pools. Where a track curls left up to and over the golf course, follow it for a shorter route or continue to a vast carpark under the clubhouse. Here (also a good place to start) walk on to the A942 at the edge of Portessie, turning left up the brae to a minor road opposite the clubhouse.

With Findochty Castle visible over fields ahead, this road breaks southwest to Rathven, once centre of a large parish, and the A98. Depending on season and if the fields (a drained loch) are sown, follow this road to the first bend, then cross the field past an old watertank, or follow the road to the 1886 railway track. Either way, at the track turn east. Elsewhere cleared for walkers but here overgrown, the field alongside is easier to follow. When south of the castle (455674), bear left to a track past the 15th-century ruin, once an L-plan keep. Back on the A942, return to Findochty by the edge of the golf course.

East of the harbour a road past the 1863 kirk descends to Sandy Creek, protected by Long Head and start of more rocky coastal scrambling towards Portknockie a mile away.

It's clear why smugglers loved this coast!

117.   Smugglers & the Revenue Men   *(History)*

With life hard and money scarce, in the 18th and early 19th centuries taxation to sustain foreign wars grew so heavy that smuggling was common and no dishonour. Cottar, seaman and laird alike combined to outwit the revenue men to profit from contraband - mostly salt, tobacco, French brandy and Dutch gin. For this the Moray Firth coast's many hidden caves and coves were ideal for landing goods unseen, its seatowns and inland moors offering endless hiding places. The French brandy landed then lost in Culbin's shifting sands (**3**) remains lost; caves between Hopeman and Lossiemouth (**35**) hid the contraband of one celebrated Burghead laird; and the rugged coast east of Buckie invited moonlit operations requiring daring and wit plus, often enough, the bribery of Preventers (excisemen).

Approaching by night and signalled by shoreline lights that no Preventers were about, the smuggler ship would stand by, approaching oarsmen offering a password; often a shouted: 'Devil, devil, devil' - this a name which, with the Kirk so powerful, only bold men dared to speak aloud, especially at night, when Auld Cloutie was up to his tricks.

Born in 1765, at the height of his career Buckie man George 'Captain' Geddes had tobacco and rum from New Orleans reshipped from Rotterdam for secret landing at Buckie. Later a wealthy man with a London address, he chartered ten ships to the government as troop carriers, but failed to insure them. Ruined by the capture of eight, hiding in a coffin on a Scots trading smack to escape his creditors, back in Buckie he found a coastguard station established. The good old days were gone. It's said he died not only broke but teetotal. The moral? He should have stuck to smuggling. Going legal ruined him.

In 1830 salt cost £3 a ton, excluding duty. Fishcurers and sea-skippers each had a salt bond cellar, double-locked, one key with the salt's owner, the other with the exciseman. No salt could be removed from bond without (as with whisky today) the presence of the gauger. Yet vast quantities were smuggled. Fisherwomen bound for Keith or Elgin hiding salt under the fish in their creels had it confiscated or scattered on the road if intercepted. Salt on the highway then (often every 400 yards) had nothing to do with icy weather.

Around 1800 Buckie innkeeper Mrs Ogilvie dealt in smuggled gin and tobacco. Once, with a grindstone-sized roll of tobacco hidden in her bed, excisemen acting on a tip-off searched her house. As they approached the bed she said: 'You can search away, but wait till I take off some of the dirty clothes,' then with the blankets scooped away the tobacco – a tale suggesting that the excisemen were not mental giants.

With 'Whisky Galore' on TV at least once a year, even the most law-abiding folk cradle an imp delighting in how our ancestors flouted Authority. Yet little changes. Then it was tobacco and gin. Now it's other stuff altogether.

118.   Portknockie: From the Bow Fiddle to Cullen   (Walk)

Founded in 1677 by Cullen fishermen attracted by its natural harbour in the lee of Greencastle Hill, with its remnants of an Iron Age fort, the clifftop fishing village of Portknockie (pop. 1200) slopes steep above a tortured shoreline, its clean bright-painted houses gable-end to the sea to protect against winter gales. Peaceful today, here a millennium ago there were ferocious battles against the Danes (see **119**).

Crossing the Moor of Findochty past a clifftop cemetery, the A942 enters the village by Station Road then passes along Church Street before turning south to the A98. For a spectacular walk past the Bow Fiddle Rock (see photo next page) to Cullen and back, at the east end of Church Street turn left down to Patrol Road and the clifftop. With the rocky harbour to the left, turn right along Patrol Road. Where it meets Addison Street bear left to park above a joinery yard. Taking the path sign-posted to Bow Fiddle Rock, follow the clifftop east above this offshore crag, the reason for its name soon obvious. Beyond, with views east to Troup Head, the dizzy

path curls south above Scar Nose, Cullen Bay's long beach below. Above a deep cut and the vast Whale's Mouth Cave, by a clifftop bench the path forks, three ways.

The right turn leads back to Portknockie.

The continuing clifftop path passes a benched viewpoint, a path down to Cullen golf links, then reaches the old railway track. There a right turn re-enters Portknockie; the left turn on the railway walk leads to Cullen.

The left turn, now described, descends via the Whale's Mouth Road to the shore, and continues past Jenny's Well and Preacher's Cave, once known as Janet's Well and Janet's Cave. A Janet Carstairs lived in the cave, but after the 1843 Schism the Free Church held secret services there, so the change in name. Round a rocky tide-swept corner the long beach opens up; the Black Rocks offshore marking where in 1738 Lord Banff drowned while bathing with Lord Deskford. To the right is Boar Craig, so-called because once a hole (now blocked) pierced it. Above the dunes the 300-year-old links offer another approach to Cullen via clubhouse and the Three Kings, rocks named after the Viking kings slain nearby in 961 (see below).

With Cullen's tight-packed Seatown ahead over the Burn of Deskford, and the main village above and east of the vast 19th century railway viaduct, from the beach-front carpark (one option) turn under the viaduct to the A98 pavement. Bear right, uphill, past a roadside knoll at the edge of the vast Seafield Estate, on it the 'Temple of Fame' (1822), a neo-classical folly suggesting the vanity of the old aristocracy. Follow the A98 up to Cullen Bay Hotel, and opposite it turn right onto the old railway track – made by Irish navvies so poor they worked for twice the work, half the pay. The route, including the double viaduct, was demanded by Seafield, who wanted no vulgar railway on *his* land.

Follow the track a mile back to Portknockie. Facing the dome of the Bin of Cullen, drive south on the A942 to the A98 over the Bauds of Cullen – pasture now, but once...

119. The Vikings in Moray   *(History)*

For centuries Viking raiders from Norway and Denmark plagued this coast, at last settling peacefully, or being driven away. Leader of the first Norse attacks on Moray was Sigurd, Earl of Orkney, who *c.*800 occupied Burghead (**29**). Thereafter battles were fought all round the coast to repel the marauders, who seized land from the Orkneys to East Anglia, Dublin to Normandy and beyond. Energetic sons of a hard land, their naked berserker warriors charging into battle intoxicated by infusions of the fly agaric toadstool, they were feared from Cromarty to Constantinople. 11th century Viking graffiti in Orkney's Maes Howe tomb boasts of a trip to Jerusalem, adding that 'Ingigerth is the most beautiful of women' and that 'Tryggyr carved these runes' – proof that Kilroy has been here a long time. Already they'd colonised Greenland and visited North America, and the 'Normans' from France who took over England in 1066 were 'Northmen' too (see **33**).

Not until the defeat of King Haco's fleet at Largs in 1263 were they driven out. By then the war had lasted almost 500 years. Thus the name of Cruden Bay north of Aberdeen comes from *croju-dane* ('slaughter of the Danes'), after the 1012 battle where Malcolm's Scots drove Canute's Danes into the sea. Near Burghead in 1040 the Battle of Torfness, against the Norse under Thorfinn, led to the death of Duncan and accession of Macbeth (**30**). Here on Bauds Moor, or Moor of Rannachie, the year 961 saw a rout of the Danes. In terms of slain leaders it was 3-1 to the Scots, the dead Danish kings still commemorated by the Three Kings Rocks on Cullen Beach. A local rhyme claims that: *'Between Rannachie and the sea, Three kings there buried be'*; and many gravemounds were once found on the high ground above Findochty. As for the mortally-wounded Scottish king Indulph, he was carried to Cullen, where he died. Various sites near Portknockie are claimed as his final resting place, including the King's Cairn (494656) east of Woodside under the Bin.

Once seizing Portknockie, the Danes held it until the Scots cut down trees and advanced behind them. Just as Macbeth was shocked to see Birnam Wood march on Dunsinane, so the pirates fled when confronted by this mobile forest. It's said many jumped into the sea and drowned off Scar Nose.

Buckie men used to dig up bones from what is now Strathlene golf course. Only a century ago lived some old men who as youths had played football on the Links, the ball a human skull they kicked all the harder in the belief that it had once belonged to a Viking...

120. Cullen: Round the Crannoch *(History, Walk)*

Snugly hugging its slope above Cullen Bay and under the Bin, the old royal burgh of Cullen (pop. 1410) began as Invercullen, a 12th century settlement on Castle Hill, its name maybe from *cuilan*, 'little nook'. In the 13th century it was moved slightly inland, but remained a rough poor place, as Dr. Johnson noted five centuries later. By 1618 its population of about 500 boasted (or hosted) 16 sellers and brewers of ale, plus a gallow tree, stocks and a busy 'common executioner'. By then the Ogilvie Earls of Findlater had left Findlater Castle (**121**) to build Cullen House (506664: not open). Sited high above Cullen Burn, after the 1858 additions this very grand house extended to 386 rooms. Hugely complex on its rock above the burn, this vast baronial pile has lately been converted into separate dwellings.

Between it and the village is the Old Kirk, dedicated to St Mary of Cullen and dating back to 1327, when 'with mad mourning and woe' Robert the Bruce endowed a chaplaincy for his wife Elizabeth, who died here. With its high-walled old kirkyard, and internal columned and canopied monument to Alexander Ogilvy, St Mary's is worth a visit.

Today, bisected by the embankment and elegant high arches of the old railway track, Cullen is postcard-pretty. From Crannoch Hill to the east or the top of Seafield Street the eye swoops down the wide streets of the new town, began by the Seafield Earls in 1820. Under the viaduct the Seatown – one of the northeast's finest – marches the sea wall from the harbour to the Three Kings rocks. The harbour, begun in 1817, now caters to pleasure craft; while the legacy of the vanished fish-curing business is 'Cullen Skink' a fish soup based on smoked haddock. Two novels by the noted Victorian fabulist George MacDonald (1824-1905) – 'Malcolm' and 'The Marquis of Lossie' - were set in the Seatown.

And there are the walks. Besides the trails up and round the Bin (**122**) there are many ways to go – along the coast west to Portknockie or east to Findlater Castle; via the Old Kirk and Lintmill southeast on lanes to Fordyce and its pocket-sized castle; or, closer to hand, the popular stroll up and round Crannoch Hill.

To start, either walk from Seafield Place via the track above the caravan park and fork right, or drive out of Cullen on the Banff A98. In half-a-mile, just past the Keith B9018, by the mileage sign Portsoy 5 turn left into a small carpark (518663). From it cross the old road (once the King's Highway to Sandend), bearing right on a path up through beechwood. At a junction over the old railway bridge keep left, up the north edge of the wood above rolling fields, fine views opening - the Bin's elegant blue dome, then the sea; Cullen rooftops and the Bow Fiddle Rock peeping over an opposite ridge of the field.

A boggy sink in the dell below - the Hough of Gillyfurry, where Cullen folk once got peat – may be where in 1562 Sir John Gordon, the Earl of Huntly's wild son, defeated the forces of Mary Queen of Scots. Having seized Findlater Castle from Sir James Ogilvie, in July he'd wounded Ogilvie in Edinburgh. Escaping jail, he fled to Findlater. Ogilvie and Mary pursued him. Ordered to surrender Auchindoun (**107**) and Findlater, and to let Mary into Findlater, he refused, defeated her, but, forced to surrender, was executed in Aberdeen.

Further up the track, a pine-needled path enters the wood to the right. (The continuing track climbs from woodland to wide views, then descends past ruined Logie House to Sunnyside Bay: see next walk.) Turn right up the pine-needled path through the wood to the Crannoch; a forested lochan (dry in summer) with a central islet. Crannogs are artificial isles, mostly Iron Age, but this dates from the 18th century, being created by the Earl of Seafield, who planted literally millions of trees from the Bin to Deskford and beyond - part of the 'Improvements'.

Past the Crannoch the path descends to join the old King's Highway. The left turn climbs out of the wood to fine views past Deskford and Durn Hill. The right turn descends to the old railway bridge, and so back to the carpark.

121. Giant Steps & Findlater Castle   *(Walk)*

This fine coastal walk east from Cullen follows a rocky path past Sunnyside Bay over the district boundary to the awesome ruin of Findlater Castle, returning by Logie House.

From the harbour start east along the shore past the old curing stations and boatyard, then via the rough Portlong road past an old salmon bothy, used from 1829 until the 1970s. Beyond the sheltered bay (once a smuggler's haunt) the ever-rougher, cliff-hugging track climbs to Logie Head, turning into a narrow path twisting up to the top of the Giant Steps, which descend the far side. Until 1989 in ruin, that summer Cullen resident Tony Hetherington rebuilt the entire flight singlehanded, levering up huge blocks from the original steps that then lay piled at the bottom.

Tony died in a canoeing accident in 1993: there is a memorial to him on a cairn below the steps (528681), but the steps themselves are his real memorial.

The path flattens out, soon reaching a tiny natural stile in the rock. Beyond it lies Sunnyside Bay, an enchanted cove of sand and rock pools, a track climbing to the clifftop: on return, this is the track to take. At the bay's east end a second track climbs the cliff, continuing over the district boundary to a viewpoint above Findlater Castle (543674) – a gaping-eyed ruin merging so well with the cliff-face that at first it's easily missed. A narrow path leads down to it. Take care! As for the castle's interior, don't try it. One slip in its open-windowed sand-filled halls could land you on sea-lashed rocks far below. Why these windows haven't been protectively barred is beyond me

Another path descends to the cove below. If the tide is out, you can scramble over the rocks to the mouth of the huge Doo's Cave. Here the rock strata of the cliff-face stand vertical, wrenched by some ancient geological cataclysm. With gulls screaming overhead, return to the viewpoint, where a track heads south past an old doocot to Barnyards of Findlater and a carpark (see below). Also from here you can follow the clifftop east to Sandend and its popular beach.

Back in Sunnyside Bay, climb the track mentioned above. At the top a well hidden in the grass bears the inscription: REST, DRINK & THINK 1895. The well may be dry, but at least you can rest and think. A tiny gate leads to a wide open field. Hug the edge of it and head inland to ruined Logie House (526673), from which (with a track breaking south to the Crannoch) a track heads west to Cullen, in sight most of the way. In time a track on the right to Cullen Caravan Site leads to a left turn past playing fields to Seafield Place, and so back to Seafield Street. The distance is about five miles, and you'll need good boots.

To reach Findlater Castle more easily, take the A98 from Cullen just under two miles towards Portsoy and turn right at a minor crossroads (536656: Findlater Castle signposted). The lane turns a sharp bend onto a long straight towards Sandend. After half a mile turn left (north again) to Barnyards of Findlater and follow the signposted track.

122.   The Bin of Cullen   *(Routes, Walks)*

Climbing the Moray coast's most conspicuous and elegant landmark is a fine way to end this tour. Smoothly conical, the Bin of Cullen (480643: 1050 ft.) rises from the Bauds of Cullen south of Portknockie. Flanked to the east by the Little Bin (802 ft.) and to the west by the Hill of Maud (900 ft.), from much of the coast it resembles some final graceful, emphatic flow of the wave of the land into the sea. And being so isolated and close to the coast, its summit offers remarkable views. So climb it on a clear day, taking maps and binoculars to identify distant landmarks.

With a maze of paths and tracks below and about it, the best approach is from the south, by a track reached via back-roads through an area not elsewhere described:

From Buckie crossroads (432642) just east of Inchgower Distillery keep straight over the A98 on the Deskford back-road. Past the Drybridge-Clochan turn (**114**) and up a steep brae by hidden Letterfourie House (1773: Robert Adam) it passes a carpark and viewpoint (452626) on the west flank of the Hill of Maud. A few yards on a track into the wood traverses this low round hill to Hillhead of Rannas and a path up the west side of the Bin – walkable but dull. Continuing past the Old Monastery Restaurant, once a retreat for the monks of Fort Augustus, this road winds west over bleak pastures to a rural crossing (475616: by a house called Rosebank) just north of the forested Hill of Clashmadin.

A left turn here soon picks up a lane which, leaving the A98 two miles east of Buckie by harled council houses (450648), crosses the saddle between the Hill of Maud and the Bin at Hillhead of Rannas. Continue east a mile past a right turn (Deskford) to Braidbog steading by the forest. Just inside the forest park left, by the gated track (492633).

Or, from Cullen, start east on the A98 and turn south on the Keith B9018. Crossing the Burn of Deskford at Lintmill, after two miles (the B9018 continuing past pretty Deskford, with its ruined Ogilvie tower and medieval church) turn east on a straight minor road by Nether Blairock steading (511633). Follow this road two miles to forestry south of the Bin and the gated track by Braidbog.

Beyond the gate start north. Soon on the right another main track breaks northwest, running two miles through Shirrald's Wood to Lintmill. Under fine mature forest continue straight, curving down over Glen Burn to a main crossing (489635. Here the right turn follows the burn northeast. The track ahead also heads northeast, but higher, in time circling the Little Bin to rejoin the track to the left on the saddle between Bin and Little Bin. Also, almost a mile up this central track, before a main forest junction (497646), to the left under gnarly beeches a rough but pretty path climbs over the Little Bin's heathery, pine-clad south slope, in a mile joining the track next described.

This, left from the crossing, is the direct route up the Bin. It climbs steadily, its bracken, heathery banks, beech, silver birch and old Scots Pine making it one of the area's prettiest woodland walks. The forest here was planted over 200 years ago by Lord Deskford, an unpopular Improving innovator and epileptic said still to haunt Cullen House, having murdered his factor. Feeling a fit coming on, he'd lock himself in his library and drop the key from the window. The fit past, the factor would let him out, but one day the poor man came too soon. Still in a fit, Deskford chased him upstairs then down into the library again, there stabbing him to death. The incident was hushed up.

Just before reaching a fork almost at the crest of the saddle (484642), near a beech carved with the name 'Claire' the path across the Little Bin's south face (see above) emerges invisibly from the heather bank. At the fork above, turn left (west). Climb out of the wood to the Bin's heathery upper slopes, where stony tracks wind up to the bare round top with its white concrete cairn...and its incredible views...

123. The View from the Bin of Cullen   *(Finale)*

So here we are, end of story, end of tale, atop the Bin looking west and south the way we came, and east to another journey not yet begun. It's said on a clear day you can see forever, but here the immense view beats forever, being here and now. Cullen and Buckie streets and coastal plain below, open sea beyond. Beyond Banff and Gamrie to the east Troup Head erupts sheer from the sea. Northeast lies Norway. Due north, the next direct landfall compass-wise is in Siberia, over the Pole near the Bering Straits. Northwest, over the Firth, low blue Caithness dwindles past Wick to an oil-rig remote in the sea, but the dog-tooth of Morven (2313 ft., Scotland's highest peak in Old Red Sandstone) turns the eye west: over dolphin firth to Dornoch Firth and remote Sutherland hills; over the Laich past Covesea Lighthouse and the Firth's narrowing tongue to the Black Isle and bulky Ben Wyvis; over Elgin and Culbin to Inverness; over Moray moors to Monadhliath brows above hidden Findhorn gorges to Lochindorb where a wolf-ghost moans; southwest over Banffshire moors past Ben Rinnes to Cairngorm ramparts above the Spey.

Then south over Strathisla and Strathbogie to Tap O'Noth and The Buck; and east of south over the glacier-scrubbed rough land below to the Bin's sister-hill, the Knock and, (on a clear clear day) to Bennachie in the Garioch and beyond to Mount Keen south of Deeside, over 50 miles away.

That's some view. I hope you enjoy it, as I hope you've enjoyed this journey…and maybe we'll meet again soon.

*The Moray Firth shore at Spey Bay (see **42**)*

Gazetteer of Places to Visit

The following lists most of the places of special visited or mentioned during this tour, doing so alphabetically within the following categories and under these heads:

Name	Location	When Open	Tel.	See Chapter
Castles & Historic Buildings				
Auchindoun Castle	near Dufftown	all year (no charge)	-	107
Ballindalloch Castle	Ballindalloch	1 April - 30 September	01807-500205	58
Balvenie Castle	Dufftown	1 April - 30 September	-	106
Brodie Castle	near Forres	Easter-October	01309-641371	5
Coxton Tower	near Lhanbryde	appointment only	01343-842225	25
Darnaway Castle	near Forres	appointment only	01309-672213	6
Duffus Castle	near Duffus	all year (no charge)		33
Elgin Cathedral	Elgin	all year; not Fri or Sun Winter	01343-547171	22
Findlater Castle	near Cullen	all year (no charge)	-	121
Lochindorb Castle	Dava Moor	all year (rowing boat hire)	01309-651270	9
Pluscarden Abbey	near Elgin	all year (no charge)	01343-890257	17
The 'Roman Well'	Burghead	all year (no charge)	01343-835559	29
Ruthven Barracks	Kingussie	all year (no charge)	-	82
Spynie Palace	near Elgin	April-Sept, weekends Oct-Mar	01343-546358	24
Crafts & Exhibitions				
Barnyards	Garmouth	workshops: call for times	01343-870202	41
Logie Steading	near Forres	workshops: call for times	01309-611278	11
Old Mills	Elgin	March-October	01343-540698	23
Spey Valley Smokehouse	by Grantown	all year	01479-873078	58
Distilleries				
Cardhu	Knockando	January-mid December	01340-810204	56
Dallas Dhu	Forres	all year	01309-676548	14
Dalwhinnie	Dalwhinnie	call for times	01528-522208	81
Glenfarclas	Ballindalloch	January-mid December	01807-500245	58
Glenfiddich	Dufftown	January-mid December	01340-820373	106
Glen Grant	Rothes	mid-March - end of October	01542-783318	49
The Glenlivet	Glenlivet	mid-March - end of October	01542-783220	104
Macallan	Craigellachie	appointment only	01340-871471	50
Strathisla	Keith	February - 30 November	01542-783044	111
Tamnavulin-Glenlivet	Glenlivet	Easter-October	01807-590285	102
Heritage & Visitor Centres				
Baxters of Speyside	Fochabers	all year (speciality foods)	01343-820393	25
Buckie Drifter	Freuchny Rd.	April-October (fisher history)	01542-834646	115
Glenmore Forest Park VC	Glenmore	all year (Cairngorm intro)	01479-861220	91
Johnstonís Cashmere VC	Elgin	all year (speciality clothing)	01309-554099	22
Landmark VC	Carrbridge	all year (history, play-areas etc)	01463-841613	64
Village Heritage Centre	Findhorn	seasonal (local history)	01309-690309	14
Rothiemurchus VC	Inverdruie	all year (crafts, etc.)	01479-810858	88
Speyside Cooperage VC	Craigellachie	Mon-Fri Jan-Dec; Sat Apr-Sept	01340-871108	51

Museums

Clan Macpherson	Newtonmore	Clan Macpherson history	unlisted	75
Elgin Museum	1 High St.	April-October; Pictish exhibits	01343-543675	22
Falconer Museum	Forres	all year: varied exhibits	01309-673701	2
Fisheries Museum	Lossiemouth	Easter-September	01343-813772	35
Grantown Museum	Burnfield Ave.	all year	01479-872478	59
Highland Folk Museum	Kingussie	all year	01540-661307	72
Nelson's Tower	Forres	May-October	01309-673701	2
Tomintoul Museum	The Square	seasonal: times vary	01807-580440	100

Sport & Recreation

Glenlatterach Fishing, near Elgin	April-October	01343-860234	27
Glen of Rothes Trout Fishery, near Rothes off A941	all year	01340-831888	49
Lochindorb Fishing, Dava Moor	March-October	01309-651270	10
Loch Insh Watersports, near Kincraig		01540-651272	68
Loch Morlich Watersports, Glenmore Forest Park		01479-861220	91
Lochnabo Fishing, near Lhanbryde	April-October	01343-842214	25
Loch of Blairs Fishing, near Forres	April-October	01309-672936	
Millbuies Fishing, Fogwatt	April-October	01343-860234	26
Strathspey Steam Railway, Boat of Garten	daily June-Sept., specials	01479-810725	64

Tourist Information Centres

Aviemore	Grampian Road (all year)	01479-810363	66
Dufftown	Clock Tower, The Square (seasonal)	01340-820501	106
Elgin	17 High St. (all year)	01343-543388	22
Forres	116 High St. (seasonal)	01309-672938	1
Grantown-on-Spey	High St. (seasonal)	01479-872773	59
Inverness	Bridge St. (all year)	01463-234353	—
Kingussie	Spey St (seasonal)	01540-661297	72
Ralia	A9 by Newtonmore (seasonal)	01540-673253	82
Tomintoul	The Square (seasonal)	01807-580225	100

Wildlife

Findhorn Bay Nature Reserve	dolphins, seals, ospreys etc.		14
Friends of the Moray Firth Dolphins	dolphin-spotting boat-trips	01542-833867	42
Highland Wildlife Park, Kingussie	drive-through	01540-651270	69
Insh Marshes RSPB Reserve, Kingussie	observation hides	01540-651270	69
The Lein, Kingston-on-Spey	bird-watching, geology	-	39
Loch Garten RSPB Nature Reserve	osprey hides & visitor centre	-	95
Loch Spynie, near Elgin	bird-watching	01343-551436	24
Moray Firth Wildlife Centre, Spey Bay	Mar-Oct, weekends Nov-Dec	01343-820339	42
Neilson, Karl; Portessie	dolphin-spotting boat-trips	01542-832289	42
Reindeer House, Glenmore	reindeer-spotting expeditions	01479-861228	91

This is by no means a complete listing but may help those of you with particular agendas to plan an itinerary to your own liking. Have fun!

To find out more about trespass, rights of way and public access, write to or call The Scottish Rights of Way Society (24 Annandale St., Edinburgh EH7 4AN; tel. 0131-558-1222) to obtain their *Rights of Way: A Guide to the Law in Scotland*.

Glossary of common place-name prefixes and suffixes

Key to abbreviations: B = Brythonic/Brittonic; E = English (OE = Old English); G = Gaelic; L = Latin; N = (old) Norse; S = Scots

Aber	Brittonic/Welsh	'estuary', 'confluence' (see inver)
Ach	Gaelic achadh	'field'
All	Early Irish all	'rock'
Allt	Gaelic allt	'burn', 'stream'
Aonach	Gaelic aonach	'ridge'
Ard	Gaelic aird	'height', 'high place', 'promontory'
Auchter	Gaelic uachdair	'upper part of', 'high ground'
Bal	Gaelic baile	'town', 'village', 'enclosure'
Ban	Gaelic ban	'white'
Barr	Gaelic barr	'crest', 'height', 'top of'
Bealach	Gaelic bealach	'pass'
Beg	Gaelic beag	'small', 'little'
Ben	Gaelic beinn	'mountain', 'horn'
Bidean	Gaelic bidean	'pinnacle'
Blair	Gaelic blar	'battlefield', 'cleared ground'
Bodach	Gaelic bodach	'old man'
Buidhe	Gaelic buidhe	'yellow'
By, Bie	Norse byr	'farm', 'hamlet'
Cam	Gaelic camas	'bay', 'bend', 'crooked'
Cardine	Brittonic cardden	'copse', 'thicket'
Clach	Gaelic clach	'stone'
Corrie	Gaelic coire	'hollow', cup-shaped depression', 'kettle'
Craig	Gaelic creag	'cliff', 'crag'
Dale	English dale (dalr:N; dol:B; dail:G)	'valley', 'field', 'haugh'
Darroch	Gaelic darroch	'oak'
Dearg	Gaelic dearg	'red' (pron. jarrag)
Dour	Gaelic dobhar	'water'
Druidh	Gaelic druidh	'shieling' (pron. drewy
Drum	Gaelic druim	'back', 'spine', 'ridge'
Dubh	Gaelic dubh	'black'
Dun	Gaelic dun	'fortress', 'castle', 'hill', 'mound'
Eagach	Gaelic eagach	'notched'
Eas	Gaelic eas	'waterfall'
Eilean	Gaelic eilean	'island'
Eilrig	Gaelic eilrig	'deer walk'
Erin	Gaelic Eireann	'of Ireland'
Ey	Norse Ey	'island'
Firth	Norse fjordr (art; G)	'sea-estuary'
Fo	Gaelic fo	'under'
Fuaran	Gaelic fuaran	'spring'

Garbh	Gaelic *garbh*	'rough'
Gart	*gardr* (N); *garth* (B); *garradh* (G)	'garden', 'enclosure', 'yard'
Glas	Gaelic; Brittonic	'grey' or 'green' (G); or 'water' (B)
Glen	Gaelic *gleann*	'narrow valley'
Gorm	Gaelic *gorm*	'bluish green'
Gowrie	Gaelic *gowrie*	'goats'
Hope	Norse *hop*	'bay', 'refuge', 'valley'
Inch	Gaelic *innis*	'island', 'meadows by a river', 'field'
Inver	Gaelic *inbhir*	'estuary', 'confluence' (see aber)
Iolaire	Gaelic *iolaire*	'eagles'
Kil	Gaelic *ceall, cill*	'monastic cell', 'church'
Kin	Gaelic *ceann*	'head'
Kirk	Scots (*kirkju*:N)	'church'
Knock	Gaelic *cnoc*	'round hillock'
Kyle	Gaelic *caol*	'slender', 'thin, 'sea-strait'
Lairig	Gaelic *lairig*	'pass'
Liath	Gaelic *liath*	'grey'
Linn	Gaelic *linn;* Brit. *llyn*	(1) 'pool', (2) 'lake'
Loch	Gaelic *loch*	'loch', also sometimes 'black'
Luineag	Gaelic *luineag*	'surging'
Mam	Gaelic *mam*	'round hill'
May	Gaelic *magh; moigh*	'field', 'plain'
Meall	Gaelic *meall*	'knob', 'hump'
Moine	Gaelic *moine*	'mossy land'
Monadh	Gaelic *monadh*	'moorland', 'flat-topped ridge'
More	Gaelic *mor, mhor*	'great', 'big'
Ness	*naes* (OE); *nes* (N)	'point', 'headland' (L. *nasus,* 'nose')
Ochil	Brittonic *uchel*	'high'
Pit	Pictish	'part', 'share', 'piece' (?)
Rath	Gaelic *rath*	'fort', sometimes 'underground house'
Rathad	Gaelic *rathad*	'road'
Ruadh	Gaelic *ruadh*	'red', 'reddish'
Sgorr	Gaelic *sgorr, sgur*	'sharp peak'
Shee	Gaelic *sithe, sidhe*	'fairies', 'fairy hills'
Shieling	Norse *skali*	'hut' (usually on high pasture)
Stob	Gaelic *stob*	'point'
Strath	Gaelic *strath*	'river valley', 'fertile valley'
Tigh	Gaelic *tigh*	'house'
Tobar	Gaelic *tobar*	'well', 'source'
Tom	Gaelic *tom*	'conical hillock', 'mound', 'knoll'
Ton	English *ton*	'homestead'
Tor	Brittonic *tor*	'hill'
Tulloch	Gaelic *tulach*	'eminence', 'ridge', 'knoll'
Uaine	Gaelic *uaine*	'green'
Uisge	Gaelic *uisge*	'water' (whisky)

Bibliography

Some books and other publications I've plundered or which you may find useful in following up topics are as follows (some out of print or hard to find):

Bord, Janet & Colin, *Alien Animals,* Panther Books, London 1985
Browne, James, *History of the Highlands,* Fullerton, Glasgow 1838
Clayton, Peter, *Guide to the Archaeological Sites of Britain,* B T Batsford, London 1985
Dorward, David, *Scotland's Place-Names,* William Blackwood, Edinburgh 1979
Francis, Di, *Cat Country: The Quest for the British Big Cat,* David & Charles, London
        1983; *My Highland Kellas Cats,* Jonathan Cape, London 1993
Gaffney, Victor, *Tomintoul: Its Glens and People,*Sutherland Press, Golspie 1976 (1970)
Gordon, Seton, *Highways and Byways in the Central Highlands,* Birlinn, Edinburgh 1995
        (1935)
Grant, Elizabeth, *Memoirs of a Highland Lady,* Canongate, Edinburgh 1988
Gray, Affleck, *Legends of the Cairngorms,* Mainstream, Edinburgh 1987
Hutcheson, George, *Days of Yore,* Provost Publications, Buckie 1997 (1888)
Ives, Edward D, *The Bonny Earl of Murray: the Man, the Murder, the Ballad,*
        Tuckwell Press Ltd., East Linton 1997
Jackson, Kenneth, *The Symbol Stones of Scotland,* Orkney Press, Kirkwall 1984
Lauder, Sir Thomas Dick, *Great Moray Floods of 1829,* Moray Books, Forres 1998 (1830)
Lockhart, J G, *Curses, Lucks & Talismans,* Geoffrey Bles, London 1938
Lynch, Michael, *Scotland: A New History,* Pimlico, London 1992
Mackie, J D, *A History of Scotland,* Penguin Books, London 1964
Maclean, Loraine, *Discovering Inverness-shire,* John Donald, Edinburgh 1988
Macpherson, James, *Poems of Ossian,* Edinburgh University Press, 1996 (1760-63)
Matheson, D, *The Place Names of Elginshire,* Eneas Mackay, Stirling 1905
Marren, Peter, *Grampian Battlefields,* Aberdeen University Press, 1990
McDowell, R J S, *The Whiskies of Scotland,* John Murray, London 1975
McKean, Charles, *District of Moray: An Illustrated Architectural Guide,* Scottish
        Academic Press, Edinburgh 1987
Peck, Edward H, *Avonside Explored,* Edward H Peck, Tomintoul 1989 (1983)
Prebble, John, *Culloden,* Penguin, London 1967
        - The Highland Clearances, Penguin, London 1969
Ritchie, Anna, *Picts,* HMSO, London 1989
Sellar, W D H (ed.), *Moray: Province and People,* Scottish Society for Northern Studies,
        Edinburgh 1993
Simpson, Eric, *Discovering Banff Moray and Nairn,* John Donald, Edinburgh 1992
Spence, Lewis, *Magic Arts in Celtic Britain,* Aquarian Press, London 1970 (1946)
Stott, Louis, *The Waterfalls of Scotland,* Aberdeen University Press, 1987
Thompson, Francis, *Discovering Speyside,* John Donald, Edinburgh 1990
Towill, Edwin Sprott, *The Saints of Scotland,* Saint Andrew Press, Edinburgh 1983
Wightman, Andy, *Who Owns Scotland,* Canongate Books, Edinburgh 1996

About the author

Born in Banff in 1947 and since 1970 (writing as Stuart Gordon) author of some 20 titles of fiction and non-fiction, when Richard Gordon returned to north Scotland in 1988 he realised he knew little or nothing of the region and its history, and set about changing that. In 1992 he published *The Complete Moray Rambler*, much of it incorporated in this present book, which is a sequel to *Round Inverness, The Black Isle and Nairn* (1998). He lives near Buckie and is currently working on a third book in this series, provisionally titled *Round Aberdeen from Deeside to Buchan.*